Contents

CW01500375

Intention and Causation in Medical Non-Killing

The impact of criminal law concepts on euthanasia and assisted suicide

Glenys Williams PhD

Routledge·Cavendish
Taylor & Francis Group
LONDON AND NEW YORK

First published 2007 by Routledge-Cavendish
2 Park Square, Milton Park, Abingdon, OX14 4RN, UK

Simultaneously published in the USA and Canada
by Routledge-Cavendish
270 Madison Ave, New York, NY 10016

*Routledge-Cavendish is an imprint of the Taylor & Francis Group, an
informa business*

© 2007 Glenys Williams

Typeset in Times New Roman by
RefineCatch Limited, Bungay, Suffolk
Printed and bound in Great Britain by
TJ International Ltd, Padstow, Cornwall

All rights reserved. No part of this book may be reprinted or
reproduced or utilised in any form or by any electronic, mechanical,
or other means, now known or hereafter invented, including
photocopying and recording, or in any information storage or
retrieval system, without permission in writing from the publishers.

British Library Cataloguing in Publication Data
A catalogue record for this book is available from the British Library

Library of Congress Cataloging in Publication Data
Williams, Glenys
  Intention and causation in medical non-killing / Glenys Williams.
    p. cm.
  Includes bibliographical references
  ISBN-13: 978–1–84472–027–9 (hardback)
  ISBN-13: 978–0–415–42302–1 (pbk.)
  1. Euthanasia—Law and legislation—England. 2. Assisted
suicide—Law and legislation—England. 3. Criminal intent—
England. 4. Causation (Criminal Law)—England. 5. Assisted
suicide—Moral and ethical aspects—England. I. Title.
  KD3410.E88.W55 2007
  344.4204′ 197—dc22   2006026518

ISBN10: 1–84472–027–6 (hbk)
ISBN10: 0–415–42302–3 (pbk)
ISBN13: 978–1–84472–027–9 (hbk)
ISBN13: 978–0–415–42302–1 (pbk)

Acknowledgements

Having completed this book at long last, there are a number of people to whom I am greatly indebted.

As it is a rewritten version of my PhD thesis, I will begin by expressing my thanks to both Professor John Williams, my supervisor, and to Dr Stephen Skinner for their significant help in the completion of my PhD. Thanks go also to my external examiners Jo Bridgeman and Dr José Miola for their rigorous examination and their subsequent suggestions for improvement. I am also grateful to those individuals with whom I conducted a series of interviews, some extracts of which appear in this book.

I am more grateful than words can say to my colleagues Gavin Dingwall, Neil Kibble and Dr Stephen Skinner (again!) for reading earlier drafts. I could not have produced a sound final version without their invaluable advice and assistance. Thanks also to Yvonne Williams for her careful proof-reading, and to Anne Kuehnel, computer wizard.

Sincere thanks also to my parents (my mother being the one who started me on this path) and friends for their unfailing encouragement and interest, and last, but certainly not least, profound thanks to my husband, Ceredig and our two sons, Benjamin and Rhys for their patience and moral support during the many years it has taken to complete the PhD and the book.

Table of cases

Table of statutes

Introduction

Judges decline to define . . . [intention] . . . and they appear to adjust it from one case to another.

(Williams 1987: 417)

Euthanasia and assisted suicide have reached a level whereby they are discussed in the media and by the public on a virtually daily basis. For example, there has been intense media coverage of the exodus by terminally ill patients from the UK who have travelled to Switzerland to commit suicide, and of recent treatment withdrawal cases from young children who are suffering from some disability. The role of doctors is central to any analysis of treatments and decisions at the end of life, but the essentially criminal law provisions with which they have to comply are far from clear. This book therefore examines the role which medical practitioners play in euthanasia, assisted suicide and withdrawing treatment, with particular concentration on the impact the criminal law concepts of intention and causation have on end-of-life decision-making.

Euthanasia is understood to be the compassionate bringing about of a death where the 'victim' is suffering from an incurable and/or painful disease. However, as an intentional killing, euthanasia comes within the 'definition' of murder and as such is punishable by a mandatory life sentence; the requisite elements of murder are present, namely the *actus reus* – that a person causes the death of another, and the *mens rea* – that he has the necessary intention.

Intention and causation are also key elements in suicide and aiding and abetting suicide, although the former is no longer a criminal offence. In a medical context, it can be suggested that a patient who refuses life-sustaining treatment comes within the traditional definition of suicide, that is, one who deliberately takes his own life. Yet, as far as causation is concerned, the 'cause' of death is deemed to be the original illness and not the patient's refusal or the doctor's withdrawal of the treatment. Similarly, although intention is the decisive factor in suicide, the court simply assumes that the intention is non-suicidal, or imposes unattainable standards of knowledge or certainty of death on the patient's part, in order to justify its decision that withdrawing treatment is not suicide.

Intention, although not itself a clear-cut concept, is the crucial benchmark by which culpability and blameworthiness are measured by the courts and is, along with causation, the main factor used to ascribe liability. However, as neither intention nor causation (nor indeed murder) are defined statutorily, reliance has to be placed on common law 'definitions'. The consequences of this have been far-reaching. Firstly, it has enabled the courts in 'medical' cases to interpret these two key criminal law concepts in a manner which is inconsistent with previous precedent in order to avoid concluding that doctors are criminally liable for their activities.[1] Secondly, it has enabled judges to make intuitive value judgments and to use preconceived ideas based on policy and the status of the actors to manipulate intention and causation[2] in a way which provides doctors with unique 'defences' (if they can be called that) which are not available to any other category of persons. These defences, namely the principle of double effect[3] and the distinction made between acts and omissions,[4] are tactical tools which ostensibly differentiate between administering pain-killing medication to a patient whose death is on the one hand intended, or, on the other, is a mere side effect, and between acting to kill and omitting to save. As a result, although administering pain-killing medication and withdrawing life-sustaining treatment both may – and usually do – accelerate patients' deaths, neither practice attracts criminal liability on the part of the doctor.

The use of these special defences results in an unequal application of the law as between lay persons and doctors, which conflicts with Dicey's traditional view of the Rule of Law (by which he emphasised the principle of equality before the law). Nonetheless, there is a compelling argument that this is fitting and right where doctors play a (proper) part in ending their patients' lives, because they perform such a special function in society. As a profession which collectively has the authority to do things which the rest of the population are not permitted to do (Rhodes 1998: 172),[5] it seems clear that they should be afforded the kind of protection which adequately reflects their special status and the duties which arise from that. In his article 'The Doctor's Defence and Professional Ethics', Tur states that '. . . if one

---

1 See, for example, Ashworth 2006: 129.   2 See, especially, Otlowski 2000: 182.

3 The principle of double effect is generally used where a doctor administers medication for killing pain where he foresees that the patient will die as a result. In such a case, the courts use a narrower definition of intention than in other cases where death is foreseen.

4 The acts and omissions distinction is generally used where life-sustaining treatment is withdrawn or withheld. In these cases, the court will interpret the withdrawal as an omission rather than as an act, as an omission does not incur liability unless there is a duty to act.

5 As Stell 1998: 245 has said, '[p]hysicians routinely do what would be criminal for non-physicians to do.'

recognises that doctors have ethical duties which differentiate them from non-doctors one may seek to have these differences recognised by the criminal law.' He goes on to say that any exception to the current homicide laws which exists in respect of doctors can quite patently be justified on the basis of their 'professional status' and their role. (Tur 2002: 91).

Although some might argue that the profession is no longer held in the same high regard as it traditionally was,[6] it is still so held by a large proportion of the population (Rhodes 1998: 173) and certainly by the older generation. Perceptions of 'superiority' have, of course, always existed,[7] and have encouraged criticism of the profession. Nonetheless, despite a growth in patient autonomy in recent years and the perceived change from paternalism[8] to (an albeit unequal) partnership between the doctor, the patient and the healthcare team,[9] the doctor, quite properly, remains the person who has the ultimate responsibility for the patient, particularly in end-of-life decision-making.

Such decision-making has become more difficult and problematic in this age of rapidly developing medical technology whereby doctors now have the ability to indefinitely and artificially maintain patients on the 'threshold of death'; as Spicer J said in the Ohio case of *Leach, Guardian v Akron General Medical Center et al* (68 Ohio Misc. 1; 426 N.E. 2d 809; 1980 Ohio Misc. LEXIS 67; 22 Ohio Op. 3d 49):

> Since man, through his ingenuity, has created a new state of human existence – minimal human life sustained by man-made life supports – it must now devise and fashion rules and parameters for that existence. That is the business this court is faced with. It is not an easy question to answer. It deals with many of our most basic legal, medical and moral concepts.
>
> (*Leach per* Spicer J at 812)[10]

The same sentiments as to the implications of developing technology and the resulting inability of the law to deal adequately with it were also recognised by the Californian Appeals Court in *N.L. Barber, Petitioner v the Superior*

---

6 Especially after, for example, Dr Harold Shipman and the events brought to light in the Bristol Royal Infirmary Inquiry at www.bristol-inquiry.org.uk (accessed 21 June 2006).
7 Although the era of so called 'iatrocracy' ('rule by doctors') is said to be over; Jacob 1988: 6.
8 'Paternalism is most often defined in terms of one person's acting in what she takes to be another person's best interests even when that other may wish to act otherwise.' Fairbairn 1991: 122–3. For a detailed discussion on paternalism, see, for example, Childress 1982.
9 See, for example, the House of Lords Select Committee (HLSC) 1993–4 (HL Paper 21–I): para 4, and the Bristol Royal Infirmary Inquiry above.
10 Although the book concentrates mainly on 'UK' cases, significant reference is made to US cases because, although not legally binding, they have been and are used as precedents by UK judges. Some reference is also made to cases from other common law systems.

Court of Los Angeles County, Respondent; The People, Real Party in interest. R.J. Nedjl, Petitioner v The Superior Court of Los Angeles County, Respondent (147 Cal. App. 3d 1006; 1983 Cal. App. LEXIS 2256; 195 Cal. Rptr. 484; 47 A.L.R. 4th 1), where Compton J said that he was '. . . forced to evaluate petitioners' conduct within the context of the woefully inadequate framework of the criminal law' (*Barber and Nedjl* at 1014). Similarly, in *Airedale NHS Trust v Bland* ([1993] 2 WLR 316), Lord Lowry said that '[e]xisting law may not provide an acceptable answer to the new legal questions raised [by] . . . the ability to sustain life artificially . . .' (*Bland* at 380).[11]

These few examples demonstrate that the criminal law simply does not cater for these new technological solutions, and that, in its present form, it is an inappropriate method by which to deal with medical end-of-life issues.[12] However, as it is necessary for the medical profession to be safeguarded during the carrying out of their functions, and as the legislature has not provided adequate statutory defences, it has been left to the judges to devise their own methods of doing so. That they have created defences which exist as exceptions to the law is incontrovertible, but that they continue to deny that this is what has been done merely perpetuates existing anomalies and inconsistencies.[13]

As a starting point, the two 'defences' need to be brought out into the open and formally acknowledged. As traditional and long-standing solutions which have been successfully used for a number of years, it is tentatively proposed here that they could provide the basis for a statutory defence in respect of homicide charges against doctors and that, in order to avoid the murder label, a new offence, of perhaps medical mercy killing, could be created which would operate under the auspices of a graded homicide law,[14] and would include *explicit* consideration of context, role and motive. Arguably, these are the factors which distinguish between euthanasia and murder, but they are also vital in the ascription of liability, which simply cannot and should not rely on intention and causation alone.

Incorporating these two defences into legislation would clarify the law; it would satisfy practical aspects in its use and validation of existing practices

---

11 This is the case where artificial nutrition and hydration was withdrawn from a young victim of the Hillsborough football disaster who had been left in a persistent vegetative state (PVS; now generally referred to as permanent vegetative state) for an explanation of which see Mason & McCall Smith 2006: 578.

12 There is substantial agreement that the criminal law of murder is inappropriate, for example, Lacey, Wells and Quick 2003: 619; Biggs 2001: 16; Otlowski (2000); and Ashworth (1996).

13 As Otlowski 2000: 182 has said, the reluctance of the courts to deal with the matter openly and providing an '. . . appropriate defence [is] . . . perhaps understandable, in that the courts do not want to be seen creating special defences for doctors . . .'.

14 Interestingly, the Law Commission has recommended a type of graded homicide law in its new Consultation Paper LCCP No. 177 (2005) *A new Homicide Act for England and Wales?* www.lawcom.gov.uk/docs/cp177_web.pdf (accessed 21 June 2006). More is said on this in the first chapter below.

and in so doing, would show confidence in the judiciary. It would also counter the medical profession's reluctance to a major change in the law. Creating a new medically-orientated offence would satisfy the principles of labelling and correspondence, and, provided its conditions were satisfied, would legally protect a class of persons who possess unique rights. These are some of the reasons (see chapter 7 for more) which explain why this would be a better alternative to, for example, legalising voluntary euthanasia or assisted suicide, as is proposed in the hitherto unsuccessful Assisted Dying for the Terminally Ill Bill (2004 and 2005). This is but one of the many developments in this area of law in recent years. For example, the Mental Capacity Act 2005 (not yet in force at the time of writing) defines persons who lack capacity and provides a checklist for ascertaining an incapacitated person's best interests.[15] The Act also introduces liability for wilful neglect, i.e. omissions liability in s 44, as does s 5 of the Domestic Violence, Crime and Victims Act 2005 (allowing the death of a child or vulnerable adult). Another new piece of legislation, the Criminal Justice Act 2003, includes aggravating and mitigating factors which can be taken into account in sentencing.

As to legislation elsewhere in the world, the Netherlands has formalised existing practices in its Termination of Life on Request and Assisted Suicide (Review Procedures) Act 2001 (which came into force in 2002), while Belgium also passed its Euthanasia Act in 2002. Both Acts provide that doctors will not be prosecuted if they comply with specific conditions. Contrary to popular belief, they do not legalise euthanasia or assisted suicide.

In the meantime, the courts in the UK have been dealing with a number of controversial and well-publicised cases. In 2003, the Court of Appeal was faced with another case in the continuing and problematic saga of what has been called 'oblique' or 'indirect'[16] intention in *R v Mathews and Alleyne* ([2003] WL 117062), where some clarification was given as to the status of the foresight direction in intention. The courts also heard more heartrending cases of requests for treatment withdrawal from young children in *Wyatt* (five cases in all: *Portsmouth NHS Trust v Derek Wyatt, Charlotte Wyatt (by her Guardian)* ([2005] 1 FLR 21 (1)); *Portsmouth Hospitals NHS Trust v Charlotte Wyatt* ([2005] EWHC 117 (Fam) (2)); *Wyatt v Portsmouth NHS Trust and Wyatt (by her Guardian) (No 3)* ([2005] 2 FLR 480 (3)); *Re Wyatt*

---

15 Where a patient is incompetent, treatment decisions must be made in the patient's 'best interests'. This is the standard 'test' used in the UK to make treatment decisions on behalf of incompetent patients. It is, allegedly, a more objective test than the 'substituted judgment' test used in the US, i.e. what the patient himself would choose if he were competent. More will be said about the best interests test in the discussion on *Bland* (1993) in chapter 3 below, but suffice it to say at this stage that the test has been criticised mainly on the grounds of its paternalism, which does nothing to promote the autonomy of the patient.

16 Commonly used to describe the foresight element of intention. See, for example, Williams (1987) and Norrie (1989).

(A Child) (Medical Treatment: Continuation of Order) ([2005] 3 FCR 263 (4)); *Re Wyatt* ([2005] 4 All ER 1325 (5)); in *Re Winston-Jones (A Child) (Medical Treatment: Parent's Consent)* ([2004] All ER (D) 313); in *Re L (Medical Treatment: Benefit)* ([2004] EWHC 2713 (Fam)) and in *An NHS Trust v MB* ([2006] EWHC 507 (Fam)). Furthermore, Leslie Burke, suffering from spino-cerebellar ataxia, successfully challenged the GMC's Guidelines on treatment withdrawal in the High Court (in *R (Burke) v General Medical Council et al* ([2004] WL 1640202 (1)) but lost his appeal in *R on the Application of Oliver Leslie Burke v the General Medical Council et al* ([2005] EWCA Civ 1003 (2)). At the same time, in what has been described as a (further) instance of 'death tourism' (Biggs 2005: 45), it was held in *Re Z (An Adult: Capacity); Local Authority v Z and Another* ([2004] EWHC 2817 (Fam)), that competent persons who wished to travel to Switzerland to commit suicide could not be prevented by the UK authorities from doing so.

Meanwhile in the USA, the case law on withdrawing treatment was and had been well settled until the contentious case of *Schlindler v Schiavo* (851 So 2d 182 (Fla 2d DCA, 2003), 17 March 2005 (Order list 544 US), US Court of Appeals for the 11th Circuit, No 05–11628, 25 March 2005). The case arose following a conflict between the patient's husband (who requested that her life-sustaining treatment be withdrawn) and her parents (who opposed treatment withdrawal) compounded by some uncertainty as to whether or not she was in a PVS. Following intervention by the Florida State Governor to prevent removal of her treatment (which intervention was subsequently held to be unconstitutional), it was nonetheless withdrawn and she died soon afterwards following this protracted litigation.[17] Cases like this demonstrate that the courts have seen an excess of defensive litigious behaviour in recent years. A new individualistic human rights culture has made patients more aware of their rights of self-determination especially when it comes to dying.

The questions surrounding euthanasia and assisted suicide are not going to go away, and while this remains the case, the law must be able to deal with these questions effectively and fairly. Continued and singular over-reliance on the problematic concepts of intention and causation at the expense of ignoring real life circumstances and complex real life factors such as emotion and motive is not the way forward. The first chapter of this book will therefore commence by examining intention, foresight and the problems associated with the mental element in murder.

17 For details of the case see, for example, Mareiniss (2005).

Chapter 1

The concept of intention

> There is no term fraught with greater ambiguity than that venerable Latin phrase that haunts Anglo-American criminal law: mens rea.
>
> (Fletcher 1978: 398)

Euthanasia and murder

A standard dictionary defines euthanasia as 'the act or practice of putting painlessly to death, *especially* in cases of incurable suffering' (*Chambers' Twenty First Century Dictionary*).[1] To the layman, this may imply two things: firstly, that it is at least a morally, if not legally, permissible activity and secondly, if it is not permissible, then it is an independent offence called 'euthanasia'. What is less evident is that any person who carries out euthanasia is liable to be prosecuted for murder, because euthanasia is the intentional taking of life. This is so, despite the fact that euthanasia is carried out with compassionate motives, because the criminal law ostensibly takes no account of motives except at the sentencing stage.

Although the subject matter here is inherently medical, the criminal law concepts of intention and causation are the governing factors in establishing blameworthiness and liability. However, the criminal law of murder, with its emphasis on intention particularly, is an inappropriate way to deal with medical end-of-life issues because firstly, it is inconsistent and indeed impossible to combine the criminal intent of a murderer with the daily life of a medical professional (Wilson and Smith 1995: 389). Secondly, the whole concept of *mens rea* itself is fraught with the inherent problems of assessing intention, and the dangers of subjectivity, semantics, 'constructibility' (Griffiths 1994: 47) and 'decontextualisation' (Norrie 1986: 221).

In the medical scenario in particular, a doctor is not thinking about the

---

1 Compare the definition in the *Oxford Dictionary of English* (2003) which defines it as 'the painless killing of a patient suffering from an incurable and painful disease or in an irreversible coma'.

implications of intention and causation when he is going about his daily work. Rather, his concern is with treating and caring for his patients in the most effective way possible. In performing this function, there are important 'situational' factors he has to take into account, such as the context in which an event occurs, the special doctor/patient relationship and the obligations and duties imposed by that relationship. It also includes the physical space where the events take place[2] (generally a hospital) together with the factors the parties would thus have to consider in making any decisions. This, in turn, would encompass the seriousness of the patient's condition, his capacity or competence, his ability (or not) to give consent and the motives of the parties concerned. As Pellegrino (1996: 180) states:

> [i]ntentions cannot be assessed in isolation from the other components of moral events. They must be related to the nature of the act in question, the circumstances under which it is performed, and its consequences.

However, the criminal law ignores both these and other elements inherent in euthanasia, and anomalies have arisen in the law of homicide as a direct result of judges, trained in criminal law, deciding issues which actually lie within the medical domain. The criminal law errs, not only in applying a criminal standard to doctors when they are making end-of-life decisions, but also in ignoring the context in which such decisions are made. A doctor is required by law to act in his patient's best interests and it is both inappropriate and contradictory to confuse that role with the criminal intent required to satisfy the *mens rea* for murder (Wilson and Smith 1995: 389).

What is murder?

There is no statutory definition of murder,[3] but there have been many unsuccessful attempts to place the offence on a statutory footing.[4] The offence therefore remains a common law one while efforts to explain its meaning continue. It has, for example, been said that murder is a 'result' crime, because a forbidden consequence – death – has to be shown as part of

---

2 See, for example, Croall 1998: 8.
3 Coke's seventeenth century definition still tends to be used: 'Murder is when a man of sound memory, and of the age of discretion, unlawfully killeth within any county of the realm any reasonable creature *in rerum natura* under the king's peace, with malice aforethought, either expressed by the party or implied by law . . .' reproduced in Ormerod 2005: 429.
4 Commencing with the Criminal Law Revision Committee Cmnd. 7844 (1980) and, since then, Law Com No. 143 (1985); the HLSC (1988–9) Law Com No. 177 (1989) (and see generally, LCCP 122 (1992) and Law Com No. 218 (1993), both of which dealt only with non-fatal offences against the person).

the *actus reus*.[5] This, however, does not define the elements of the offence and indeed, it has been suggested that it would be futile to attempt to do so.[6] However, we do know that the *actus reus* element of the offence is that a person causes death by an unlawful act or omission, and that the *mens rea* element is 'malice aforethought'. This presently encompasses not only an intention to kill (or cause grievous bodily harm),[7] but also a much wider concept of indirect or oblique intention (foresight of virtual certainty). Essentially, this means that a person can be guilty of murder where he has foreseen that a virtually certain consequence of what he does is that someone will be killed, but it is not his intention to cause that consequence.

In the medical setting, this can be seen when a doctor withholds or withdraws life-sustaining treatment from a patient, and where he increases pain-killing medication to a patient which has the potential to hasten death. In both situations, the doctor foresees that the patient will die following his act or omission, although that is not his intention. As the legal meaning of intention has been extended to include foresight, this could therefore result in a doctor being found guilty of murder when he withdraws life-sustaining treatment, or increases medication which he foresees will hasten death. However, it will be seen that the courts use 'tactics' which, together with the adoption of a narrower definition of intention, avoid liability on the part of the doctor.

What is intention?

Psychologists and philosophers[8] have often discussed the concepts of 'intention' and 'intentionality', but in the same way that defining murder is problematic, so also is the concept of intention. Jefferson, for example, adopts a layman's understanding of the term in saying that 'intention covers the state of mind where the accused aims or decides to kill' (Jefferson 2006: 88).

---

5 Compare with a 'conduct' crime, where one does not have to prove anything other than that the prohibited conduct took place; see Jefferson 2006: 46. The distinction is useful because it explains the link between intention and causation in murder; where a result is required as part of the offence definition '. . . implicit in that result element is a causation requirement'. Robinson 1995: 199.

6 See, for example, Lacey 1993: 642.

7 'Presently,' because the law may change in response to the recommendations contained in the new LCCP No. 177 (2005): paras 1.38 and 1.39. The recommendation is that intentional killing (which includes oblique intention) should be confined to an intent to kill and not to do serious harm. This is categorised as first degree murder and carries the mandatory life sentence. Second degree murder on the other hand would cover the situation where the offender intended to do serious harm, but not to kill. This would carry a discretionary life maximum penalty.

8 Such as Searle 1983: 84–99; Anscombe 1976; and Hart 1968: 116 *et seq.*

Aiming towards, or indeed making it our purpose to achieve a certain consequence, encompasses the idea of a plan or an objective the agent aims for in order to do something, or even the idea of doing something with a view to bringing about that which he wants or desires. Intention should not, however, be confused with desire, as anyone can intend a consequence, even if he does not desire it (Moore 1987: 246). Alternatively, it has been suggested that something can be intended if it is chosen, or if it is within the actor's control (Hart 1968: 121–2) and more controversially, it has been said that intention is the reason for acting. Certainly this is incorrect because motive, and not intention, is the reason for acting (Horder 2000: 173).[9]

None of these enable a clearer understanding of the concept and meaning of intention, and neither does identifying its purpose. We know that the purpose of *mens rea* is to gauge blameworthiness; the more deliberate an act, the more blameworthy it is. Horder has said that one of the roles that intention plays is to constitute the criminal wrong (Horder 1995: 681). He is correct in so far as the guilty act taken together with deliberateness constitutes the crime and that therefore, to a certain extent, intention, once found, does play an (albeit limited) role as an indicator of blameworthiness. It also indicates that a greater degree of blame or culpability is at stake than in a reckless or (grossly) negligent act. However, it is also true that assessing blame or culpability more fully depends on other contextual issues which the criminal law (seemingly) excludes. Horder acknowledges this when he concedes that the degree of blame or culpability is measured by factors other than intention, such as sanity, maturity, voluntariness and control.

It has also been said that intention determines criminal liability for the consequences of actions (Duff 1989: 76). If so, then any imputation of intention must link the agent's mental attitude with the results of his conduct. This definition ascribes responsibility for an intentional action. However, a person acting unintentionally can be just as responsible for wrongs as one who acts intentionally. While saying this is not fatal to the argument, it does nonetheless tell us that there is no point in relying solely on a definition of intention to demarcate the limits of criminal responsibility (Horder 1995: 680). Where euthanasia is concerned, other considerations, such as those noted by Horder above, together with the motive of the actor, the consent of the 'victim' and the status of the parties, are also relevant in the ascription of liability. These are the very important factors which distinguish euthanasia from murder and the cases examined in the following chapters show that the courts do consider these, although they would not admit to doing so. The consequence of this is that the concept of intention is applied inconsistently according to a judicial

---

9 For contrasting views on this, see, for example, Begley (1998); Lord Hailsham in *Hyam v DPP* ([1975] AC 55): 73; and LCCP 131 (1993): para 2.59, where the Law Commission confirmed that 'good motive' operated as the reason for the accused's acting as he did.

discretion which is arguably dependent on the status of the actor and the reasons for his actions (that is, his motives). This, in turn relates to preconceptions as to the blameworthiness and culpability of the actor and the role he plays in society.

The courts, intention and foresight

Where it can be adequately proved that the defendant intended to kill (that is, in cases of 'direct' intention) no problems arise, but defining the foresight element of intention has created problems for the courts since *DPP v Smith* ([1961] AC 290), *Hyam*, and *R v Moloney* ([1985] AC 905). In the latter, it was held that the *mens rea* of murder is the intention to cause death or really serious bodily harm. However, the court said that no elaboration should be given as to the meaning of intention in this context except in rare cases and that if such elaboration was considered necessary, the jury should be asked to consider two questions. Firstly, was death or serious injury a natural consequence of the defendant's act and secondly, did the defendant foresee it as a natural consequence of his act? If the answer to both these questions was 'yes', then it could be inferred that he intended that consequence. Lord Bridge explained that unless foresight of the probable consequences was 'little short of overwhelming', it was not intention, but could only be evidence from which intention could be inferred. Thus, although he confirmed that foresight was not the same as intention, he unfortunately did not define what intention was.

In *R v Hancock*, *R v Shankland* ([1986] AC 455), as in *Moloney*, it was again noted that foresight was not the same as intention. However, Lord Lane, reading the judgment of the court, saw the *Moloney* guideline on the meaning of 'natural consequence' to be misleading; he explained that what it meant was '. . . that it must have been highly likely that the defendant's act would cause death or serious injury before the inference can be drawn that he had the necessary intent' (*Hancock* and *Shankland* at 460–1). On appeal (which was dismissed) it was said that the judge, if he had to explain to the jury at all, should only explain that the greater the probability of the consequences, the more likely it was that the consequence was foreseen and that if it was foreseen, the more likely it was that it was intended.

The case of *R v Nedrick* ([1986] 3 All ER 1) followed, in which it was held that where a defendant performs an act resulting in death, and the primary desire or motive was not to harm the victim, the judge should explain that intention is not desire. The judge should then ask two questions of the jury: how probable was the consequence that resulted from the defendant's act, and did the defendant foresee that consequence? If death or really serious injury were foreseen as virtually certain consequences, the jury could infer that the defendant intended to kill or harm. In setting out his decisive test for intention, Lord Lane said:

... the jury should be directed that they are not entitled to infer the necessary intention unless they feel sure that death or serious bodily harm was a virtual certainty (barring some unforeseen intervention) as a result of the defendant's actions and that the defendant appreciated that such was the case.

(*Nedrick per* Lord Lane at 4)

Again this does not define intention, but rather, simply reiterates that foresight, even of virtual certainty, does not constitute intention.

The case of *R v Walker and Hayles* ((1989) 90 Cr App R 226) did nothing to cast light on its meaning either. As in *Moloney, Hancock* and *Nedrick*, it was explained that there was no need to elaborate in straightforward cases on the meaning of intention, because the relevant intention is an intention to kill. It was agreed that the difficulty only arises when the defendant brings about a result he is not trying to achieve and does not want. Only in these rare cases does the judge need to elaborate. The Court of Appeal (rather surprisingly) confirmed that 'very high degree of probability' as used in the lower court, was not a misdirection, but that 'virtual certainty' (as used in *Nedrick*) would be better. In this case, intention could be inferred from a 'very high probability of death'.[10] The court went on to say that if and when the two questions posed in *Nedrick* were answered in the affirmative, one would be entitled to draw an inference that the defendant was intending or trying to kill the victim.

Five years later, in *R v Scalley* ([1995] Crim LR 504), it was again confirmed that foresight was no more than an evidential guide. It was also noted, as in *Walker and Hayles*, that once the two questions posed by Lord Lane in *Nedrick* had been asked, there was a third question to be asked, namely whether in light of all the circumstances, including the question of foresight, the intent to kill or cause serious harm was made out.

The meaning of intention in the 'foresight' cases arose again in the case of *R v Woollin* ([1998] 4 All ER 103)[11] but, despite hopes to the contrary,[12] was not resolved by the House of Lords. In this case, a father threw his three-month-old son against a wall in a fit of temper. The child suffered a fractured skull and died. Woollin's defence was based on his having had no intention to kill or alternatively, on provocation. He was found guilty of murder. The Court of Appeal dismissed his appeal but his subsequent appeal to the House of Lords was allowed because of a misdirection by the Recorder at first instance. He initially instructed the jury according to the classic *Nedrick*

---

10 Jefferson 2006: 95 rightly criticises the court's equation of high probability with virtual certainty, as they are not the same – one is more likely to occur than the other.

11 Much of the analysis to the end of this section can be found at Williams and Dingwall 2004: 72–3.

12 By, for example, Norrie 1999: 533, and Wilson (1999).

direction, but the following day in continuing his summing up, he directed the jury in terms of 'substantial risk'. The court, in endorsing and applying *Nedrick*, held that 'substantial risk' unacceptably expanded the scope of the mental element of murder because it was wider than 'virtual certainty' as understood in *Nedrick*. The Crown accordingly alleged either that *Nedrick* was wrongly decided or that Lord Lane's guidelines in that case did not apply.

Lord Steyn in his answer to this contention reviewed previous cases and conceded, unsurprisingly, that they did not adequately resolve the law. He followed Lord Lane's direction (subject to changing 'infer' to 'find'), but then totally misunderstood its meaning by confirming that '[its] effect . . . is that a result foreseen as virtually certain is an intended result' (*Woollin* at 110).[13] As noted earlier, the previous understanding of this passage has been that foresight of virtual certainty of a consequence allows the jury only to infer intention; it is not actually intention. The direction does not say that the jury must find intention; it merely confirms that they are entitled to do so (Williams 2001a: 43).[14]

The misdirection in *Woollin* was then unfortunately maintained in *Re A (Children) (Conjoined Twins: Surgical Separation)* ([2000] 4 All ER 961)[15] where both Ward and Brooke LJJ also '. . . misinterpreted the *mens rea* element of murder by holding that death *is* intended where it is foreseen as a virtual certainty' (Williams and Dingwall 2004: 73). Moreover, Robert Walker LJ then complicated matters further by adopting yet another approach to the question of intention. He held that *Woollin* was inapplicable because, following Lord Scarman's direction in *Gillick v West Norfolk and Wisbech AHA* ([1986] AC 112) – which in itself was inconsistent with the standard approach to intention – criminal intent is incompatible with the *mens rea* of a physician who is bona fide exercising his clinical judgment.[16]

Based on these decisions, therefore, what then is the definition of intention? What is the magic or 'mystery ingredient' that converts foresight into intention? (Card 2006: 96)[17]. As Allen asked: '[I]f foresight of a consequence as a virtual certainty is not equivalent to intention, by what process is the jury to convert it *into* intention?' (Allen 2005: 63).

While this question was not directly answered in *R v Mathews and Alleyne*,[18]

---

13 Note the contrasting views held by Smith 1998a: 891 (that a result foreseen as virtually certain should be intended) and Griew 1987: 82 (that suggestions that virtual certainty may be evidence from which intention can be inferred is an '. . . unnatural way to talk, and we ought to give it up'.)
14 See also Wilson 1999: 456.
15 Hereinafter referred to as *Re A (Children)*. This is the well-known case where the Court of Appeal granted a declaration that an operation to separate conjoined twins would be lawful despite the fact that it was known the weaker twin would die during the operation.
16 See text to, and footnote 30 in Williams 2001b: 186.
17 A question asked by others, such as for example, Griew 1987: 81.
18 And see Williams and Dingwall 2004: 76.

the last case in the series to date, the Court of Appeal nonetheless clarified the status of Lord Lane's 'entitlement to find' direction in *Nedrick* by correctly adopting the opinion expressed by Norrie who said that the word ' "entitled" is permissive rather than obligatory' in the sense that it '. . . suggests that the jury may . . . identify intention, but, alternatively may not do so' (Norrie 1999: 537). According to Wilson, the terminology in the direction is set out '. . . in the conditional negative':

> . . . it does not say '*you must* find intention *if* the defendant foresaw the consequences as certain'; rather it says '*do not* find intention *unless* the defendant . . . foresaw the consequence as certain'.
>
> (Wilson 1999: 456)

In *Mathews and Alleyne*, the victim had been forced into the appellants' car, was driven to the nearest river and thrown over the parapet of a bridge into the wide and fast-flowing water and left to drown. Counsel for the appellants argued that Lord Steyn's comment in *Woollin* had moved the court 'away from a rule of evidence to a rule of substantive law'. In denying this, Rix LJ said that '[i]n our judgment . . . the law has not yet reached a *definition* of intent in murder in terms of appreciation of virtual certainty' and that there was '. . . very little to choose between a rule of evidence and a rule of substantive law' (*Mathews and Alleyne* at paras 43 and 45) particularly in this case where the appellants' omission to rescue the victim reinforced the inference of their intention to kill. As a result of this decision (and indeed its predecessors, *Nedrick* and *Woollin*) juries have been provided with a 'get-out clause' whereby they may decide that although the defendant foresaw death as virtually certain, he or she did not intend it (Wilson 1999: 456).

What does the intention/foresight distinction mean?

The decision in *Mathews and Alleyne* effectively gives the jury the opportunity to distinguish between intention and foresight by finding that a defendant may well have foreseen, but did not intend, a consequence. This reflects the common sense view that, despite what the law implies, we do not necessarily intend what we foresee. A simple, but effective example given by Jefferson explains:

> . . . intention and foresight, even of a certainty, can be completely different concepts. By imbibing alcohol you may foresee a hangover as a certain result, but one would not say that you intend to have a hangover.
>
> (Jefferson 2006: 89)[19]

---

19 And see generally his chapter 3.

This does not, of course, assist juries when they have to make decisions unaided by judges, who merely give advice as to how intention can be found rather than saying what it really means. However, Norrie's analysis of direct and oblique intention might assist. He sees two approaches to intention which he calls the 'orthodox subjectivist approach' (the dominant approach in the UK, which he asserts is supported by Glanville Williams and in Smith and Hogan), and the 'morally substantive approach' (which he claims is shown in Duff, Gardner and Horder's work). The former is a factual approach to intention in the sense of aiming or meaning, while in the latter, 'the emphasis is not on whether the individual actually did conceive an intention but rather, on . . . whether [a] person's intention was *in its intrinsic quality* morally good or bad.' To the moral substantivist, the approach is concerned with moral values; '[t]he moral quality in the act is more important than a precise distinguishing of different psychological states' (Norrie 2001: 50) which is why this approach would recognise mercy killing, but the orthodox subjectivist would simply see mercy killing and murder in the same light. The latter would see nothing artificial in holding that a consequence foreseen as virtually certain can be an intended consequence as long as it is necessary for the desired end, because foresight of virtual certainty is as much of a certainty that one can expect, barring the intervention of the unexpected. Yet as Norrie goes on to say:

> The unexpected may defeat the achievement of our purpose or render our calculations of means and side-effects wrong, but it does not cancel our intentions and purposes whether those are either direct or indirect.
>
> (Norrie 2001: 48)[20]

The 'morally substantive approach' is the most accurate, realistic and less arbitrary of the two approaches and is the one the courts adopt – albeit unadmittedly – in the medical context, where intention is interpreted in a way which is not only totally inconsistent with other criminal cases, but is also contrary to the 'test' established in *Nedrick*. Cases such as *Gillick*,[21] *Re A (Children)* and *R v Moor* (*The Times* 12 May 1999)[22] show how the courts have tailored the legal definition of intention in order to absolve the doctor through a 'morally substantive' analysis which looks to the medical practitioner's motive.

In *Gillick*, a parent objected to a circular which permitted a doctor to prescribe the contraceptive pill to a minor without her parents' consent.

---

20 And see generally: 47–50.
21 The same idea was expressed in *R v Bourne* ([1939] 1 KB 689) (although now superseded by legislation).
22 For which see the next chapter.

Mrs Gillick claimed that if he prescribed the Pill, the doctor would be aiding and abetting the commission of unlawful sexual intercourse under s 28 of the Sexual Offences Act 1956. Lord Scarman said that the essential ingredient of the offence was a 'guilty mind' but that as long as the doctor was exercising his clinical judgment in a bona fide manner, then that sufficed to negate the possibility of any guilty mind. As was noted earlier, the direction would be completely inconsistent with the *Woollin* direction.

In *Re A (Children)*, by saying that the extended meaning of intention (which includes foresight) was 'not appropriate' (*Re A (Children) per* Brooke LJ at 1050) and that it 'was to be given its "natural ordinary meaning" ',[23] the court employed a direct intention argument[24] in order to acknowledge the moral element in the case. Again in *Moor*, Hooper J confined the intention direction to 'purpose' alone rather than giving the relevant *Woollin* direction (see next chapter).

All three cases support a number of points. Firstly, they are examples of cases where the courts have manipulated intention to achieve a result that more closely matches the judges' perception of justice in response to their sympathy for certain types of defendant perceived as being non-culpable; looking at the status of the actor in this way by implication involves a pre-judgment based on motive. Secondly, that despite foresight of a consequence as a virtual certainty, the defendant can nonetheless be found not to have intended that consequence and thirdly, they show how ill-equipped criminal law concepts are in dealing with medical cases where moral dilemmas are raised (Ashworth 1996: 174–5). As Ashworth states:

. . . the courts have striven to exculpate doctors for decisions taken in medical contexts which would probably, in almost all other situations, lead to the imposition of criminal liability . . . Rather than commit themselves to one view or the other . . . judges seem to have shifted between

---

23 That is, purpose; the point is made by Norrie 2001: 58. There is a difference between intention and purpose which is set out by both Ormerod 2005: 436 and the LCCP No. 177 (2005): para 4.32, where it is said that '. . . a purpose is a reason for doing something . . . in contrast to an intention, which accompanies the action . . .' Quoting White, the Commission goes on to observe that 'we may do things *with* an intention but *for* a purpose . . .' Purpose here is therefore more like motive than intention.

24 Such as appeared in *R v Steane* ([1947] KB 997). This is also an example of a case (although not 'medically' based) where the court adopted a narrow, inconsistent definition of intention (and accounted for motive). Steane appealed against a conviction of assisting the enemy under wartime regulations by making daily broadcasts on the radio on behalf of the Germans. It transpired that he had done so under threats to his family and himself. The court held that the act was not carried out with the specific intention required (essentially because his motive was to save his family and not assist the enemy), but there is no doubt that while Steane was ostensibly acting to save his family, he must have realised the 'virtual certainty' of his assisting the enemy by so doing.

narrower and broader meanings of intention in order to distinguish between those with 'worthy' and those with 'unworthy' motives.

(Ashworth 1996: 192 and 182)[25]

In cases involving a 'worthy' or good motive, the courts have departed from the standard definition of intention and, in order to reflect a doctor's good motive and his 'status and role' in society, have then invoked the relevant 'medical' defences (Tur 2002: 91).

Thus, despite contentions that the law in the UK does not differentiate between doctors and non-doctors[26] and despite claims that they are not treated in any way differently to any other class of persons (British Medical Association (BMA) 1993: 157),[27] the narrow interpretation of intention in medical cases shows discrepancies between the law as applied to doctors on the one hand and to lay persons on the other (Wilson 1995: 137).[28] While there is a conscious feeling that although the conclusions in these cases are exactly what we would desire them to be, the methods used to reach them are based on considerations such as social acceptability, motive, intuition, and the patient's condition, none of which have anything at all to do with intention.

It would seem, therefore, that in these cases of 'moral threshold' (Norrie 1999: 538)[29] and in any such cases that arise in the future, the court would have a number of options:

(a) it should use the so-called 'doctrine of entitlement' which originated in *Nedrick* to emphasise that the right to (infer or) 'find' intention does not mean the jury has to find it;

(b) it could go with the 'bolder alternative' of following Scarman in *Gillick* (as Walker LJ did in *Re A (Children)*), by giving a direction which excludes the standard test of intention (Wilson 1999: 458); or

(c) it could opt for direct intention only, as occurred in, for example, *Steane* and *Moor* and as the majority did in *Re A (Children)*.

25 Ashworth states that the courts appear to adopt a different definition depending on the circumstances of each case.

26 As alleged by Farquharson J in *R v Arthur* ([1981] 12 BMLR 1): 5. See also Otlowski 2000: 182.

27 See also *R v Adams* (1957) Crim LR 365 and Devlin J's summing up in the case, reproduced in Devlin 1986: 171.

28 Witness those cases involving doctors found not guilty, such as *Adams* (1957); *Arthur* (1981); *Bland* (1993); *Dr M. Irwin* (*The Sunday Times* 20 July 1997); *Dr D. Watson* (*The Scotsman* 11 June 1991); *R v Carr* (*The Sunday Times* 30 November 1986); *R v Lodwig* (*The Times* 16 March 1990) and *R v Moor* (1999).

29 Norrie (1999) defines this as 'such that even though the accused could foresee a result as virtually certain, it is so at odds with his moral conception of what he was doing that it could not be conceived as a result that he intended.'

All three options have been successfully used by the courts to date, and all three will continue to be viable options for as long as there is no clear definition of intention in its wider legal meaning.[30] Moreover, simply providing a statutory definition of intention would not supply an answer to the problem of the inability of the criminal law to deal appropriately with end-of-life issues. Similarly, the problem of the innate dangers in assessing a subjective notion such as intention will remain for as long as the criminal law continues to ignore the context in which decisions are made. The myriad factors which a doctor has to consider in the proper treatment of his patient, together with the problems inherent in a subjective concept such as intention, therefore form the basis of the remaining discussion in this chapter.

Some basic problems with intention

Subjectivity

The House of Lords in *Woollin* expressly noted that 'the mental element of murder is concerned with the subjective question of what was in the mind of the man accused of murder' (Lord Steyn at 108), but the subjectivity of intention was recognised long before this. For example, Stephen Brown J in *Moloney* said that, '. . . you cannot take the top of a man's head off and look into his mind . . .'[31] We have no evidence of and cannot prove intention because the only person who knows what is going on in his mind is the individual himself. Nonetheless, juries are expected 'to assess intention in all sorts of cases' (HLSC 1993–4: para 243) and in this, they are assisted by s 8 Criminal Justice Act 1967. The section states that:

> A court or jury in determining whether a person has committed an offence,
>
> (a) shall not be bound to infer that he intended or foresaw a result of his actions by reason only of its being a natural and probable consequence of those actions; but
> (b) shall decide whether he did intend or foresee that result by reference

---

30 See LC Report No. 290 (2004): para. 2.48 on this. www.lawcom.gov.uk/docs/lc290(2).pdf (accessed 22 June 2006). Also relevant here are the Law Commission's ongoing proposals in LCCP No. 177 (2005) to either adopt the definition of intention in the Draft Criminal Code (their Model 1) or to codify existing common law principles which would, in their view, retain the permissiveness not to find intention (their Model 2).

31 This is cited as an example by Duff 1990: 29 and see the comparison between 'dualism' and other mentalistic concepts in his chapter 6. Essentially, dualism distinguishes the mind from the body; humans are made up of two distinct elements – physical bodies and non-physical minds. Whereas bodies are public and observable, minds are private and inaccessible to public observation; see *Cambridge Dictionary of Philosophy* (1995).

to all the evidence drawing such inferences from the evidence as appear proper in the circumstances.

However, two criticisms can be made of the section. Firstly, it is concerned with how intention is proved if required and not with when intention or foresight is required (Card 2006: 143). Secondly, s 8 provides for a subjective test, which may cause difficulties for juries because while the test is subjective, the method of proof is objectively based on probability, natural consequences and the reasonable man (Carson 1995: 284).[32] At the end of the day all that the section and the common law doctrine of entitlement do is to permit the jury to infer (or find) that the accused intended the consequence. The advantage always lies with the accused because, as Devlin J noted in *Adams*, only he can say what he intended[33] and there is no one to know if he is lying or not and, other than considering the evidence, no way of disproving his claims.

Each individual may have more than one intention or purpose in acting

Quill has said that in most end-of-life situations there are 'multi-layered intentions'. In his account of his treatment of 'Diane', he lists seven different intentions he had when prescribing her barbiturates (Quill 1993: 1040). However, the law is concerned only with the presence of the intention required for a particular offence. Ashworth expresses this as follows:

> It is quite possible – indeed quite normal – to do things with more than one intention in mind . . . The approach of the criminal law, however, is generally not to ask with what intentions D committed the act, but to ask whether one particular intention was present when the act was committed. The law . . . is interested in the presence or absence of one particular intention – that specified in the definition of the offence charged – and not in conducting a general review of D's reasons for the behaviour in question.
>
> (Ashworth 2006: 175)

The quotation neatly and concisely expresses the uncompromising position in

---

32 The new 2nd edition of Carson and Bull (previously Bull and Carson's) *Handbook of psychology in legal contexts* was published in 2003, but the editors themselves concede that most chapters and authors in the 2nd edition are new, as its emphasis is different; *preface: xv.*

33 As Devlin 1986: 142 said, '. . . the real fight is about the intent. It is always the stronghold of the defence. It is the ground on which the accused has the advantage. The prosecution can only invite the jury to draw inferences . . . But . . . [the accused] . . . can assure them of what was truly in his mind.'

the UK, where intention forms the yardstick upon which judgments are made by the courts. This is in direct contrast to the Netherlands, where a new category of intention was recognised following an investigation which eventually formed the basis of the Remmelink Report.[34] It was found that a doctor acting with the primary intention of relieving pain could also act partly with the intention of hastening death. Despite an acknowledgement that intention was one of the most difficult concepts that had to be applied to the investigation, the investigators nonetheless recognised three categories of physician intention:

i.   (acting with) the explicit purpose of hastening the end of life;
ii. (acting) partly with the purpose of hastening the end of life;
iii. (acting while) taking into account the probability that the end of life will be hastened.

(Van der Maas *et al* 1992: 21)[35]

In their explanation of these categories, the investigators noted that the middle category was created specifically by them following responses from doctors that their intention did not fit into the other two categories. This solution was felt to solve the problem that doctors were not always able to show what their intention actually had been in a specific case. More importantly, the intermediate category of intention was aimed at the situation where '. . . death of the patient was not foremost in the physician's mind but neither was death unwelcome' (Van der Maas *et al* 1992: 21). There is an inherent honesty here on the part of both the investigators and the respondents that is patently lacking in this country.

'Constructibility' and 'directing the intention'

Griffiths has devised the notion of 'constructibility' (Griffiths 1994: 147),[36] in order to explain that doctors may 'construct' what is really a case of euthanasia into something entirely different according to what is allowed. This idea has been alternatively explained by Ann Davies thus:

When we are in circumstances in which . . . there is no possibility of independent verification of what our intentions were, and we want very much (not) to do a particular thing . . . we may be tempted to misrepresent our

34 Background information to which can be found in Keown 1995: fn 23. (The original Report was not translated into English, although the concurrent survey by Van der Maas *et al* (1992) was).
35 There has since been a more recent investigation by the same team for which see Fenigsen (2004).
36 See also Skene (2005) on the significance of this in the *Schiavo* case (2005).

own mental states in a way that misleads both ourselves and other people into thinking that it is permissible for us (not) to do it.

(Davies 1996: 118)[37]

This is similar to the idea that has been otherwise expressed as 'directing the intention' – that a person can '. . . change the nature of an action merely by shifting one's way of thinking about it' (Jonsen 1996: 44).[38] Anyone who is unhappy with his true intention can choose one intention rather than another (Anscombe 1976: 43) and thereby deny the truth of what he is doing. This is a well-recognised phenomenon known as a 'psychological defence mechanism' (Docker 1996: 142).[39] In the case of a doctor, for example, he could say that when he is switching off a ventilator, he is doing his job as a doctor and not performing an act (or an omission) that means a patient will die. Duff simply explains that:

> [a]ctions and events are identified and individuated only by our descriptions of them: what someone does can be described in various ways . . . and which of these . . . descriptions we offer depends . . . on our own interests . . .

(Duff 1990: 41)

There is nothing new in this sentiment. It is a truism in all cases where the cause of a consequence is questionable.

You may not intend all the consequences of your action

As noted earlier, unless it can be claimed that all the consequences of behaviour are absolutely certain (and this would be doubtful because of the intervention of unforeseeable events), then it would be virtually impossible to intend all the consequences of any act (or omission). The 'accordion effect' is an effect described by sociologists to show how an agent can perform many actions under the one description and yet not intend all of them.[40] Essentially this means that there are additional components to any action other than the more obvious bodily movements, and that these components result in the accordion effect. In medical terms the effect could be described as a doctor filling a hypodermic with a substance; he plunges it into the patient, he kills the pain, he kills the patient, he leaves himself open to prosecution, he gains

---

37 Compare Harris's 'argument from self-deception' in Harris 1985: 38.
38 Jonsen (1996) adopts Pascal's formulation.
39 Referring to Hunt, R., and see Grossman (1995). The Consultant Neurologist interviewed said that although this was a 'comfortable' way of looking at the issue, it was nonetheless ducking the issue to pretend that the patient's death was something else.
40 For a recent (and complex) analysis of the accordion effect see Bratman (2006).

publicity and he may implement a change in the law.[41] His intention may simply have been to help his patient with his pain, although it must, of course, be conceded that he may have foreseen some, but not necessarily all, of the consequences, especially where unexpected events occur. Nonetheless, it is patently easier to find responsible a person who intended a consequence, than it is where the actor simply foresaw that a consequence might occur.

As evidenced by the cases mentioned in this chapter, adopting a narrow interpretation of intention is one method by which responsibility (and liability) for consequences can be avoided and as will be seen in chapter 4 below, the principles of causation also place a limit on what consequences one is responsible for.

You can intend an action without intending to bring about the result

This is based on the argument made by some writers that there is a distinction between an intended action or omission (intending a result) and intentional actions or omissions (bringing about a result intentionally). As Duff explains:

> I do not intend the expected side effects of my actions, but I may be said to bring them about intentionally . . . [t]he concept of intention both does and does not encompass . . . side effects; it does in that they are brought about intentionally; it does not, in that the agent does not act with the intention of bringing them about.
>
> (Duff 1990: 76 and 80)

The distinction can be illustrated by an example given by Davis of pressing the brake of the car when a child runs out in front of it (Davis 1979: 59). This is obviously an intentional action carried out to avoid hurting the child, but is not an intended action because in no way was it part of what the driver was intending to do that day.

Another explanation for the distinction is based on the difference between future and immediate results; when acting intentionally, '. . . one is concerned . . . only with the immediate or concurrent results of those actions: in colloquial terms, with what the agent is, or was actually doing' (Buxton 1988: 485). Contrarily, an intended action is concerned with the future results of actions, in other words, aim or purpose. This suggests that in order for an activity to be intended, there must be some kind of plan (Anscombe 1983: 179–80) and that conversely, therefore, an intentional action can be performed without forming a prior intention or making a plan. However, it has

41 This is based on a formula used by Searle 1983: 98–9.

to be said that thinking of the distinction in terms of whether the actor has planned an event or not does not help to explain what at first glance appears to be a seemingly semantic problem. To say that the distinction is simply linguistic, as suggested by Devettere, is insufficient. He explained that the grammar of the word 'intentionally', when it is said that someone 'intentionally' caused death, does not support its meaning because:

> '[i]ntentionally' is an adverb and hence modifies the verb 'cause', not the noun 'death'. 'Intentionally' applies to the action of causing and not to the effect that is caused – the death.
>
> (Devettere 1990: 268)

While this is a correct grammatical explanation, it does not grasp the importance of the distinction which does, after all, differentiate between intending to perform an act (or omission) that causes death, and intending the death itself. The distinction emphasises the difference between acting *because of* an event, rather than *in spite of*, some event;[42] the reason the driver pressed his brakes in the example given earlier was because the child had run out in front of the car and not in spite of it.

There is no difference between an intention not to keep the patient alive and to end a life

In making the above claim, Fletcher disagrees with those who would argue that there is a moral distinction between an intention not to keep the patient alive and to end a life. In his view and following Kantian principle, there is no difference because if the end is the same, then the means are irrelevant (Fletcher, J. 1969: 68). In legal terms, of course, the difference is acknowledged in the distinction made by the courts between acts and omissions and killing and 'letting die'. A clear illustration of this can be seen by how carefully Lord Goff formulated the question as to whether or not it was justifiable to withdraw artificial nutrition and hydration from Anthony Bland:

> [t]he question is not whether it is in the best interests of the patient that he should die. The question is whether it is in the best interests of the patient that his life should be prolonged by the continuance of this form of medical treatment or care.
>
> (*Bland per* Lord Goff at 371)[43]

---

42 See Rehnquist CJ in *Vacco v Quill* (521 U.S. 793; S. Ct. 2293; 1997 U.S. LEXIS 4038; 138 L. Ed. 2d 834) at 15. This is fully discussed in the context of foreseen and intended effects in the section on choice, control and responsibility in chapter 2 below.
43 The case is more fully analysed in chapter 3.

As Lord Donaldson had previously done in *Re J (A Minor) (Wardship: Medical Treatment)* ([1990] 3 All ER 930: 936) in effect, he 'reversed' the way in which the question was asked in order to justify withdrawing the treatment, but it has to be said that the distinction relies to a great extent on semantics and linguistics. Nonetheless, it is a very convenient way in which liability can be avoided, although it can be contended that the intention in withdrawing treatment which is keeping the patient alive (that the patient dies) and the consequences (that the patient does die) can be the same in both situations.[44] Accordingly it must be factors other than intention which make a difference; certainly intention alone, especially bearing in mind the problems analysed above, is insufficient in itself to deal with the issues raised in the medical domain.

The distinction between foresight and intention does not aid in the determination of whether an agent or his action is right or wrong, good or bad

But the question must be asked – does it have to? A consequentialist[45] would say that '. . . actions are right and wrong only in so far as their consequences are good or bad' (Duff 1989: 87). Whether the action is intended or foreseen is therefore not important to a consequentialist; it is only the outcome, the benefit accruing from the action that categorises it as good or bad. Conversely, a non-consequentialist argument would hold that there is a distinction between direct and indirect intention and that only directly intended killing is the paradigm of murder. From this point of view, therefore, acts are right or wrong in themselves, irrespective or independently of their consequences.

When you come to a decision, '. . . *the rightness or wrongness . . .* [of what you are about to do] . . . *is determined by the reasons for and against it*' (Rachels 1986: 95); intention does not come into your consideration of the reasons. Accordingly, labelling the actor's mental state would not provide an absolute guide to the blameworthiness of his actions, but accounting for motive would. Admittedly, it does not explain whether a person acted intentionally or not, but it does explain why a person did what he did, and this can be used to assess a person's character as being either 'good' or 'bad'. This could be one explanation as to why, if we try to distinguish between a doctor who withdraws life-sustaining treatment and a 'malicious interloper' who does the same thing, we would find the latter liable, but the former not.[46]

---

44 Lord Mustill in *Bland* (1993) at 397 conceded that the intention was to cause death.
45 A consequentialist holds that there is no distinction between intention and foresight as long as the consequence is good; Reese (1980).
46 This is a comparison made by Lord Goff in *Bland* (1993) at 369 and is used extensively

Consideration of motive reinforces perceptions of non-blameworthiness and non-culpability and this is precisely why motive is central to the decision-making process. Sole reliance on and manipulation of intention in order to reach a 'correct' decision, together with the problems listed above, simply provide more evidence of the inappropriateness of applying criminal law concepts to medical decision-making. Moreover, the numerous factors a doctor has to consider when treating his patients, some of which will be briefly mentioned below, certainly have nothing to do with the 'criminal' intention discussed earlier in this chapter. Indeed, none of the considerations discussed are *per se* based upon the mental element of intention at all, but they do nonetheless form a central part of the way in which a doctor treats his patients and performs his role. They also reinforce the importance of situational factors.

Intention and context

Medical decisions are made and must be seen in the context in which they occur, because people's thoughts and behaviour are influenced by their environment:[47]

> [o]ur wishes are never formulated without a thought for the world in which we live . . . they are shaped partly by the constraints imposed upon us by that world.
>
> (Donnison and Bryson 1996/7: 162)

This would be especially true in a hospital environment where behaviour is significantly affected by the social arrangements, traditions and customs of such an institution (Wilson and Hernstein 1986: 24).[48]

Issues of context such as these were discussed at length by the medical experts and by Butler-Sloss P in the case of *B v An NHS Hospital Trust* ([2002] WL 347038),[49] where a tetraplegic patient being maintained on a ventilator which was keeping her alive, successfully applied for a declaration that the machine be switched off. Butler-Sloss P praised the evidence given by Dr Sensky in particular and it is useful to reproduce his views here, as they impress upon us the importance of taking surrounding circumstances into account when making a decision whether or not to proceed. He said:

throughout this book as it demonstrates the impossibility of relying solely on intention. Similar comparisons have been made by others to a stranger, an enemy or to a 'greedy nephew', for example, Brock 1989a: 343–4.

47 For more on this see, for example, Meier 1989: 131.
48 See also Hinkka *et al* (2002); Biggs 2001: 99, and Mann 1998: 17–20.
49 *Sub nom Re B (Consent to Treatment: Capacity)* ([2002] 1 FLR 1090) and *B (Adult: Refusal of Medical Treatment)* ([2002] EWHC 429 (Fam)).

... the clinicians ... looked too much at the decision, which was contrary to their advice and which they would not endorse, and not enough at the surrounding circumstances.

(B v An NHS Hospital Trust at 17)

Decisions as to appropriate medical treatment are not taken in isolation and it is precisely the circumstances surrounding end-of-life decision-making which differentiate them from the truly criminal scenarios envisaged when contemplating murder and the concept of intention. Situational pressures imposed by the circumstances,[50] such as a doctor's own perception of his professional competence and actual experience, particularly in treating terminally ill patients,[51] environmental factors like the attitude of family and friends (Kelly and Varghese 1996: 3), the quite natural instinct of self-protection and self-interest (Battin 1998: 38), fear of publicity (Solomon *et al* 1993: 19), the threat of sanctions (both disciplinary and legal), apprehensions that some acts were 'killing' the patient (Fried *et al* 1993: 726),[52] or simply that hastening a patient's death is inconsistent with a doctor's healing role[53] (Dickinson *et al* 1997–8: 207), are all relevant factors, the impact of which should never be underestimated.

Autonomy v paternalism

Doctors have always played a very specific role in society and despite recent bad publicity following, for example, the events leading to the Bristol Royal Infirmary Inquiry and successful criminal convictions against some doctors, changes in the way medical services are delivered, the growth in patient autonomy and advances in medical technology, patients – particularly the older generation – still look upon their doctor with some measure of respect for the function doctors perform for and in society. Doctors have certain ethical and moral duties which no other persons are permitted to exercise[54] (Rhodes 1998: 172) and whereas this has led to paternalistic practices in the past, there are signs that this is changing in recent times; in an

---

50 For example, having to make quality of life judgments; the 'psychological discomfort' of stopping life-sustaining treatment, Solomon *et al* 1993: 19; and the fear of 'burnout' syndrome (characterised by emotional exhaustion, diminished empathy and lack of personal accomplishment), Portenoy *et al* 1997: 278.

51 Evidence shows that doctors tend to 'withdraw [both] physically and emotionally' from terminally ill patients. This was recognised in the Report of the Council on Ethical and Judicial Affairs of the American Medical Association 1994: 97.

52 See also, Edwards and Tolle (1992) and Kass (1989).

53 Even Ward LJ in *Re A (Children)* (2000) at 987, noted the doctor's instinctive response to saving a patient's life if it could be saved; their 'collective conscience' would not let them do otherwise.

54 Three paradigms of the doctor's role are set out in Sheldon and Thomson 1998: *viii*.

age when autonomy and self-determination are on the increase, the patient's wishes must be considered. This has led to some conflict, but usually only when the patient wishes to exercise his autonomy in a way which is contrary to the doctor's clinical advice. In *B v An NHS Hospital Trust*, Ms B was granted a declaration allowing her life-sustaining treatment to be withdrawn, but only after the court had decided that she was competent to make the decision. This is not to say, however, that patient autonomy is absolute; a patient cannot tell a doctor what to do and expect him to do it. This very question arose in *R v Portsmouth Hospital NHS Trust ex p Glass* ([1999] Lloyds Law Rep (Med) 367 (1))[55] and more recently in the cases of *Burke* (*R (Burke) v General Medical Council et al* [2004] WL 1640202 (in the High Court) and *R on the Application of Oliver Leslie Burke v the General Medical Council et al* [2005] EWCA Civ 1003 (in the Court of Appeal) and *Re Wyatt* (5).

In *Glass*, a disabled child's mother made an application for Judicial Review against a hospital's decision not to provide life-saving treatment for her son if he were to be admitted to hospital in a life-threatening condition in the future (and also that the hospital administered diamorphine to him and entered a Do Not Resuscitate Order against him, both without her consent). The Court of Appeal refused Mrs Glass's application, Scott Baker J saying '[N]o-one can *dictate* the treatment to be given to a child – neither court, parents not doctors' (*Glass* (1) at 371).

In the recent case of *Burke*, Leslie Burke applied for Judicial Review of the General Medical Council (GMC)'s Guidance *Witholding and Withdrawing Life-prolonging Treatment* on the basis that whereas it emphasised the right of a competent patient to refuse treatment, it said nothing about any right to require treatment. Mr Burke suffered from a debilitating disease which would in time mean that he would have to receive artificial nutrition and hydration and he did not want this to be withdrawn. Munby J in the High Court said that certain factors had changed the original position whereby a doctor could not be placed under an obligation do to anything which was against his clinical judgment of what was in the best interests of his patient. These factors were the coming into effect of the Human Rights Act 1998 and the broadened scope of best interests (*Burke* (1) at 17–24).

Whilst Munby J was prepared to accept that the court would not grant a mandatory order requiring an individual doctor to treat his patient, he said that this did not mean that a doctor could simply decline to go on treating his patient merely because his views as to what was in his patient's best interests differed from those of the patient. There were limits to a doctor's discretion

---

55 Mrs Glass subsequently took her case to the European Court of Human Rights. The Court held there had been a breach of Article 8, but no mention was made of any right to demand treatment. *Glass v United Kingdom* (Application No. 61827/00) (2).

in exercising his clinical judgment about best interests; they were no longer simply what a doctor believed them to be.

Lord Phillips' judgment in the Court of Appeal was highly critical of the manner in which Munby J dealt with the issues raised in the case. He said that Munby's suggestion (that it is the duty of the doctor to provide treatment which complies with the wishes of the patient) did not mean that a doctor was obliged to provide treatment to a patient:

> Munby J was not . . . concerned with the extent to which, in general, a patient has a right to insist on particular treatment. He was concerned with the choice of whether or not to receive life-prolonging treatment . . .
>
> (*Burke* (2) at para 50)[56]

He went on to say that just because a patient has the autonomy to refuse treatment does not mean he has the corollary right to demand treatment. 'Autonomy and the right of self-determination do not entitle the patient to insist on receiving a particular medical treatment regardless of the nature of the treatment' (*Burke* (2) at para 31).[57]

The *Wyatt* cases (5 in all between October 2004 and October 2005) commenced with a successful application by the Portsmouth NHS Trust for a declaration confirming that it need not continue to treat Charlotte, who was severely disabled, if an emergency arose in the future. The declaration remained in force until, following an improvement in Charlotte's condition, her parents applied for it to be removed and when it was, the hospital feared that the treating doctors would have to comply with the parents' wishes as to their daughter's treatment. The Trust therefore applied to the High Court for a 'novel' declaration that, in the event of a disagreement between themselves and Charlotte's parents (and there had been numerous altercations already) the treating doctors should have the last word. In *Re Wyatt* (5), Hedley J held that a declaration was unnecessary as doctors do not take orders from the family: '. . . where a clinician concludes that a requested treatment is inimical to the best interests of the patient, and . . . his professional conscience, intuition or hunch, confirms that view . . . he may refuse to act and cannot be compelled to do so . . .' (*Re Wyatt* (5) at para 36).

The *Burke* and *Wyatt* cases are prime examples of the conflict which can arise between the exercise of patient autonomy, a doctor's clinical judgment, and the sometimes dubious benefits of advanced technology.

56　And see generally paras 50–5. Mr Burke's application to the European Court of Human Rights has been declared inadmissible. Application no. 19807/06.

57　That doctors cannot be compelled to treat was reiterated by Holmes J in *An NHS Trust v MB* (2006) at para 54.

The 'technological imperative' and 'technical rationality'

The invention of machinery that can prolong life (albeit not necessarily to cure illness) is one of the factors that has changed both doctors' and patients' ways of thinking about medical treatment (Solomon *et al* 1993: 14). However, just because the technology exists does not mean that it must be used; despite a tendency to over-use all things new, to follow the 'technological imperative' (Somerville 1993: 34), and to treat a patient if treatment is available irrespective of the consequences, decisions must be made as to when it is not appropriate to use them (Landsman 1986: 145). The advent of technological solutions should not replace the doctor's good judgment as to when it is, or is not, appropriate to treat a patient. A particular danger is what has become known as 'technical rationality', a practice said to be exercised by a doctor where his training and experience leads him to acquire fixed attitudes and set ways of thinking and doing. He does not have to do any fresh thinking in a given situation, since the result is a foregone conclusion. Instead, he relies on his training and experience to come to a decision. In this way, decision-making becomes almost automatic (Still and Todd 1998: 138–40).[58]

This is a very dangerous situation in so far as familiarising oneself with a particular form of activity, to such an extent that it will be performed automatically, precludes any consideration of its possible implications. While this does not necessarily mean that performing that activity will get any easier, it does nonetheless mean that certain, previously unacceptable activities will, over time, become acceptable.[59] The growth in patient autonomy has curbed this to some extent, as competent patients are permitted to request withdrawal of life-sustaining mechanisms and that request must be complied with.

Resources and rationing

As well as possible conflicts between himself and his patient, a doctor also faces other battles of a more practical, economic and personal nature. In these days when there is a severe lack of funding to maintain the National Health Service (NHS) and when technology is able to prolong life indefinitely, one of the main considerations which influence a doctor in making decisions about his patients is the lack of resources and the need for rationing. On a practical level, basic resource issues such as a shortage of beds,[60] which will govern which patient can have treatment and which not, have no connection with the concept of intention and neither does rationing. The HLSC on

---

58 This is, however, true of all decision-making processes; see, for example, Thompson, Melia and Boyd 1994: 171–3.
59 The dangers of this are emphasised by Gillet (1988), and see final chapter below.
60 The relevance of which was pointed out in the interview with an Accident and Emergency Consultant.

Medical Ethics recognised the rationing of finite resources as an inevitable 'fact of life' (HLSC 1993–4: paras 274–5), but rather naively thought this was a decision that doctors did not have to make.[61] Doctors do have to consider resources but in what ways are they qualified to allocate resources and upon what basis do they do so? Random selection? Age?[62] 'QALY'?[63] Likelihood of success?[64] Past contributions to society?[65] Present and future worth? Social class?[66] 'Salvageability'?[67] As Logue has said:

> [a]gain and again, decisions are based on biographical potential, using unarticulated criteria. The demented, the decrepit and others who have outlived their capacity for meaningful social interaction are all low priority.
>
> (Logue 1996: 103)

On a more personal level, there may be a simple conflict of interest between a doctor's personal feelings on the one hand, and his professional duty on the other. He will not simply be a product of his vocation, because all individuals play more than one role – a '. . . nurse may be a man . . . union member and Roman Catholic. The doctor may be a young woman, feminist, keen golfer and atheist' (Thompson, Melia and Boyd 1994: 189). As Reinhardt J said in *Compassion in Dying v Washington* (79 F. 3d 790; 1996 U.S. App. LEXIS 3944):

> One's philosophy, one's experiences, one's exposure to the raw edges of human existence, one's religious training, one's attitude toward life and family and their values, and the moral standards one establishes and seeks to observe, are all likely to influence and to color one's thinking . . .
>
> (*Compassion in Dying v Washington per* Reinhardt J at 799)

Religion and conscience

A number of studies have shown that religion also plays a part in decision-making; for example, in a study of doctors' attitudes towards physician-

---

61 The point is made by McLean and Britton 1996: 71.
62 Known as 'ageism' – a tendency to regard older persons as debilitated and unworthy of attention. The interview with a Social Worker stressed the importance of the patient's age as a deciding factor. New legislation on age discrimination has come into force on 1 October 2006.
63 Quality Adjusted Life Year, based on age – 'the older the patient, the fewer the life years that can be achieved by therapy', Harris 1985: 77–9.
64 McLean and Maher 1983: 195. Interview with Accident and Emergency Consultant confirms.
65 Dworkin 1995: chapters 7 and 8.
66 A study by Crane worryingly found that doctors may well base their decisions on a patient's social class, simply because the patient has contributed more to society; Crane 1975: 23.
67 That a patient is only worth treating if he is capable of resuming his social role and interacting with others; Crane 1975: 1 and 5.

assisted suicide and euthanasia, Dickinson *et al* concluded that of those who thought euthanasia and assisted suicide were never justified, it was their religion which influenced them (Dickinson *et al* 1997–8: 207). However, in an increasingly secular society, it can be contended that this plays less of a part than other basic moral scruples, such as conscience. Defined as 'the intentional recognition of the moral quality of one's motives and actions . . .' (*Shorter Oxford English Dictionary* 1993),[68] obviously, the strength of each person's conscience is different; a person with a greater sense of conscience is less likely to commit a crime than one who does not have a conscience.[69] Whatever one's view, no one should be forced to act against his conscience. It was made clear in *B v An NHS Hospital Trust* that it was the duty of a doctor who was unable to carry out a patient's wishes to find another doctor who would do so (*B v An NHS Hospital Trust* at 24).[70]

Conclusion

This chapter has shown the problems inherent in the whole concept of intention. Firstly, in the absence of a statutory definition (which would not necessarily help anyway) the courts have been able to interpret intention differently in each individual case. This has led the way to a clear manipulation of core criminal law principles in cases where doctors are involved.

Secondly, intention as a concept is open to criticism as to its meaning and to its identification, and thirdly, situational factors which doctors have to consider do not feature intention (or indeed causation). In the medical scenario, it is particularly pertinent to realise that the doctor's first and foremost concern is to act in the best interests of his patient (and indeed he has a duty to do so); he is not going to be preoccupied with intention, the subjectivity of which causes other complex problems of interpretation, application and manipulation. The courts have recognised this, and as Otlowski has quite rightly noted, they are reluctant 'to impose criminal liability on doctors' (Otlowski 2000: 78).

This is particularly evident where the doctrine of double effect has been invoked as a 'defence' following the administration of pain-killing medication to a patient who has subsequently died. This then is the subject of the next chapter.

---

68 Also defined as 'the moral sense of right and wrong that determines someone's thoughts and behaviour' *Chambers Twenty First Century Dictionary* (1999) and as an 'internal inhibitory factor' by Farrington 1995: 307.
69 See the paradox of this in Schopp 1998: 13–14 and 155–6 (his 'crimes of conscience/personal moral obligation') and Horder's 'demands of conscience partial excuse' in Horder 2004: 209.
70 See also HLSC (2005): paras 113–16.

Chapter 2

The principle of double effect

[In] ... the double effect principle ... the intention of the agent ... is not the morally specifying feature of the action ... the principle ... is mis-stated if it is held to differentiate between acts on the agent's intention alone.

(O'Keefe 1984: 360 and 362)

Introduction

As has been seen, the mental element for murder has been widened to include oblique or indirect intention whereby a result may be intended in certain circumstances when it is not the actor's specific purpose to cause it, but rather when he may foresee that it is a virtually certain consequence of what he does that someone will be killed. The problematic distinction between intended and foreseen consequences is well illustrated by the principle of double effect, a 'defence' invoked by and for doctors, usually when increasing pain-killing medication to a suffering terminally ill patient where a possible side-effect of that increase would be to hasten the patient's death. Such a situation thus has both a good and a bad consequence (killing the patient's pain as against possibly killing the patient). In a case like this, it is permissible to relieve the pain, even if life is incidentally shortened,[1] but killing in order to relieve pain is not permitted.

Briefly, the principle's conditions can be expressed as follows:

1) The nature of the action must be morally good . . .;
2) The bad effect . . . must not be a means of achieving the good effect . . . [that is, the end can never justify the means];
3) The good effect is directly intended; the bad effect is merely foreseen and tolerated;
4) Proportionally, the reasons for performing the good action must

---

1 Devlin 1986: 171.

> outweigh the unintended bad consequences (the actor must have a justifying reason for acting rather than refraining from acting).
>
> (Williams 2001a: 45)

This chapter examines the cases and, in the context of the intention/foresight distinction, provides an analysis of the principle by looking particularly at the elements of choice, proportionality, justifiability and causality, which are its crucial components. The principle allows the courts to manipulate the intention/foresight distinction to absolve doctors in circumstances where, technically, they do foresee the patient's death with the virtual certainty required in *Nedrick* and approved of both in *Woollin* and *Mathews and Alleyne* (albeit as evidence of intention). In reality, double effect operates as a justificatory (non-statutory) defence which exculpates one particular category of person simply because of what they do, but despite the resulting inequality, the availability of this 'defence' is to be commended as it avoids unimaginable consequences for suffering patients. However, it should be placed on a formal basis in order to avoid allegations of misuse.

The cases

As the cases of *Adams, Cox* and *Moor* in particular show how the principle of double effect is used in practice, they will be examined in some detail with a view to ascertaining the reasoning upon which they are based. Although the principle of double effect was raised in all three, not only did the courts adopt different routes to arrive at the decision in each case, they also omitted to apply the standard intention (and causation) 'tests'.

A further two cases, *Carr* and *Lodwig*, also show doctors being acquitted of attempted murder and murder respectively even though the principle of double effect was not specifically invoked in those two cases.[2] In *R v Carr* (*The Sunday Times* 30 November 1986), the doctor was found not guilty of attempted murder following an overdose given by him to a terminally ill patient. The doctor's defence was simply that the overdose was a 'ghastly mistake'. Despite Mars Jones J's unreceptive summing-up, the jury acquitted, obviously feeling that a mistake was a sufficient defence to a charge of attempted murder in this case.[3]

In *R v Lodwig* (*The Times* 16 March 1990), the doctor was charged with murder after administering a combination of an anaesthetic drug and potassium chloride (a substance which has no curative properties, and is not an

---

2 The case of *R v Arthur* (1981) is sometimes used as an example of the application of the principle of double effect, but it is a problematic case which has been criticised as being 'something best forgotten' by Mason 1993: 116.

3 Generally, a mistake is only considered to be a defence where it prevents the defendant from having the necessary *mens rea* for the offence.

analgesic) to a patient suffering from terminal cancer. Ongoing experiments had, however, shown that the combination of the two drugs had the potential to accelerate their analgesic effect. It would accordingly have been difficult to prove that the doctor's intention was not to ease his patient's pain (Ferguson 1997: 369).[4] On this basis, the prosecution offered no evidence and Dr Lodwig was cleared of the murder charge.

Some years later, in what was claimed to be a 'landmark court battle' (although it never actually went to court), Annie Lindsell, a Motor Neurone Disease sufferer, made an application for a declaration that her doctor could administer drugs to hasten her death when her condition deteriorated, but she withdrew her application when the lawyers agreed that the principle of double effect was appropriate to relieve the 'mental distress' and not just the pain associated with the disease.[5]

More recently, in *R (On the Application of Pretty) v DPP* ([2001] WL 1171775 (1)), Dianne Pretty, another Motor Neurone Disease sufferer, made an application for Judicial Review to the High Court following a refusal by the Director of Public Prosecutions (DPP) to undertake that he would not prosecute Mr Pretty for assisting in his wife's suicide. The case was a direct challenge both to human rights provisions and to the Suicide Act 1961, but in reality, there was no real need for the case to have been brought to the courts at all; the principle of double effect would have enabled Mrs Pretty's doctors to lawfully prescribe sufficient medication to relieve the mental suffering which is obviously allied to the physical symptoms of this degenerative disease. Lord Steyn hinted at this when he suggested that Mrs Pretty could be sedated in the final stages of her illness (*Pretty* (1) at 20).[6]

R v Adams (1957) Crim LR 365

Murder is the cutting short of life, whether by years, months or weeks. It does not matter that Mrs Morrell's days were numbered. But that does not mean that a doctor who is aiding the sick and the dying has to calculate in minutes or even in hours, and perhaps not in days or weeks, the effect upon a patient's life of the medicines which he administers . . . If the first purpose of medicine, the restoration of health, can no longer

---

4 As it transpired, the prosecution offered no evidence because their main medical witness was no longer convinced that Mr Spratley, the patient, had died of a potassium chloride overdose. There was a possibility that he had died from natural causes, although he did have one of the highest recorded records of morphine in his body.

5 http://news.bbc.co.uk/1/hi/health/background_briefings/euthanasia/332464.stm (accessed 20 February 2006).

6 Mrs Pretty died in a hospice on 11 May 2002, duly sedated, shortly after the European Court of Human Rights' judgment was delivered on 29 April 2002; see *Pretty v UK* (Application No. 2346/02 (3)) upon which more is said in chapter 6 below.

be achieved, there is still much for a doctor to do, and he is entitled to do all that is proper and necessary to relieve pain and suffering, even if the measures he takes may incidentally shorten life.

(Devlin 1986: 171)

Devlin J in his account of the case in his book *Easing the Passing* (1986) set out what many regard as the definitive statement on the principle of double effect. On the facts of this particular case, however, and on the basis of the evidence of one of the medical experts, doubt was raised as to whether there was a legitimate reason for the amount of medication given, as the patient was in a coma during the last days of her life.

Dr Adams was charged with the murder of his patient of two years, Mrs Morrell, following the administration of two abnormally large doses of heroin, morphia, and paraldehyde. His defence was that the treatment was designed to promote comfort. Devlin J noted that Dr Adams had a reputation as a legacy hunter and was a beneficiary in no less than 132 wills executed by his patients. According to Devlin, the general feeling among the police and the prosecution was that he was a mass poisoner. However, Devlin J's account also reveals that the prosecution encountered problems with inconclusive medical evidence and divided expert medical witnesses which, together with allegations that their reliance on a paltry legacy to Dr Adams was 'ludicrous' (Devlin 1986: 153), may explain why the jury found him not guilty after only 46 minutes.[7]

Devlin went on to say that the reason doctors are authorised to proceed in such a way is not because they have a special defence, but because they are simply not the cause of death:

> . . . no act is murder which does not cause death. We are not dealing here with the philosophical or technical cause, but with the commonsense cause. The cause of death is the illness or injury, and the proper medical treatment that is administered and that has an incidental effect on determining the exact moment of death is not the cause of death in any sensible use of the term . . .
>
> (Devlin 1986: 171–2)

Although Devlin J's emphasis here is on causation, the case is nonetheless authority for the proposition that a doctor whose primary intention is to

---

7 In reality, a *nolle prosequi* prevented his acquittal (Devlin 1986: 181); it only became public knowledge subsequently that the police had prepared a second indictment which was abandoned following this verdict.

relieve pain, even if life is incidentally shortened, has an exceptional defence to murder (Stauch, Wheat with Tingle 2006: 645–6).

R v Cox [1992] 12 BMLR 38

Dr Nigel Cox was charged and convicted of the attempted murder of Lillian Boyes, his patient of 13 years. His defence, based on the principle of double effect, was unsuccessful, as he had injected his patient with a mixture of a slow-acting tranquilliser and potassium chloride.[8] In contrast with the causation-based judgment in *Adams*, this is very much an intention-based judgment. Ognall J said:

> What can never be lawful is the use of drugs with the primary purpose of hastening the moment of death.
>
> And so, in deciding Dr Cox's intention, the distinction the law requires you to draw is this. Is it proved that in giving the injection, in that form and in those amounts, Dr Cox's primary purpose was to bring the life of Lillian Boyes to an end?
>
> If it was, then he is guilty. If, on the other hand, it was, or may have been, his primary purpose in acting as he did to alleviate her pain and suffering, then he is not guilty. That is so even though he recognises that, in fulfilling that primary purpose, he might or even would hasten the moment of her death.
>
> (*Cox per* Ognall J at 41)

Grubb, although contending that Dr Cox acted to relieve his patient's pain, criticises the very foundation upon which the decision is based, saying that the principle of double effect 'has no place in the English criminal law' (Grubb 1993: 233) as, following *Nedrick*, there is no distinction between side-effects and the desired consequence. This ignores the fact that the test in *Nedrick* is permissive in the sense that it allows the jury to find an absence of intention where circumstances permit. Also, Grubb's criticism of the doctrine fails to acknowledge the necessity of this informal defence which, although it causes discrepancies in the law, nonetheless enables doctors to deal sympathetically with suffering patients without the fear of legal repercussions.

---

8 Note the similarity with *Lodwig* (1990) who was acquitted for using a combination which included potassium chloride.

R v Moor The Times 12 May 1999[9]

Dr David Moor, a general practitioner, was charged with murder after the cremation of his patient, George Liddell, was halted by the coroner. He was first questioned in November 1997 over the death, which he consistently claimed was the result of an administration of diamorphine for the purposes of pain relief and the defence relied squarely on this.

George Liddell had been sent home to his daughter's house following an operation to remove cancerous cells. His health deteriorated rapidly and he suffered significant pain, which Dr Moor fully believed was due to remaining cancer cells in his patient's body. Following the administration of morphine via a syringe driver, Dr Moor claimed that he subsequently administered 60 mg of the drug directly by injection. His patient died 20 minutes later. On post mortem, up to six times the claimed amount of the drug was found in his body, but because of problems with some of the medical procedures which raised doubt as to the amount of morphine in various parts of his body, Hooper J informed the jury that they should not rely on this. Further tests also showed that George Liddell was not terminally ill, although the prosecution did not dispute the fact that Dr Moor fully believed that he was.

Hooper J set out four questions to help members of the jury to come to their decision. The first related to the amount of diamorphine given, but the second asked them to consider whether the prosecution had satisfied them that Dr Moor had caused his patient's death (the causation question). The remaining two questions related specifically to intention: was the jury satisfied that Dr Moor's purpose in giving the injection was not to give his patient treatment which would relieve his pain and suffering, and lastly, was the jury satisfied that the injection he gave to his patient was intended to kill?[10] Following an 18-day trial, he was found not guilty after only 65 minutes.

Analysis of Adams, Cox and Moor: a special defence?

Devlin J seemingly based his judgment in *Adams* on both intention and causation principles, yet his directions in respect of both do not fit the standard tests for either. As to causation, Hart and Honoré used *Adams* as a basis for trying to explain the distinction between accelerating and causing death (Hart and Honoré 1985: 344),[11] but the distinction (if it exists) is difficult to maintain here because, as Ashworth notes in his analysis of the case, Devlin

---

9 Details of the case are set out in an article by Anthony Arlidge QC, defence counsel: Arlidge (2000), and in an account of a speech by the trial judge himself at the British Academy of Forensic Sciences: Hooper J (2000).

10 The four questions are more fully explained by Arlidge 2000: 39.

11 For more on this, see the section on causality below and chapter 4's conclusion.

J's causation direction implies that '. . . causing death means accelerating death . . . that leads to the conclusion that Dr Adams did cause the death . . .' (Ashworth 1996: 174). Certainly therefore, the case did not rely on the normal understanding of causation. Dr Adams could equally have been acquitted simply on his lack of direct intention, but, as Ashworth continues, the jury were not given the 'standard' intention direction either. As a result, the case is widely considered by, for example, Tur (although his reasoning is different), Cooper, Smith and Hooper J himself, as providing a special defence for doctors (Tur 2002: 90; Cooper 2000: 1258; Smith 2000a: 42) and is a classic example of the court's reluctance to convict doctors (Lacey, Wells and Quick 2003: 694).[12]

In *Cox*, the direction was made solely on the question of intention and similarly seems to provide doctors with 'a special defence' (Arlidge 2000: 37) in so far as, providing the primary purpose was to alleviate suffering, it was immaterial that the doctor foresaw death as virtually certain (Cooper 2000: 24). The rather worrying problem with the intention test in *Cox* is the suggestion that if he had used pain-killing medication, he would have been found not guilty regardless of his intent and even if the results were identical (Brahams 1992: 2). This is precisely why intention cannot be the sole determining factor in cases involving the principle of double effect.

Hooper J in *Moor*, raised both causation and intention questions but, mindful of what he perceived as the constraints of the causation question, he only gave the jury a 'standard causation direction' (Hooper 2000: 192) which was simply to say that if someone 'contributes significantly' to the death, then he causes that person's death. By omitting to elaborate further, Hooper J provided the jury with an opportunity for them to acquit on the basis of uncertainty as to Moor's guilt (Smith 2000a: 42).[13]

As to the two intention questions, Hooper J himself conceded that the way in which he phrased them provided doctors with a defence even when the doctor knew that his actions were virtually certain to cause death. By restricting the direction to 'purpose' alone rather than giving the relevant *Woollin* direction, Hooper J influenced the jury into returning a verdict that was favourable to a doctor–defendant, although it can equally be suggested that they would not have needed much persuasion to acquit.

The principle of double effect in the courts abroad

In the US, the principle of double effect has received recognition in two landmark cases. In *Quill v Vacco* (80 F. 3d 716; 1996 U.S. App. LEXIS 6216),

---

12 The case can be compared with *R v White* ([1910] 2 KB 124), where the Court of Criminal Appeal held that a man who intended to kill his mother was guilty of attempted murder, even though he had not caused the death (she died of a heart attack first).

13 Smith makes the same comment in relation to the intention questions.

three doctors (three terminally ill patients originally parties to the action having died) claimed that two New York statutes penalising assisted suicide violated both the equal protection and due process clauses of the Fourteenth Amendment to the Constitution. It was claimed that the patients suffered discrimination because, as they were not on life support machines, they did not have the option of requesting their withdrawal. The New York Appeals Court held that doctors *should* be allowed to prescribe drugs to be self-administered by competent patients who asked to end their lives during the final stages of terminal illness, Miner CJ holding that '[p]hysicians do not fulfil the role of "killer" by prescribing drugs to hasten death . . .' (*Quill v Vacco* at 730).

At the same time, a challenge was brought against the constitutionality of Washington legislation in *Compassion in Dying v Washington* (79 F. 3d 790; 1996 U.S. App. LEXIS 3944). That case arose when four doctors, three terminally ill patients and an organisation called Compassion in Dying claimed that there was a constitutionally protected liberty interest in hastening death, and that a Washington statute prohibiting doctors from prescribing life-ending medication for use by terminally ill patients at their request violated the due process clause of the Fourteenth Amendment. The Appeals Court upheld both claims, Reinhardt J presenting a controversial interpretation of the principle of double effect[14] in holding that when a doctor administers palliative medication which shortens life, the doctor and not the illness causes the patient's death (*Compassion in Dying v Washington* at 823).[15]

As expected, the US Supreme Court, in *Vacco v Quill* (521 U.S. 793; 117 S.Ct. 2293; 1997 U.S. LEXIS 4038; 138 L. Ed. 2d 834) and *Washington v Glucksberg* (521 U.S. 702; 117 S. Ct. 2302; 117 S. Ct. 2258; 1997 U.S. LEXIS 4039; 138 L. Ed. 2d 772), reversed both decisions (on the same day). The court rightly rejected the relevance of the principle of double effect to both cases where, after all, the clear intent was to assist suicide. As such, the proposed course of action breached the first three conditions of the principle. Nonetheless, its existence was acknowledged and approved on the basis that it was perfectly reasonable to accept that a doctor's intention could be simply to ease a patient's pain.

In Canada, had the case gone to trial, the principle could well have been raised as a defence by Dr Nancy Morrison, who was arrested and charged with the murder of a patient suffering from oesophogal cancer. It was alleged that she had injected her patient, Paul Mills, who had already been disconnected

---

14 An interpretation which has subsequently been severely criticised by, amongst others, Brody 1996: 40–1.

15 Two comments arise from this – firstly, that in seeing no difference between providing medication with a single or with a double effect, he rejected the principle of double effect (see Annas 1998: 206) and secondly, his conclusion presumes that analgesics are themselves capable of causing death, which, as will be seen below, is open to question; see, for example, Wall (1997).

from a ventilator, with a combination of nitroglycerine and potassium chloride, neither of which have any analgesic effect. At the preliminary hearing, it was disclosed that the patient's intravenous line was not functioning properly so the potassium chloride allegedly injected could not reach the bloodstream and therefore could not possibly have caused Mills's death (this was the reason why the pain-killing medication previously administered had not been effective either). The Provincial Court judge, Judge Hughes Randall, accepted this and dismissed the charges on the basis that there was insufficient evidence to put Dr Morrison on trial (Sneiderman and Deutscher 2002: 1).

Following an analysis of the cases and commentaries, it can be concluded that there are substantial grounds for suggesting that the principle of double effect is used by the courts as a special defence to absolve doctors from criminal liability.[16] The next part of this chapter will therefore move on to analyse the principle in greater depth by firstly highlighting the implications of the intention/foresight distinction; secondly by examining the issues of choice and control in that distinction and finally, by providing an in-depth view of Helga Kuhse's analysis of double effect in her book *The Sanctity of Life Doctrine in Medicine. A Criticism* (1987), which in itself raises a number of related issues.

The principle of double effect: an analysis of its components

The intention/foresight distinction

The main problem with the principle of double effect lies in the distinction between intention and foresight. Normally, people are held responsible for the reasonably foreseen consequences of their actions because the criminal law generally holds that a foreseen consequence is intended. It is precisely because of this that it is then contradictory to hold that doctors are not held responsible when they are prosecuted, if indeed they are prosecuted at all (President's Commission 1983: 78–9). As has been argued elsewhere:

> . . . the logical legal conclusion is to hold doctors liable when they have foreseen their patient's death as a virtual certainty of the treatment. But, while the courts have held on the one hand that doctors are not entitled to special consideration . . . on the other hand, they have avoided the logical legal conclusion that a doctor's conduct may amount to murder by adopting a 'deliberately narrow' definition of intention where a doctor gives life-shortening or death-accelerating drugs, 'to avoid responsibility accruing.' We have only to look at the case of *Adams* . . .

16 As acknowedged by the Law Commission in LCCP No. 177 (2005).

and *Gillick* as evidence that, contrary to the norm, 'doctors are not normally presumed to intend all the foreseen consequences of their actions.'

(Williams 2001a: 44 (footnotes excluded))

Thus, whereas in 'criminal' type cases intention has been extended to include foresight, in 'medical' type cases involving doctors who foresee a patient's death, the courts contrarily accept a narrower definition of intention which does not fit into the conventional criminal law.

Traditionalists such as Kenny and Frey (see below) take the view that while there may well be moral differences between intention and foresight (which is exactly what the principle of double effect maintains), it is quite reasonable that '... where an evil effect is foreseen as certain it is quite reasonable it should in law be treated as if it had been intended' (Kenny 1978: 90). While this may be true in a truly 'criminal' scenario, in a medical scenario that moral difference is upheld in law by the invocation of the principle of double effect as a totally exclusive defence for doctors which appropriately acknowledges their role.

Choice, control and responsibility in the distinction between foresight and intention

In cases where an agent foresees the consequences of his action, but chooses to proceed in spite of those consequences, some, such as Hart and Kuhse, suggest that the agent is nonetheless responsible for the patient's death because a deliberate and voluntary choice has been made '... to bring about a state of affairs that includes the ... consequence, in preference to another state of affairs which does not' (Kuhse 1987: 165).

Hart expresses this idea by virtue of the notion of control (Hart 1968: 121–2)[17] as does Frey. His theory of 'control responsibility' means that a doctor has the choice whether to proceed or not. If he does decide to administer the drug, he is a '... causal factor in a death, *whether* he ... directly intends the patient's death or knowingly brings it about' and must accordingly accept responsibility for that (Frey 1996: 73). This consequentialist view treats a doctor who foresees death as a side-effect in the same way as one who intended it, because according to that view, the action is judged solely by its consequences.

The contrasting view held by, for example, Gormally, Finnis, Price and Boyle, is that:

(a) One intends only the consequences that one chooses to produce (Gormally 1994b: 769);

---

17 That a person who has consciously chosen an option which leads to death has control over that death.

(b) '[t]o choose . . . is . . . to *adopt a plan or proposal'* (Finnis 1991: 36);
(c) 'side-effects are not part of an agent's plan or proposal' (Price 1997: 328) because
(d) while the agent will no doubt consider side-effects as foreseen consequences while making a choice, '[t]hey are not a part of what . . . [he] . . . chooses to bring about' (Boyle 1980: 536).[18]

Both arguments concede that the doctor has to choose whether to proceed or not; if he proceeds with the intention of killing the patient in order to end that patient's suffering, then he acts because of the consequences; if he proceeds with mere foresight that the patient may die, he does so '*in spite of*' the consequences (Boyle 1980: 535). What the principle of double effect therefore does is to distinguish 'actions taken "because of" a given end . . . [in the case of euthanasia, this would be causing death as a means of relieving suffering and would accordingly breach condition two of the principle of double effect] from actions taken "in spite of" their unintended but foreseen consequences' (*Vacco v Quill* at 15). In the case of the principle of double effect, the intent is to '. . . relieve suffering despite the fatal side-effects . . .'[19]

As was noted in the previous chapter, this distinction between acting despite the consequences on the one hand, and because of the consequences on the other, can help to distinguish between whether a person has intended to act, or has simply acted intentionally. There is therefore a distinction between acting with intention and acting simply with foresight of the patient's death. However, because the end result is the same, those who advocate no distinction between direct and oblique intention can argue that the moral, if not the legal, responsibility for each is the same (Duff 1990: 76, analysing Bentham).

Campbell and Collinson's understanding of the principle of double effect is not that it tells us '. . . whether certain actions are right or wrong . . .' but that 'it tells us whether performing them makes us responsible for foreseen consequences that may follow from performing them' (Campbell and Collinson 1988: 159). However, as it is obvious that no one can (or should?) be responsible for all the foreseen consequences of their actions, a line must be drawn to mark the limit of responsibility:

> What you have to ask is, am I responsible for all the results of my actions? If I am, life is impossible. People go on about the principle of double effect as though it was something intended to get you off the hook. You

---

18 A more sophisticated version of this argument can be seen in Begley (1998).
19 '. . . while the intent [in euthanasia] is to cause death as a means by which relief of suffering is achieved'. The quote, taken from the Report of the Council on Ethical and Judicial Affairs of the American Medical Association 1992: 2231 is interesting because it would breach Condition two of the principle of double effect (Kuhse's Condition 3).

can't live without it; you need it to narrow what you are responsible for and for what goes on in the world.[20]

Duff has said that an agent is held 'properly responsible' only for those side effects he is morally certain of (Duff 1990: 95). This takes us a step nearer to understanding the principle of double effect because while responsibility might be admitted, this does not automatically ascribe blameworthiness, as blame for the action can be avoided if the agent can justify his action on the basis that death may sometimes justifiably be caused (Duff 1990: 78).[21] Lay people rely on the doctor to exercise his discretion and judgment. As such, there is an expectancy that given a choice between letting a patient suffer and alleviating that suffering, he will choose the latter and will be justified in doing so. By selecting the option which causes the least harm – which is the essence of justification – he is absolved from blame, but not on this basis alone. Other components of the principle of double effect, in the form of proportionality and motive, are equally relevant in the non-ascription of blame. Kuhse analyses these and other components of the principle in *The Sanctity of Life Doctrine in Medicine* and an examination of this analysis forms the remaining part of this chapter.

Kuhse and the principle of double effect

Kuhse, a strong supporter of the principle of double effect, contends that the 'conditions' of the principle lay down that sometimes a bad effect is 'allowed or permitted' to occur, but must not be intended. Her four conditions are:

(a) Condition 1 – (the most problematic and confusing) which states that the nature of the action must be good;
(b) Condition 2 – (the 'intentionality condition') which states that the good effect is directly intended and the bad is merely foreseen and tolerated;
(c) Condition 3 – (the 'causality condition') states that the bad effect must not be a means of achieving the good effect; and
(d) Condition 4 – (the 'proportionality condition') states that the reasons for performing the good action must outweigh the unintended bad consequences.

The intentionality condition allows for the permissibility of an action, so that an action is 'prima facie *permissible*' if it meets both this and the causality condition. The proportionality condition provides for justification, upon

---

20 Interview with Roman Catholic Priest.
21 Saying that the principle of double effect is justificatory entails accepting that some deaths are therefore justified; there is nothing new in this as some deaths are already justified, for example, deaths caused while acting in self-defence.

which the principle of double effect is based, so that, once the action is permissible for meeting the intentionality condition, it is also justified if it meets the proportionality condition. Condition 2 must be fulfilled before the agent initiates the causal chain of events (in Condition 3) because it determines whether the proposed action is permitted or not. Only when the intentionality condition is satisfied will the proportionality condition come into play. As Kuhse explains, '[i]f an agent infringes the intentionality conditions, she is not *permitted* to perform the intended action': if she infringes the proportionality condition, '. . . she is not *justified* in bringing about a death . . .' (Kuhse 1987: 156). The crux of the doctrine is therefore that of justifiability.

Kuhse claims that any disproportionality should be measured against the patient's medical condition[22] but that the patient's medical condition – even if dying – is not relevant to the intentionality condition and neither is motive, because neither tell us whether the agent terminated life intentionally. What is relevant, however, is the concept of 'deliberate and voluntary choice' because what matters is that the agent has chosen to produce a set of circumstances which includes (foreseen) consequences over and above a set of circumstances which do not. As there has been a choice deliberately to produce the death of a person, the agent is responsible for that foreseen consequence.

The constraints of the situation, however, provide excusing or justifying conditions, so that, while she is responsible, this does not mean that she is to blame.[23] This in turn depends on the all-important criteria of proportionality and whether the agent can justify her behaviour under Condition 4. Therefore, where two doctors administer pain-killing medication, one intending to relieve suffering and the other intending the patient's death, both are responsible for the consequences because both have brought about the death intentionally, but only one of them is to blame – for directly intending it. 'Thus, what seems to be the same thing can apparently be done differently by different people, with one . . . deemed blameworthy and the other not' (Kuhse 1987: 158).

Condition 1 states that the action must be a 'good' action, while Condition 2 (the intentionality condition) stipulates that the goodness or badness of the action (and so its permissibility) is determined by what the agent intends. Yet, the principle of double effect does not differentiate between the goodness or badness of agents and the rightness or wrongness of their actions. This is a criticism which causes immense problems for advocates of the principle. Kuhse however insists that the answer still lies in the intentionality of the agent's action:

---

22 Although she admits that treatment may also be disproportionate to other criteria, such as that medical equipment may be put to better use elsewhere: 126–7.
23 As Duff 1990: 78 puts it: '[t]o ascribe responsibility is not yet to blame the agent; it is rather to say that he must justify or excuse his action . . . if he is to avoid blame for it.'

... although *why* what a man does what he does may be of interest to our assessment of his character, it does not change the nature of his action. [If he] ... voluntarily and deliberately brings about a bad effect, he brings it about intentionally and is responsible for it.

(Kuhse 1987: 163)[24]

Four areas of discussion arise from this analysis: firstly, the importance of justification and proportionality, secondly the issue of motive, thirdly, the question of right and wrong/good and bad and finally, the relevance of causality.

Justification and proportionality

As Kuhse points out, as long as her proportionality condition (Condition 4) is not infringed, then an agent can claim that he was justified in bringing about a death. As a justification focuses on the nature of the action (rather than on the individual actor)[25] and because it accepts that the act can be carried out with the intention necessary to satisfy an offence definition, it is easy to see why the principle of double effect is widely perceived as a justificatory defence.[26]

The principle is based on choice and proportionality; Kuhse herself advanced the premise that a treatment choice has to be made according to whether it is proportionate to the patient's medical condition.[27] It follows therefore that '[t]he more severe ... the patient's pain, the greater the justification for risking an earlier death' (Quill *et al* 1997: 1769). If death as a side-effect of treatment is justified:

... it is justified ... because ... hastening death is a price worth paying for the relief of pain. It's not the fact that the side-effect is unwanted that makes it permissible, but rather that the total package of consequences including unwanted side-effects is morally preferable to the alternative.

(Harris 1985: 46)

24 This is only correct to a point, as it must be conceded that we do rely on our assessment of character in order to provide a doctor with the principle of double effect 'defence'. Compare Rachels (1986) in the **Right and wrong/good and bad** section below at page 48.
25 As an excuse does when it excuses the agent from liability for conduct which is unlawful; Card 2006: 65. See also Laing 1990: 112–13; Schopp (1998); and Fletcher 1978: 459.
26 For example by Begley 1998: 871 and Skegg 1988: 133. However, to say that it is a 'defence' is misleading, as claiming that an action is justified is to claim that it is lawful, so a 'defence' would not by definition be required.
27 Including whether or not the patient is dying; it is only irrelevant to the intentionality condition, see above. Interestingly, it was stated hypothetically in *Latimer v R* ([2001] SCR 1) that it would never be proportionate to kill, although in that case the child's condition was operable. Obviously, therefore, the conditions of proportionality would not be satisfied in all circumstances; see the poisoned edible oil example given by Foot 2002: 22.

The quotation acknowledges that justification is also founded upon the law's preference for one course of action rather than another (Smith 1978: 99–100), that is, its rationale is that while the defendant caused the harm or offence, given the justifying circumstances he should be exculpated not just because of the harm he has avoided, but also because, after balancing one choice against another, the benefits of treatment (relief of pain and suffering) sufficiently outweigh the risk of the side-effect of the patient dying (Buchanan 1996: 27). As Ognall J said in *Cox*:

> We all appreciate that some medical treatment . . . carries with it a serious risk to the health or even the life of the patient. Doctors are frequently confronted with, no doubt, distressing dilemmas. They have to make up their minds as to whether the risk . . . is, or is not, medically justified. If a doctor genuinely believes that a certain course is beneficial to his patient . . . then even though he recognises that that course carries with it a risk to life, he is fully entitled, nonetheless, to pursue it.
>
> (*Cox per* Ognall J at 41)[28]

Balancing the risk of treatment against the benefit to the patient forms the essence of justification, and this justificatory element has a vital part to play in a suggested formalisation of this double effect defence. More will be said on this in the final chapter.

Motives

As we know, and as Kuhse concedes in her analysis of the principle of double effect, motives do not tell us whether a person acted intentionally or not. In fact, motives – even if good – do not 'displace' a person's intention[29] (Wilson 2002: 151), but then, they are not meant to. As such, they do not make a person any less responsible for doing something because, contrary to intention – which is a condition of responsibility – motives are relevant only to questions of culpability and justifiability (Sistare 1987: 307–12).

Assessing motive does, however, perform a number of other important functions. Firstly, motive provides a reason as to why a person acted in the way he did. In fact, it could be said that alleviation of pain could really be a motive and not an intention, because if we were to ask a doctor why he was administering analgesics to a patient, he would reply that it was in order to

---

28 Compare Butler-Sloss LJ's approval of Lord Donaldson's judgment in *Re J* (1990) in *Bland* (1993) at 344–5.

29 However, a good motive can enable juries to exercise the foresight/intention get-out clause by holding that foresight of virtual certainty is not intention; Norrie (1999) and in his chapter on 'Motive and Intention' (2001).

deal with that patient's pain (Jonsen 1996: 51). Indeed, we have already seen the relevance of motive in a number of cases, such as *Gillick, Re A (Children)* (especially Walker LJ's judgment where the doctor's conduct was not seen as criminal if he had acted upon his clinical judgment), *Moor, Steane*[30] and *Adams*.[31]

Secondly, motives are relevant in assessing the 'good' or 'bad' character[32] of the agent; you would perhaps be more favourably disposed to a person who acted with a good motive than one who acted with a bad one, even if they were performing the same action.[33] A contrary argument – that if the action itself is an inherently bad action, then no amount of good motive or intention can make the act a good one[34] – misses the point and ignores the truth that cases where the principle of double effect may be invoked are not considered to be inherently bad. Rather, they are simply cases of the doctor performing his duty to treat his patient in the best possible way.

Right and wrong/good and bad

It has long been recognised that although motive may help in telling us whether actions are right or wrong, the distinction between intention and foresight does not. The important thing is, however, that it is never claimed that it does. The distinction is not a test to determine whose behaviour is right and whose is wrong, or that someone who kills intentionally is a 'worse person' than someone who brings about death as a foreseen side-effect;[35] if the action itself is permissible (Condition 1 of Kuhse's analysis) and 'if there is a serious reason for undertaking it' (Condition 4 of Kuhse's analysis) then it may be carried out regardless (or in spite of) what the foreseen consequences will be (Boyle 1980: 533).

---

30 Compare *R v Le Brun* ([1992] 94 Cr App R 101) and see Smith, J.C. 1989: 61.
31 For example, Jefferson 2006: 50 suggests that motive could have provided Dr Adams with a defence. See also Biggs 1996a: 882 on motive and its implications in *Arthur, Adams, Carr* and *Cox*.
32 On character and criminality generally, see Gardner 1998: 575.
33 Yet this causes a problem: can it be said that a doctor whose motive is to alleviate pain and suffering by means of the patient's death is a 'bad' person, bearing in mind that what he does is to decrease the amount of time for which a patient suffers? Is he a morally worse person that a doctor who intends only to relieve pain where death is a possible side-effect? Begley 1998: 872 has disagreed with this argument on the basis that in the case where two doctors act in the same way, except that one directly intends a patient's death and the other only indirectly intends it, can one seriously say that this has any bearing on the morality of the agent's action because in order to ascertain that the doctor's intention reflects his moral character, enquiries would have to made into the doctor's motive. In this she questions the very foundation of Rachels's argument as discussed below.
34 For more on this, see Pellegrino 1996: 169.
35 For discussion on this see Frey 1996: 68–9.

Rachels finds the distinction which is made between intention and foresight to be totally unacceptable. He tells the story of Jack and Jill, two young people who visit their lonely grandmother one afternoon. Jack, while knowing that his grandmother is going to make her will, merely visits her to cheer her up. It is no part of his plan to influence her in any way, but he does realise that his grandmother may be influenced by his visit. Jill visits because she wants to be included among her grandmother's heirs. Both do exactly the same thing – they keep their lonely grandmother company one afternoon – and while the consequences of what they do may also be the same, their intentions are entirely different (as are their motives). However, because they did the same thing, Rachels contends that we cannot say that one acted wrongly and the other acted rightly, because '[i]f . . . [an] . . . act is wrong with one intention, how can it be right with another?' (Rachels 1986: 92). The relevance of intention in this context is not to decide whether an act is right or wrong; rather, its relevance is in assessing the character of the person who does the act, which is a totally different thing. He goes on to say that supposing you are trying to decide what to do in a given situation, for example, whether to continue treatment:

> . . . the rightness or wrongness of an act is determined by the reasons for and against it . . . The intention you would have, if you decided to cease treatment, is not one of the things you need to consider. It is not among the reasons for or against the action. That is why it is irrelevant to determining whether the action is right.
>
> (Rachels 1986: 95)[36]

Based on the principle that the reason for or against an action is the motive, this reinforces the argument for taking motive into account.

Causality

The final area of discussion arising from Kuhse's analysis is the relevance of causality (it will be remembered that her Condition 3 states that the bad effect must not be the means of achieving the good effect and as has been seen already, the principle of double effect does not permit killing in order to relieve pain).

Briefly here – because causation is the topic of a later chapter – it is obvious that in situations where pain-killing medication is administered and the principle of double effect is invoked, causality is as relevant as it is in situations where treatment is withdrawn (the subject of the next chapter), albeit administering pain-killing medication is an 'act' whereas the withdrawing treatment

36 And see generally 93–5.

is interpreted as an 'omission'. This is because in all of these cases, there is potentially more than one cause of death and it is one of the court's functions to ascertain what *the* cause of death is. Thus, where a doctor administers palliative medication, there are potentially three causes of death:

(1) The patient died from the underlying disease and the medication had no part to play in the death. This was seen in, for example, *Adams*, where Devlin J made it clear that death was caused by the illness and not by the administration of any medication (but as in *Moor*, neither case relied on the normal or 'standard causation direction').[37]

(2) The medication accelerated a death which would otherwise have occurred later. This raises two distinct points for further discussion. Firstly, the link between accelerating and/or causing death and the *de minimis* requirement in causation,[38] and secondly, whether it can be categorically claimed that increasing pain-killing medication can cause death. There is significant disagreement among the profession as to whether or not this is so; on the one hand, the invocation of the principle of double effect as a defence in itself implies that increasing medication can kill the patient on the basis that '[t]here would be no need to apply . . . [it] . . . if death was not hastened by the treatment' (Hunt 1999: 440). On the other hand, however, there is significant literature which claims that pain-killing medication simply does not and cannot have this effect.[39] This can be because of the development of tolerance by the patient (Edwards and Tolle 1992: 255), because minimising the incapacitating effects of pain prolongs and improves the patient's quality of life (Skegg 1988: 134), or because of the nature of the medication and the variability between individuals – which depends upon such things as the patient's general condition, metabolism and weight – make it impossible to predict whether one particular dose in a long series will be the last one; '[t]he dosage required by one patient may be hundreds of times greater than that required by another . . .' (National Council for Hospice and Specialist Palliative Care Services 1998: 372). Eventually the patient will die, but whether this is as a result of the pain-killing medication or not, the fact that the patient may be too ill and fragile to withstand any more medication does not necessarily mean that it was the medication which accelerated his death. There is therefore only 'a risk' that the next dose might

37 Interviews with both Consultant Neurologist and General Practitioner confirmed that, in their view, it is the disease that is killing the patient; the big dose of pain-killer is an 'accessory' to the original condition.
38 See Hart and Honoré (1985) in the analysis of *Adams*, above. This first point is analysed in detail in the causation chapter below at pages 111–12.
39 Brownstein (2001) explains how empirical evidence shows that death is not hastened. See also Brock 2004: 136.

hasten the patient's death; there is no certainty that it will (Lineacre Centre 1994: 79). This is the '. . . gray area between euthanasia and bona fide treatment' recognised by Beezer CJ, dissenting in *Compassion in Dying v Washington* (Beezer CJ at 839).

(3) By administering the medication, the doctor caused the death. In fact, Kuhse concedes that this will be so in some cases (Kuhse 1987: 101), as Reinhardt J did in *Compassion in Dying v Washington* above. Generally, however, doctors will not be held to be the cause of death either in administering pain-killing medication or in withdrawing treatment, but, as will be seen in the next two chapters, there is certainly room to argue that the doctor's behaviour may be *a* cause of death, or at the very least, that he is the part cause.

Conclusion

A report on the results of a study of 300 general practitioners appeared shortly after the decision in *Moor*, in which one in seven doctors admitted to helping patients to die (*The Sunday Times* 15 November 1998). The report confirmed that many doctors deployed double effect, and in general, it is a principle supported by the medical profession (Fried *et al* 1993: 727). It has also been supported in the Appleton Conference (1992: 3), by the Council on Ethical and Judicial Affairs of the American Medical Association (1992: 2231), the New York Multi Society Task Force (1994: 6 (preface)), and the HLSC (1993–4: para 242). It has been said that it is of '. . . immense practical importance in the care of dying patients . . .' (Sulmasy and Pellegrino 1999: 545) and it has been called '. . . an ethical cornerstone in the medical treatment of the terminally ill' (Quill 1993: 1039).[40]

The principle does make it hard to maintain the line between intention and foresight, and to maintain the same line between killing and administering palliative care (Grubb 1993: 367) and, as Richard Huxtable wrote in a letter to *The Times*, in principle of double effect cases 'there appears to be . . . manipulation of the facts to enable the "right" resolution' (*The Times*, 18 May 1999). The cases discussed here are proof that this is correct. The courts have, quite properly, created an exception to the law of murder but all the people concerned, the patient, medical professionals, and society are best served by acknowledging that doctors, in their medical role, and acting in their patients' best interests, have a 'special dispensation' (Stauch, Wheat with Tingle 2006: 646) when treating a terminally ill patient with palliative medicine.

In *R v Arthur* [1981] 12 BMLR 1, Farquharson J said that '[t]here is no

---

40 However, criticisms of the principle have been made by, for example, Begley (1998); Price (1997); Glover (1986); and Clarke (1997).

special law in this country that places doctors in a separate category and gives them extra protection over the rest of us' (*Arthur* at 5).[41] Such statements hide behind rose-tinted spectacles. Doctors are and should necessarily be treated differently because of the context in which they work. We find their activities acceptable (barring some exceptions) because they are acting in the course of their duties; in *Compassion in Dying v Washington* Reinhardt J said:

> In the case of 'double effect' we excuse the act or, to put it more accurately, we find the act acceptable, not because the doctors sugarcoat the facts in order to permit society to say that they couldn't really know the consequences of their action, but because the act is medically and ethically appropriate even though the result – the patient's death – is both foreseeable and intended.
>
> (*Compassion in Dying v Washington per* Reinhardt J at 823)[42]

The principle of double effect has to be viewed in its context; medical professionals work in an environment where they have to consider the consequences of their activities and weigh up risks and benefits on a daily basis.[43] In such an environment, hurtful actions simply cannot be avoided (Quill *et al* 1997: 1768). In exercising their duty, doctors have to be able to treat their patients humanely and adequately. A 'legitimate and lawful' way of fulfilling that duty has always been through the provision of medication to control pain, 'even if death . . . is risked' (Annas 1998: 213).

In the previous chapter, it was noted that the Van der Maas investigation on *Euthanasia and Other Medical Decisions at the End of Life* (1992) introduced the category of acting partly with the purpose of hastening the end of life. This category was included specifically to allow for the situation where, while death was not unwelcome, neither was it foremost in the physician's mind.[44] This acknowledges the truth that a doctor can determine never to intend to kill, and yet he can be glad that a patient's suffering has been relieved by virtue of his death (Finnis 1991: 52). Marcia Angell recognised this when she treated a cancer patient at whose request she increased the dosage of morphine. She confessed that her intention was both to relieve her patient's pain and bring about death (Angell 1998: 4).[45]

Most treatment choices a doctor has to make have undesirable consequences, but defining a doctor's responsibilities so as to prioritise his goal – of which relieving suffering forms but one small part (President's Commission

---

41 Expressing the same sentiment as Devlin in his summing-up in *Adams* in *Easing the Passing* 1986: 171 and by the BMA 1993: 157.
42 Compare Tur (2002).   43 A fact acknowledged by the HLSC (1993–4): para 244.
44 And because this situation was not covered by the other categories; Van der Maas *et al* (1992).
45 And compare Quill and his patient 'Diane' 1993: 1040.

1983: 79) – enables acceptance of his ultimately beneficent behaviour as justified in the circumstances, despite criticisms of an unequal application of the law. While it may be thought therefore that there are no benefits to the intention/foresight distinction, it represents a way of recognising that we must sometimes acknowledge that some side-effects we do not want are brought about simply by virtue of the 'practical constraints' imposed by the situation (Carse 1996: 88).

The principle of double effect has been used here as an example of one of the problems associated with the concept of intention and its relevance to murder in the medical domain. Equally important and the subject of the next chapter is the distinction made by the courts between acts and omissions in withdrawing life-sustaining treatment. The patient's death is most certainly foreseen (especially if the life-sustaining treatment being withdrawn is artificial nutrition and hydration) but the doctor's omission to continue treatment is deemed not to have 'caused' the patient's death. The act/omission distinction is thus a further example of the way in which intention and causation have been manipulated to provide doctors with another 'defence'.

Chapter 3

Acts and omissions

> ... even if there is sense in the distinction the current state of the law is
> unsatisfactory both morally and intellectually ... [however] the distinction
> between acts and omissions exists, and ... we must give effect to it.
> (*Airedale NHS Trust v Bland per* Lord Mustill at 394)

Introduction

In ordinary language, and in this context, the distinction between acts and
omissions is the distinction between a person who acts positively to bring
about a death and a person who omits to intervene in a course of events in
which he could have prevented death. However, the term 'omission' has also
been legally interpreted to cover the situation where a doctor has to perform
what is ostensibly an action in order to withdraw (life-sustaining) treatment
from a patient. This facet of the distinction is one created by the courts as a
tactic to provide doctors with a defence against a murder charge where death
is the certain, or even foreseen consequence of a patient's death. The distinction is inextricably linked with intention, with causation and with the perceived difference between killing and letting die. This is because if the doctor
'acts' he would be deemed to have the intention required to kill (cause the
death of) the patient. Conversely, if he has merely omitted to act, the intent to
kill is considered absent and he would be regarded as having allowed or
permitted the patient to die of his pre-existing illness or injury.

In the UK, there is no general liability for omissions unless there is a duty
to act. One example of such a duty is that of a doctor to care for his patients;
thus he would breach that duty if he omitted to provide for those in his care.
On this basis, therefore, if the patient's death follows as a consequence of
treatment withdrawal, why is the doctor not held to have caused the death?
Although treatment withdrawal is interpreted as an omission, surely the presence of the prerequisite duty would entail finding the doctor to be liable for
the demise of the patient?

This conclusion was avoided in *Bland*, where life-sustaining treatment in the form of artificial nutrition and hydration was withdrawn. The House of Lords followed the formula of finding that the conduct was an omission and not an act, and held that any duty ceased to exist when it became obvious that it would not be in Anthony Bland's best interests to continue treatment. The absence of a duty by the doctor was thus used to permit withdrawal of treatment without criminal liability arising for the death of the patient.

The formula raises a number of questions as to the role of causation and intention in the acts/omissions distinction. That it is legally problematic can be seen in the case itself with Lord Goff's statement that whereas a doctor's conduct in switching off a life-support machine would be construed as an omission, this would not be the case where an interloper did exactly the same thing. The semanticism and linguistic sophistry used in the distinction, and the 'acute unease' (*Bland per* Lord Mustill at 388) attached to reliance on it, has been conceded by judges in the British courts, but this has not prohibited their continued – albeit reluctant – use of the distinction.

However, despite criticisms as to its vagueness, obscurity, elusiveness and inadequacy,[1] considerations of public policy suggest that the acts/omissions distinction should be maintained. If it were not, and as withdrawing treatment from patients occurs on a daily basis in all our hospitals, liability would be unfettered and there would be widespread 'killing' by doctors of their patients. The distinction thus enables the 'right' resolution, but the method by which that result is achieved is defective when it is based on an untenable fabrication which relies, to a great extent, on judicial intuition and preconceived categorisations of what is acceptable and what is not.

What are acts?

> . . . an act consists of events or states of affairs for which a person might be responsible according to the principles of responsibility that guide such judgments; and so an act has taken place when such events occur or when such states of affairs exist.
>
> (Gross 1979: 56)

Hyman Gross ventured to provide a definition of sorts (and it has to be conceded that it does not assist much) where other philosophers have made it clear that it is nigh impossible to provide a definitive explanation of what an act is (Duff 1995: 104). However, we do know that actions occur when we perform some activity or we 'do' something (Hornsby 1980: 2–3). Generally we can see if someone acts because it usually involves moving some part of the body, although it must be emphasised that acts are not *exclusively* based

---

1 See, for example, Kuhse 1987: 38; Gormally 1994a: 127; Brock 1993: 190; Fletcher 1973: 121 Begley 1998: 865 and Anderson 1978: 102.

on bodily movement.[2] Social scientists and philosophers claim that an action always has a corresponding intention,[3] but this is only true in so far as it is easier to prove intention in the case of acts than it is in the case of omissions (but this does not mean that omissions are not intended).

Even in everyday language, there is more than one way of describing an action. We can choose a description which gives what we do an interpretation which best suits the circumstances and the nature of our enquiry (and perhaps which also best describes our intention as well), and very often, we will explain what we did in a way which makes what we did seem to be the right thing both in our eyes and in the eyes of others (Duff 1990: 41–2).[4] Take withdrawing treatment, for example; such an incident can be explained as either an act or as an omission. From a purely factual point of view, one would have to *act* to turn a respirator on or off in the same way one would switch a light or a television on or off (Mason and Laurie 2006: 639–40). This clearly involves a physical movement which can be described as an act, and yet a doctor who switches off a respirator is seen as omitting to provide further treatment (and letting the patient die from his existing disease) rather than acting in a way which 'kills' the patient. Contrarily, however, we know that an interloper who does exactly the same thing is interpreted as performing an act which would attract liability for killing the patient. The fact that both 'do' the same thing cannot therefore be the distinguishing factor; on the contrary, the distinction between them is reliant on preconceptions which are based on the nature of the inquiry being made, and on the context, identity and motive of the actor. The following observation by Fletcher is a classic example of the value-laden way in which we reach our conclusion:

> . . . [the] test . . . is whether . . . we should be inclined to speak of the activity as one that causes harm or merely that permits harm to occur . . . Because we are prompted to refer to the activity of turning off the respirator as an activity permitting death to occur, rather than causing death, we may classify the case as an omission, rather than as an act.
>
> (Fletcher, G.P. 1969: 77)[5]

2 As has been said, '. . . there can be cases of killing in which the killer does nothing (e.g., killing by starving to death), and there can be cases of letting die which involve doing something (e.g., hiding the lifeline that could save the drowning person)'; Steinbock and Norcross 1994: 24.

3 For example, Searle 1983: 82; Brand (1984); Thomson (1977); and Davis (1979).

4 Anscombe's (1976: 37 *et seq*) tale of the various activities of the plumber who is pumping poisoned water into a household's water supply is comparable here.

5 Fletcher 1978: 421, later refers to an omission as a 'passive abstention', but also (in his chapter 8), distinguishes between two types of omissions – breach of a duty to act (this involves direct liability) and failing to intervene, namely, commission by omission – this involves what he calls 'derivative liability', that is, where a person's conduct is 'insufficient in itself to constitute a violation of the norm under which he is punished'. This derivative liability is based on some independent process of events over which the doctor has minimal control.

Categorising an activity which 'permits death to occur' as an omission (and conversely that an omission is an activity which permits death to occur) is simply a descriptive expression which does not actually exist in definitional terms. It is a construction devised to provide some kind of explanation for the distinction between acts and omissions.

What are omissions?

A dictionary definition of an omission describes it as 'forbearing to perform', the 'non-performance or neglect of an action or duty'[6] (*Shorter Oxford English Dictionary* 1993). In order to omit to do something, there must have been an obligation or a requirement to do it. Not doing it must therefore involve a conscious decision not to do it. Kuhse describes an intentional omission as a '*refraining*', which she defines as a deliberate non-intervention in a course of events where '. . . an agent . . . has the *ability* and *opportunity* to perform an action . . . that she *believes* would, if performed, save or prolong . . . life' (Kuhse 1987: 43).[7] It can be seen, therefore, that an agent cannot accidentally refrain from preventing death; there must be an intention to refrain. Logically, therefore, it must be possible to intend death through an omission, even if the link between intention and omission is weaker than that between intention and an action (so that it would be more difficult to prove intention in the case of omissions than it would be in the case of an act) (Smith 1984: 97).[8] Therefore, to say that death is the result of an omission and not a commission is not of itself sufficient to remove it from the category of killing. As Gormally has said, '. . . a "decision to terminate someone's life" may be carried out by a planned course of omissions as well as by a positive act' (Gormally 1994a: 185). Indeed, this can be seen in *Bland* where their Lordships, despite holding that withdrawing artificial nutrition and hydration from Anthony Bland amounted to an omission, nonetheless freely admitted that the intention behind the proposed course of treatment was that the patient should die (Lord Browne-Wilkinson: 383).[9]

Thus the fact that behaviour is construed as an omission does not mean that it is not possible to intend to omit, and neither does it mean that an omission does not have a consequence. A consequence still arises after an omission; the patient does not go into a state of suspended animation simply because something has not been done. It is clear that an omission is more than just not doing something; according to Fletcher:

6 Interestingly, it is also described there as 'the *action* of omitting'.
7 Compare Lord Goff's 'desisting' in *Bland* (1993) at 369.
8 See Ashworth (1989) for more on this.
9 In fact, three of the Law Lords in *Bland* (1993) said this, and the other two did not disagree. What this means is that even if a doctor had the intention to kill, as long as there is no duty, the law does not concern itself with or pursue that intention; see Skegg 1988: 174 and 176.

It is naïve and superficial to suppose that because we do not do anything positively to hasten the patient's death, we have thereby avoided complicity in his death. Not doing anything is doing something; it is a decision to act every bit as much as deciding for any other deed.

(Fletcher 1973: 121)

As with an act, an omission to act can therefore also 'cause' a consequence. As will be seen in the next chapter, Hart and Honoré make a distinction between a cause and what they describe as a 'mere condition'.[10] A mere condition cannot be a cause if we are specifically answering the question of why did what happened happen now – why did this man die at this time? Using the example of a gardener failing to water flowers, they show that an omission can be a cause; the flowers died because the gardener failed to water them. We know that flowers die if not given water, but it is the gardener's omission to water these flowers now that causes them to die.

In ordinary life, the requirement for a causal explanation is most often prompted by a deviation from the norm; '. . . in such cases, we are not looking for the cause of "death", but for the cause of death *under circumstances which call for an explanation*' (Hart and Honoré 1985: 39–40). In the case of the flowers, what made this difference was the gardener's omission.

Thus, although intention and causation are the factors the criminal law uses to distinguish behaviour and ascribe liability, it is not possible to maintain the distinction between acts and omissions on the basis of either of these because an omission can, like an act, be intended, can have intended consequences and can be a cause. This seems to obviate any distinction between the two, and yet it is evident that there is a distinction which is capable of providing doctors – but not others – with a defence.

The reason for this is because of who the doctor is and because of what he does. Although on the one hand the law should not condone inequality of treatment between categories of persons; on the other hand, if we permit and expect doctors to carry out life and death functions which no one else is allowed to perform, then they should be given corresponding protection when a patient dies following the proper carrying out of those functions (Tur 2002: 91–3). If doctors are 'killing' their patients when they administer pain-killing medication or when they withdraw life-sustaining treatment, it is (barring some exceptions such as Harold Shipman) not the same as other types of more heinous killings and should accordingly not be punished in the same way (Ashworth 2000: 245). This principle, together with the absence of formal defences which the medical profession can and could rely on, have meant that the courts have had to resort to constructions such as the

---

10 Mere conditions are factors which we know or assume exist and which are 'present as part of the usual state or mode of operation . . .' Hart and Honoré 1985: 34–5; see next chapter.

acts/omissions distinction (and the principle of double effect) in order to exonerate doctors in situations where lay persons would be found liable.

Acts and omissions: a contrived distinction?

Sophistry and semantics

The distinction between acts and omissions relies to a great extent on a strictly semantic analysis, where events can be described as either an act or as an omission depending on the circumstances. It is interesting to note that whereas judges in the UK have used the distinction to great effect, their counterparts in the US have not relied on it to such an extent. In *Conroy* (*In the Matter of Claire Conroy* 98 N.J. 321; 486 A. 2d 1209; 48 ALR 4th 1 (1985)) for example, the court rejected what it saw as a 'nebulous' and 'elusive' distinction as being of limited use (Schreiber J at 41). In *Compassion in Dying v Washington*, Reinhardt CJ commented that it was a 'distinction without a difference' (Reinhardt CJ at 822), a sentiment also expressed by Lord Lowry in *Bland*. All but one of the judges in that case categorised removing artificial nutrition and hydration as an omission[11] (and indeed, they had to do so in order to find the proposed course of action lawful), yet it is clear that their Lordships were left with a sense of 'profound misgiving' (Lord Mustill at 400) and that they themselves doubted what they called the 'morally and intellectually dubious distinction between acts and omissions', but that because it existed, they had to apply it.

The *Bland* case shows that the courts were trying to absolve doctors by using a doctrine that even they admitted was of doubtful validity. However, the Court of Appeal quite rightly questioned its appropriateness in *Re A (Children)*, a case easily distinguishable on its facts from the treatment withdrawal cases such as *Bland*. Johnson J, the judge at first instance, concluded that the operation to separate the conjoined twins was lawful because it represented the withdrawal of the blood supply from one twin to the other, a perfectly plausible conclusion after *Bland*. In other words, he tried to justify the intervention on existing *Bland* principles. It was hardly surprising that he was not prepared to break new ground and interpret the operation as a positive act, rather than as an omission.

The judges in the Court of Appeal had no such qualms though, and all three not only (unfairly) criticised this aspect of Johnson J's judgment, but also verified categorically that the procedures carried out in the operation

---

11 Lord Browne-Wilkinson (*Bland* 1993 at 384) said it was 'undoubtedly a positive act' but that it should not be construed as such, because this would introduce 'intolerably fine distinctions' and the tube itself did nothing, so removing it – even if it was a positive act – would not cause the death. This ignores the relevance of the tube; without the need to provide food through it, it would be unnecessary.

would be intended '. . . positive acts and they would directly cause Mary's death' (Brooke LJ at 1027).[12] Watson has said that the decision '. . . appears to drive a coach and horses through the pretence that a valid distinction can be drawn between permitting a patient to die . . . and taking positive action to cause death . . .' (Watson 2000: 5). It has to be said that this would seem to be a more honest approach, but the facts of the case are exceptional.[13]

Practical distinctions?

Although there may not be a tenable distinction between the opposing concepts of acts and omissions, the practical consequences which arise from the categorisation are significant enough to show that despite criticism of the distinction,[14] there are nonetheless a number of clear and valid policy reasons as to why events which are undoubtedly acts can and should be interpreted as omissions.

Firstly, in these days of technological dependence, if there was no distinction between acts and omissions, the consequences would be that '. . . doctors . . . [would] . . . actually cause the death of the majority of their patients' (Randall 1997: 374). In fact, categorising an event as an omission rather than as an act is, for a number of reasons, a most effective way in which to remove liability and responsibility from the medical professional to the disease process (Brock 1992: 13). As the link between omission and outcome is weaker than it is for acts (Wilson 2002: 190), categorising an event as an omission makes it easier to say that the consequence arose as a result of something other than the failure to act (Fincham and Jaspars: 1980: 122). In 1986, Sugarman conducted an empirical study, using vignettes and a questionnaire, to ascertain the way in which the public judged doctors engaging in euthanasia. The results of the study showed that the participants appreciated the presence of two perceived causes of death – the doctor's action and the patient's illness – as this enabled them to ascribe the death of the patient to his illness and not to the doctor (Sugarman 1986).[15]

Secondly, as omissions limit what a person can be liable for (through the common law requirement of a duty to act), the distinction avoids placing an 'intolerable' burden on people who would otherwise be liable without limit (Glover 1986: 93).[16]

---

12 See also Walker LJ at 1062, and Ward LJ at 1003.
13 Although it has been applied in *State of Queensland v Alyssa Nolan and Anor* ([2001] QCS 174), in so far as it was possible for the court to find comparable provisions in the Queensland Criminal Code.
14 By, for example, Kuhse, Begley and Gormally (already mentioned) and, for example, Brock (1993).
15 More is said on this in the next chapter.
16 See quotation in the second chapter above by the Roman Catholic Priest.

Thirdly, human nature would suggest that '[w]e have much stronger inhibitions against active wrongdoing than against wrongfully omitting' (Williams 1991: 88). Categorising withdrawing treatment as an omission therefore satisfies our sense of justice.

Fourthly, it is seen as more psychologically 'comforting' particularly for doctors not to be perceived as the cause of death of their patients (Lynn and Childress 1986: 57);[17] evidence suggests that members of the medical profession do see a great difference between acts and omissions if only because, on a personal level, it is easier to live with the consequences of what they are required to do:

> Most doctors have an emotional attachment to the acts/omissions idea; acts or omissions have no moral validity . . . it is about how human beings find it easier to agree with an omission than to carry out an act . . . Doctors . . . feel more comfortable with the . . . doctrine even though there is no difference, because the consequences are the same.[18]

In the case of *B v An NHS Hospital Trust*, the doctor in whose care B had been placed was unable to switch off her ventilation because '[s]he felt she was being asked to kill Ms B' (Butler-Sloss P at para 57). This same perception of killing the patient has also been expressed by other practitioners;[19] thus, while common sense would suggest that the distinction between acts and omissions is spurious at best, if it helps the medical profession to continue carrying out their medical role and if it helps society to think that doctors are not killing their patients, then the distinction should be maintained, but on a more formalised basis.

The duty of care as a distinction

As has been seen, omissions liability is based on a prerequisite duty (and thus can be avoided in the absence of that duty), whereas liability in the case of acts is simply based on the sanctity of life (Elkington 1968: 744) (and can only be avoided if the court finds an excuse or justification as it did in *Re A (Children)* for example).

What, therefore, is a duty? It can arise as '. . . an incident of some special relationship where there is dependence on one side and support on the other' (Steinbock and Norcross 1994: 29). This definition acknowledges the fact that generally a duty arises by virtue of the relationship between people (such as between a parent and a child) or where responsibility has been assumed for

---

17 This is the psychological defence mechanism mentioned in chapter 1 above.
18 Interview with Consultant Neurologist.
19 For example, Edwards and Tolle 1992: 256.

another.[20] However, the courts have debated whether or not a duty could (or should) arise in more tenuous circumstances. In *R v Khan and Khan* ([1998] Crim LR 830), the defendants supplied a 15-year-old girl with heroin. She fell into a coma and subsequently died after taking an excessive amount of the drug, but the defendants left her to die without helping her or summoning medical assistance (which the evidence suggested would 'probably' have saved her life). The judge felt that the facts supported a conviction for 'manslaughter by omission' (on the basis that the *actus reus* here was the omission to summon help rather than the supply of heroin). However, the appeal was allowed because the judge did not give any direction to the jury on the required duty of care for omissions liability. On the possible existence of a duty of care, it was said that it could well be right that a duty was owed in such circumstances, but that this would obviously widen the ambit of persons to whom a duty of care was owed (Swinton Thomas LJ at 831).[21]

A similar factual situation arose in *R v Sinclair* ([1998] WL 1044437), where the victim and Sinclair each injected themselves with methadone, after which the victim became unconscious. Sinclair and the flat owner both made some effort to revive him, but did not call an ambulance until 16 hours later. In the Court of Appeal, Rose LJ held that the flat owner, who was not medically qualified and who had not previously met the deceased victim, did not owe him a duty of care but that Sinclair, who had been his close friend and who had lived with him almost as a brother, could well have been found to have owed the victim a duty, had the jury been properly directed (Rose LJ at 6). Unlike *Khan*, however, the appeal was not allowed on this point. Although in both cases the Crown put their case on the basis of failure to summon medical assistance and not on the provision of the drug, unlike *Khan* where it was said that summoning medical assistance would probably have saved the victim's life, in *Sinclair*, the medical expert was unable to confirm that conclusion with the same degree of certainty. Therefore, the appeal was allowed on the ground that a fuller direction on causation should have been given '. . . as to whether acceleration of the moment of death was other than minimal' (Rose LJ at 3).[22]

Another definition of a duty reiterates the existence of a relationship, but confines it to '. . . relationships that require people to intervene to prevent the

---

20 There are many examples, including *R v Gibbins and Proctor* ((1918) 13 Cr App R 134) and *R v Stone and Dobinson* ([1977] QB 354).

21 Upon what basis could such a duty rest? The court looked at *R v Miller* ([1983] 2 AC 161) (that the defendant created the danger) but J.C. Smith, in his comment on *Khan* 1998: 832–3, notes that Smith and Hogan (he does not specify the edition) suggest a possible duty based on engaging in a hazardous activity.

22 On causation and acceleration, see previous chapter, the section on causation-based argument at page 67 and the conclusion to chapter 4 below at page 111.

death of others' (Fletcher 1978: 372).[23] It is this definition which more precisely reflects a doctor's duty towards his patients (and which perhaps makes it harder to accept that no duty was owed to Anthony Bland) as it emphasises the necessity of being in the vicinity to be able to act, or at least potentially being able to control what could happen. This is illustrated in *Reeves v Commissioner of Police* ([1999] QB 169 (HC) (1)); *Reeves v Commissioner of Police* ([2000] 1 AC 360 (HL) (2)) where a prisoner committed suicide while in police custody. Those officers guarding him had been made aware that he was a suicide risk and, as such, the House of Lords held that, although 'unusual', both police and prison authorities nonetheless owed a duty of care to prevent a prisoner from committing suicide, which arose 'from the complete control' they had over prisoners in their custody (Lord Hoffman at 369).[24]

The judgments in *Sinclair* and *Reeves* illustrate the importance of relationships in the formation of a duty, but the idea of a duty of care serves other functions as well; for example, Fletcher has also described duty as a device which – very much like a causal inquiry – narrows a sphere of liability which would otherwise be too wide (Fletcher, G.P. 1969: 80). This definition rightly concedes that without this concept of duty, we would all be impossibly responsible. In fact, duty and responsibility are linked together in two senses. Firstly, a person who owes a duty to care for another has commensurate responsibilities over and for that person and secondly – following on logically from the first proposition – in the context of omissions, if there is no duty then an omitter is not responsible for the consequences of omitting, whereas an actor would be.

Choice, control and responsibility in the distinction between acts and omissions

Put simply, Simester argues that '. . . the moral distinction between act and omission . . . depends upon questions of responsibility'; if there is a duty, then a person would be just as responsible for omitting to comply with that duty as he would if he was an actor for whom the duty requirement was not a prerequisite condition (Simester 1995: 311).

Similarly, Frey's theory of 'control responsibility' (explained in the context of the principle of double effect in the previous chapter) states that in the context of acts and omissions, a doctor is as causally responsible for an

---

23 This is not strictly true where the patient is already dying, because the most that can be done is to delay and not prevent death.

24 The case is analysed more fully in the next chapter. There is no doubt that the concept of duty has been widened here, as it has in s 5 of the Domestic Violence, Crime and Victims Act 2005, which imposes liability for omissions by introducing a new offence of causing or allowing the death of a child or vulnerable adult in some limited circumstances. Compare s 44 Mental Capacity Act 2005.

omission as he is for an act, because it is his decision to proceed in that way. In such cases Frey asserts that because death does not arise from '. . . a mistake, an accident, ignorance, negligence, or recklessness', then it must be a 'chosen' death (Frey 1996: 73).[25]

The importance of choice and control in omissions is also reiterated by, for example, Singer, who notes that doctors are responsible for the consequences of letting their patients die because they could have chosen to continue postponing the death (Singer 1994: 219), and Kuhse who states that an agent '. . . is just as responsible for a consequence she refrains from preventing as she is for a consequence she brings about by a deliberate action' (Kuhse 1987: 60).[26] According to her notion of 'refraining' from preventing death, the doctor's omission is the 'morally significant cause of the patient's death.'

Whereas in choosing to increase pain-killing medication (an act), it can be plausibly argued that neither the medication nor the doctor is the cause of death (even if it is foreseeable), where a choice is made to withdraw life-sustaining treatment (an omission) it is indisputably more than mere foresight that the patient will die. In fact, it is even more than a virtual certainty. Therefore, we may well go a step further than Kuhse and claim that the doctor is more than morally responsible and is more than simply a moral cause of the patient's death. In other words, we can argue that he is *the* cause of death in the sense that he kills the patient and does not simply let him die.

Killing and letting die

The link between killing/letting die and acts/omissions can clearly be seen in the formula set out earlier, that one kills when performing an action, but one merely lets die in omitting to act. The tie with intention is that whereas one can intend to kill, the same intent is said not to be present in letting die. Similarly, the causative connection is formulated on the premise that killing causes death, whereas letting die does not. Although intention and causation are the only supposed legitimate and legal bases for distinguishing behaviour and ascribing liability in the distinction between killing and letting die, the distinction cannot be maintained on the basis of either of these because letting die (like an omission) can be intended and can cause death.

Upon what is the killing/letting die distinction based?

A brief and basic explanation of killing and letting die would suggest a clear distinction between them; for example:

---

25 See Carse's chapter in response; 'Causal Responsibility and Moral Culpability' (1996).
26 Although as noted earlier, to say that a person is responsible does not mean to say that he is to blame.

(a) A dictionary definition of 'kill' is to 'cause the death of, to deprive of life, to destroy' (*Oxford Concise English Dictionary* 1995).[27] There is no dictionary definition of letting die, but it is nonetheless a term which is '. . . often used to communicate *approval* of accepting that death will occur, rather than simply to describe the behaviour' (President's Commission (1983: 64).

(b) Generally, killing is confined to 'affirmative' words (Fletcher 1978: 602), such as 'shooting' 'strangling' or 'stabbing'. While there is no such equivalent in letting die, this does not mean that it cannot also be 'affirmative'.

(c) The word 'killing' implies that doing it is wrong, whereas letting die does not (Beauchamp and Childress 2001: 140–1).

(d) Saying 'you have killed' assumes both intention and causation because killing uses positive words, but saying 'you have caused the death' does not imply either the presence of intention or causation and saying 'allowed to die' certainly does not (Williams 1989: 396).

These comparisons suggest that killing and letting die are two opposing concepts, but in the examples below, certain moral factors between them are indistinguishable. In fact, in some instances, such as in the illustration given by Rachels, it could be contended that the letting die is as reprehensible as, if not worse than, the killing (in fact, even letting die is relative in the sense that there are some cases of letting die that are worse than others). By comparison, in the doctor/interloper illustration used earlier, there are moral factors – such as motive and consent, for example – which do separate what the doctor did from what the interloper did.

An example used by Fletcher to show that there is a distinction between killing and letting die is that drowning a person is different from standing by and letting that person drown (Fletcher 1978: 601). Rachels on the other hand argues that there is no real difference and illustrates this by relating the story of Smith and Jones. Smith pushes his young cousin under the water to gain his inheritance, while Jones, for the same reason, watches his cousin drown in the bath but does nothing to save him (Rachels 1975: 79). Can it really be said that in letting his young cousin drown, Jones did not play a causal part in his young cousin's death? Can it equally be said that the intention in the drowning was different from the letting drown?

For those who contend that there is a distinction, their argument is twofold – that in letting die, the actor did not have the necessary intent to kill and that he did not cause the patient's death. We will briefly look at each of these in turn.

---

27 Compare the definition in *Attorney-General's Reference (No. 3 of 1994)* ([1998] AC 245): 264.

Killing and letting die – an intention-based distinction?

There tends to be an assumption that a doctor does not directly intend to kill his patient when he withdraws life-sustaining treatment, but this is an insufficient ground on which to base any definitive argument. When a doctor withdraws (particularly) life-sustaining food and water, he cannot fail to foresee that the inevitable conclusion of this is that the patient will die. Rachels asks:

> . . . what is the cessation of treatment . . . if it is not 'the intentional termination of the life of one human being by another?' Of course it is exactly that, and if it were not, there would be no point to it . . .
>
> (Rachels 1975: 79–80)

If this proposition is accepted, it leads to the following conclusions. Firstly, that letting die, like killing, can be intentional and intended; secondly, one person can 'kill' another by intentionally allowing that person to die; and thirdly, that killing can occur by omission as well as by commission. The argument that one kills when one acts and that one simply lets die when omitting to act is flawed because one can kill by standing still just as one can let die by moving. Thus it can be said that intention is not the decisive factor in distinguishing between killing and letting die.

Killing and letting die – a causation-based distinction?

The second argument used by those who contend that there is a distinction between killing and letting die is that killing causes death, but that in letting die, the patient's death is caused by his underlying disease or illness.[28] The only claim that could possibly be considered persuasive in upholding this argument is one based on making a distinction between an event initiated by or of the doctor's own making, and one which is already in progress. As Brock explains:

> If you kill someone, what you do is to initiate a deadly causal process that leads to the person's death. If you allow someone to die, you allow a deadly causal process which you did not initiate to proceed to its result of a person's death.
>
> (Brock 1993: 189)[29]

In this account, Brock claims that a respirator is holding at bay a deadly

---

28 The distinction assumes that a doctor can save the patient's life; it has to be possible for the doctor to do that before he can be said to allow the patient to die. As Glover 1986: 116, says: '[t]o kill is to shorten a life while to save a life is merely to extend it.'

29 See text to footnote 41 chapter 5 below.

disease process and that by a positive action of turning off the respirator, the doctor allows the disease to proceed. Kuhse, however, disagreeing, claims that whereas a doctor has not 'killed' if he did not initiate the event, he is nonetheless the 'causal agent' if he refrained from intervening in a course of events which will, coupled with his refraining, lead to death (because his refraining is intentional) (Kuhse 1987: 72).[30] She calls this a 'letting die requiring a positive action'; the doctor allows the patient's death to occur as a causal consequence of a medical condition not of his making. This argument is a cunning compromise in the distinction between acts and omissions because it concedes that although turning the machine off is an act, it incurs no liability because the event leading to death was not set off by the doctor.

The same argument can be taken a step further if we think of the medical intervention as a *novus actus interveniens*.[31] This is examined in detail in the next chapter and, as will be seen from the cases analysed there (and indeed those examined in the previous chapter), where a number of causes are operating simultaneously, even though a doctor is (or can be) a causal factor, the courts have held that simply being one cause out of many does not mean he is *the* legal cause. In treatment withdrawal cases, this has been done by naming the same events as 'acts' (killing) in some cases and as 'omissions' (letting die) in others. The distinction between them is based on value judgments as to what is acceptable and justified and what is not. Essentially it is this, and not intention and causation, which is what distinguishes between the doctor and the interloper and between killing and letting die.

Killing and letting die – a justification-based distinction?

It is evident that neither intention nor causation can provide a clear basis for the distinction between killing and letting die, but the question must be asked, do they really have to? If we take the view that these spurious distinctions are creations of the court which serve to provide doctors with a defence for the consequences of their professional activities, then they serve their purpose.

As with the principle of double effect, the basis for the omissions 'defence' is justificatory, so the presence of the requisite intention – be it a case of killing or letting die – is not problematic because justification acknowledges that the offence is carried out with the requisite intention to satisfy the offence definition (Price 2001: 637). Further, if behaviour is justified, it does not matter whether it is an act (killing) or an omission (letting die); as McLachlin J said in *Rodriguez and Attorney-General of British Columbia*

---

30 Compare Hoffman LJ in *Bland* (1993): 356.

31 This is '[a]n act or event that breaks the causal connection between a wrong or crime committed by the defendant and subsequent happenings and therefore relieves the defendant from responsibility for these happenings', Martin (2003).

([1993] 107 DLR (4th) 342), '[i]f the justification for helping someone to end life is established, I cannot accept that it matters whether the act is "passive" ... or "active ..." ' (McLachlin J at 420).

There is no doubt that withdrawing life-sustaining treatment is justifiable in some cases[32] and it is this sense of justification which provides another explanation for the distinction between the doctor and the interloper; if the doctor has acted justifiably in response to a particular set of circumstances by selecting an option which causes the least harm, his conduct is perceived as being correct and right in those circumstances and there is simply no question of any wrongdoing arising.

Again, as with the principle of double effect, in saying that it is justified to withdraw treatment, we once more have to counter the argument that it can never be justified to end another person's life, but that argument holds no weight here where a justified death has already been conceded in those cases categorised by the courts as 'letting die'.

As will be seen in greater detail in the next chapter, it is a person's moral judgment about what is justified and what is not which determines what is killing and what is allowing to die in a given scenario. The categorisation often depends on acceptance or non-acceptance of certain behaviour. Withholding or withdrawing treatment is not considered to be killing, so it is not judged as such. However, if it was thought unacceptable to withhold or withdraw treatment, it would be referred to as killing. In those types of cases illustrated earlier where letting die is indistinguishable from killing, calling it one or the other is unimportant, but in medical cases, the distinction – even if it is a fabrication – is important because it illustrates the relevance of moral factors which distinguish between people who are seen as either good or bad.

An analysis of relevant case law reveals these issues in operation and shows how the courts have approached medical end-of-life scenarios with the overwhelming tendency to exculpate doctors.

The cases

The incompetent adult patient in the US

Although US cases are dealt with under federal legislation and/or the Constitution, US courts' decisions in treatment withdrawal cases – generally involving terminally ill or PVS patients – have nonetheless provided a basis upon which the UK courts have formulated their judgments. The US courts

---

32 And there is much support for this, see especially Beauchamp and Childress (2001) in their chapter on nonmaleficence; The President's Commission 1983: 70; The Appleton International Conference 1992: 6; Institute of Medical Ethics Working Party 1991: 97 and Ashworth 1989: 437.

were the first to hold that withdrawing (even life-sustaining) treatment is permissible and lawful and were the first to hold that artificial nutrition and hydration is medical treatment.

The classic reasoning in US courts is firstly to confirm the patient's right to self-determination. This includes the right to refuse treatment, which is not lost even when the patient becomes incompetent, and can be exercised by a surrogate based on (usually) a substituted judgment (rather than a best interests) test. This test means that a decision will be made on the basis of what the patient himself would have chosen had he been competent to choose. The patient's rights are then balanced against categories of state interests in order to come to a decision. The traditional state interests are the preservation of life, the prevention of suicide, the protection of innocent third parties, and the preservation of medical integrity.

In the majority of cases,[33] no mention is made of the acts and omissions distinction, except to discount it. Likewise with intention, save in the context of the patient's intention in refusing treatment (for which see chapter 5). As to causation, the courts for example in *Quinlan, Leach* and *Conroy*, specifically held that as the cause of death would be the underlying disease, then termination of life by the doctor would be lawful.

Nonetheless, exceptions to these general conclusions can be found in the cases of *Guardianship of Jane Doe* (411 Mass. 512; 583 N.E. 2d 1263; 1992 Mass. LEXIS 10) and *Barber and Nedjl*. In the former, the Supreme Court of Massachusetts did not dispute that both competent and mentally incompetent patients had a right to refuse treatment. The majority held that Doe's decision, had she been competent (she was in PVS, but had been severely mentally handicapped throughout her life), would have been to have the treatment withdrawn. Nolan J criticised this aspect of the decision in his dissenting opinion when he said '[t]here is absolutely no basis on which to conclude that Doe would choose to die by starvation and dehydration if she were competent.' Moreover, he (rightly) confirmed that the substituted judgment test was 'completely inappropriate' where the patient was, and always had been, incompetent (Nolan J at 1272).[34]

---

33 Such as, for example, *Quinlan* (*In the Matter of Karen Quinlan* 70 N.J. 10; 355 A. 2d 647 (1976)); although 25 years have passed since the case was heard by the Supreme Court of New Jersey, it can still be considered as the key decision from which the law relating to withdrawing treatment derives. See, for example, *Brophy* (*P.E. Brophy v New England Sinai Hospital Inc.* 398 Mass. 417; 497 N.E. 2d 626; 1986 Mass. LEXIS 1499); *Saikewicz* (*Superintendent of Belchertown State School and another v Joseph Saikewicz* 373 Mass. 728; 370 N.E. 2d 417; 1977 Mass. LEXIS 1129); *Cruzan* (*Nancy Beth Cruzan, by her parents and co-guardians, Petitioners v Director, Missouri Department of Health et al* 497 U.S. 261; 111 L. Ed. 2d 224; 110 S. Ct. 2841 (1990)) and *Leach* (1980).

34 The use of the substituted judgment test in *Doe* and in *Saikewicz* can be criticised on the grounds that in neither case had the patient ever been competent to make a decision. See Grubb and Kennedy in their commentary on *Bland* 1993: 362.

O'Connor J, also dissenting, was even more damning when she accused the majority of 'involuntary euthanasia' and criticised the way in which the decision had been reached. In referring to causation particularly, she said:

> Quoting Brophy . . . the court claims that 'death which occurs after the removal of life sustaining systems is from natural causes, neither set in motion nor intended by the patient.' That surely is '[a] situation contrived by the law to permit a court to dispose of a matter.' The court employs a device, a pretence, contrived for the purpose of authorising the termination of Jane Doe's life. It is clear that, but for removal or non-use of the nasoduodenal tube, Jane Doe will live for the indefinite, perhaps considerable future. Without it she will promptly die. That is proximate causation according to any recognized definition of that term.
>
> (*Doe per* O'Connor J at 1276)

The quotation recognises that the court uses deliberate ploys which have been fabricated in order to enable termination of a patient's life.

The distinction between acts and omissions was also raised in *Barber and Nedjl*. Here doctors, with the family's permission, removed life-sustaining mechanisms to which the patient had been attached following cardio-respiratory arrest suffered after undergoing an operation. Compton J in the Californian Appeal Court, while feeling it '. . . unnecessary to deal with the . . . issue of whether petitioners' conduct was . . . the proximate cause of . . . death' (Compton J at 1022), nonetheless held that withdrawing treatment '. . . is not an affirmative act but rather the withdrawal or omission of further treatment'. As such, '. . . the petitioners' omission to continue treatment under the circumstances, though intentional and with knowledge that the patient would die, was not an unlawful failure to perform a legal duty' (*Barber and Nedjl* at 1016 and 1022). Compton J further noted that the 'emotional symbolism' of artificial nutrition and hydration did not mean that it was in any way different from any other form of medical treatment, especially as it had to be provided via medical procedures (*Barber and Nedjl* at 1014).

The reasoning in *Bland*, where exactly the same logic was followed 10 years later, is strikingly similar to that in *Barber and Nedjl* which remains the only case in the US where doctors have been indicted for withdrawing life-sustaining mechanisms.[35]

---

35 See also the New Zealand case of *Auckland Area Health Board v AG* ([1993] 1 NZLR 235) and contrast the German case of *BGH (Withdrawal of Artificial Nutrition and Hydration)* ([1993] 3 Med LR 311) where the patient's son and doctor were acquitted of attempted manslaughter.

The incompetent adult patient in the UK: Airedale NHS Trust v Bland

As the foundation of treatment withdrawal cases in the UK rests with *Bland*, the next sections of this chapter will specifically look at aspects of that case (concentrating particularly on intention and causation) before briefly considering the impact on later cases of the decision and the principles formulated in it.

The *Bland* case has been described as '. . . the most famous passive euthanasia case in English Law . . .' (Stauch, Wheat with Tingle 2006: 675) and has attracted much debate. As to the medical issues in the case, the Court of Appeal and the House of Lords both reinforced existing principles and formulated new ones, namely that:

(a) no one may consent to treatment on behalf of a mentally incompetent adult;
(b) a patient's right to refuse treatment extends to an incompetent patient;
(c) the correct test is best interests (and not substituted judgment);[36] and
(d) sanctity of life is not absolute when measured against both quality of life and self-determination.

More controversially it held that:

(a) artificial nutrition and hydration is medical treatment;
(b) treatment which is not in a patient's best interests can be discontinued without breaching a doctor's duty to his patient; and reluctantly,
(c) withdrawing artificial nutrition and hydration is an omission and not an act.

As to the last three points, it had to be so held in order to justify the treatment withdrawal and exclude liability (Andrews 1995: 1437).

1. The criminal law implications: intention and causation

The criminal law implications are not fully or adequately analysed by all the judges. In the Court of Appeal, Bingham MR discussed the submissions argued by Mr Munby, the guardian *ad litem*, who cited *Cox* and *Adams* in support of his first submission – that withdrawing the tube is an act which will cause and is intended to cause Anthony Bland's death. Bingham MR

---

36 Although Butler-Sloss LJ conceded that assessing a patient's best interests would involve a 'subjective element'; *Bland*: 343. Inclusion of subjective elements has been considered important in subsequent cases and in the Mental Capacity Act 2005. This can be construed as a kind of 'modified objective standard', as was used in the Canadian case of *Latimer* (2001).

conceded that he found both cases contextually problematic, because they involved drugs that were deliberately administered (as opposed to treatment withdrawal). He admitted that comparing the scenario in *Cox* and *Adams* 'does not meet the theoretical argument' (and he was right, it does not), but essentially gave no satisfactory rationalisation for his view. In fact he evaded the causation question by presenting three hypothetical scenarios (all variations on life-threatening situations in a PVS case where consideration would have to be given whether to continue treatment or not) to 'test' Mr Munby's submission that withdrawing treatment would cause Anthony Bland's death. He stated baldly that the patient lacked the necessary intent, the doctor lacked the necessary intent, and that the patient's underlying condition caused the death, but gave no explanation why. He went on, '[f]or present purposes, I do not think it greatly matters whether one simply says that it is not an unlawful act, or that the doctor lacks criminal intent, or that he breaches no duty, or that his act did not cause death' (Bingham MR at 339–41). He did not however then go on to say what did matter. He simply dismissed these fundamental concepts as 'not compelling' but gave no reason or explanation why. He rejected Mr Munby's other submissions (that withdrawing the tube was a breach of the doctor's duty of care, and that there was no justification for withdrawing treatment in any event) 'for the reasons he had already given' – but he had not given any. This is a very disappointing judgment which does not get to grips with the possible criminal issues involved.

Like Bingham MR, Butler-Sloss LJ's discussion of the criminal issues is kept to the last one or two pages of her judgment and is very cursory. The crux of her argument was that because there was no duty of care to continue feeding, '. . . there is no actus reus and no unlawful act or omission. The issue of mens rea does not arise.' In support of this she cited *Barber*, distinguished *Cox* and confirmed that:

> The effect of the cessation of artificial feeding is to place the patient in the position he would have been in before the nasogastric tube was inserted. Without the tube he would have died from his medical condition and with it he has been artificially kept alive despite that condition until now. Whether this is an act or omission carries the matter no further.
>
> (*Bland per* Butler-Sloss LJ at 348–9)

In the House of Lords, Lord Browne-Wilkinson implied that murder would have to be redefined as a result of developing technology, and despite conceding that the intention was to bring about the patient's death and that removing the tube was an act, he nonetheless reluctantly felt that the doctor's conduct should be interpreted as an omission. As long as the treatment was not in the patient's best interests, it would thus be unlawful for the doctor to continue with it.

Lord Mustill also doubted the acts and omissions distinction, and similarly felt that withdrawing artificial nutrition and hydration was an omission which did not attract criminal liability. According to him the doctor's conduct was causative of the patient's death but was lawful because there was no breach of duty; if unlawful, '. . . the conduct will be, *as it is intended to be*, the cause of death' (Lord Mustill at 397; emphasis added). He conceded that what was happening in the case was that '. . . the authority of the state, through the . . . court, is being invoked to permit one group of its citizens to terminate the life of another', but nonetheless was quick to confirm that the court was not creating '. . . a new exception to the law of murder' (Lord Mustill at 387–92). The tide of opinion and criticism would seem to suggest otherwise.

The main criticism of the decision is that it lawfully permitted a doctor to stop treating a PVS patient even where the intention was to end his life.[37] Peter Singer, while accepting that argument, nonetheless praised the Law Lords for being honest. He noted that they could have used 'patently artificial strategy' either to argue that discontinuing treatment was not an intention to bring about death, or that death was a foreseen but unintended side effect in order to hide the true nature of their decision, but they did not. He concluded that as a result of the case, the intention element of the law of murder was re-written and that doctors may now lawfully stop tending patients in order to end their lives (Singer 1994: 72–3 and 80). A further consequence of the case is that the law has been twisted into strange – but convenient – new shapes that enable judges to avoid grasping the nettle of permissible motives.

2. The medical law implications

(a) BEST INTERESTS

The House of Lords faced severe criticism in its examination of best interests in *Bland*. This is hardly surprising in light of the problematic nature of the best interests test and considering its link with the dubious acts/omissions distinction. The judgments have been criticised both for their sophistry and for the contradictions arising from the analysis of best interests. Firstly, Lord Goff, in formulating the question as to what would be in the patient's best interests, said that whereas treatment can be administered to a patient in his best interests, so also it can be withdrawn for exactly the same reason. In other words, withdrawing life-sustaining treatment and the consequent death

---

37 A view widely held by a number of commentators, for example, Finnis 1993: 331; Lacey, Wells and Quick 2003: 695; and Keown (1997).

are in a patient's best interests.[38] Secondly, if, as was stated in *Bland*, a PVS patient has no interests, how can it be in his best interests to withdraw treatment? (Wade 2001: 352).

More will be said about the development of the best interests test in the analysis of *Burke* later in this chapter. That case confirms that best interests remains an objective test, but also shows that common law decisions in the period since *Bland*,[39] together with new legislation,[40] do and will permit subjective considerations to be taken into account in ascertaining an incompetent patient's best interests.

(b) SANCTITY OF LIFE AND QUALITY OF LIFE

An assessment of a patient's quality of life will be made whenever decisions regarding withdrawing or withholding treatment from a patient are concerned. In the case of a competent patient, quality of life (like sanctity of life) must be balanced against that patient's autonomy. The danger lies, however, in introducing quality of life as a deciding factor where patients are incompetent. In *Bland*, the patient's quality of life was included in an assessment of his best interests. Both in the Court of Appeal and in the House of Lords, it was agreed that sanctity of life is not absolute; indeed, in a conflict between sanctity of life and quality of life, sanctity of life and self-determination, sanctity of life must give way.[41]

In his renowned article 'Restoring Moral and Intellectual Shape to the Law After *Bland*' (Keown 1997), John Keown distinguishes between quality of life and Quality of life, sanctity of life and 'vitalism'. Whereas quality of life is concerned with assessing the worthwhileness of treatment, Quality of life involves assessing the worthwhileness of a person's life. If it falls below a certain threshold, it becomes a life not worth living (on grounds of futility).[42]

---

38 Walker LJ similarly held that it would be in Mary's best interests to have the operation which would result in her death, in *Re A (Children)* (2000).

39 Such as *Re Y* ((1996) BMLR 11); *Re MB* ([1997] 8 Medical Law Reports 217) and *Re SL (Adult Patient: Sterilisation)* (2000) Lloyd's Law Rep (Med) 339.

40 Section 4 Mental Capacity Act 2005 sets out a non-exhaustive, non-definitional list of matters which should be considered.

41 Butler-Sloss LJ at 341–9, Hoffman LJ at 354–5, and Lords Keith and Goff in the House of Lords. For a detailed discourse on sanctity of life, see Kuhse (1987). In other words, this is a 'qualified' sanctity of life principle where quality of life considerations can determine whether to prolong life or not; Stauch, Wheat with Tingle 2006: 634.

42 Although Keown does not define futility, in his comparison of sanctity v quality of life, he refers to the dangers of using degrees of disability as 'arbitrary criteria' to decide whose life is 'worthwhile' and whose is not, Keown 1997: 487. As Andrews has argued, '[t]ube feeding . . . [is not futile] . . . it achieves all the things we intend it to do. What is really being argued is whether the patient's life is futile – hence the need to find some way of ending that life.' Andrews 1995: 1437.

In Keown's view the House of Lords in *Bland* opted for Quality of life because it perceived its choice as being between that and vitalism – that preserving life is absolute. Sanctity of life, on the other hand, allows withdrawing treatment by taking into account the worthwhileness of *treatment*. This, in turn, involves assessing the patient's quality of life, which is not the same as subjectively assessing the worth of the *patient*.

Despite this view (with which it is difficult not to agree), quality of life judgments are unavoidable if decisions are to be reached humanely (Brody 1992: 168). This is reflected in *Bland* itself, and in cases such as *Re C (A Minor) (Wardship: Medical Treatment)* ([1989] 3 WLR 240), *Re J (A Minor) (Wardship: Medical Treatment)* (1990), *Re C (Adult: Refusal of Medical Treatment)* ([1994] 1 All ER 819), *Re R (Adult: Medical Treatment)* ([1996] 2 FLR 99) and *Re A (Children)* where it can be seen that it is acceptable to take the patient's quality of life into account in making a treatment decision.

(c) ARTIFICIAL NUTRITION AND HYDRATION AS MEDICAL TREATMENT

The categorisation of artificial nutrition and hydration as medical treatment has had a significant impact upon both intention and causation. It is more difficult to allege that a doctor who withdraws artificial nutrition and hydration does not intend or cause the patient's death when its withdrawal is absolutely certain and inevitable to lead to that end. In ordinary, non-medical circumstances, not providing food and water to a relative for whom one has a duty of care would amount to murder (as, for example, in *Gibbins and Proctor*), but this is not so in the case of artificial nutrition and hydration which can be withdrawn in the same way as any other treatment when the duty of care to the patient no longer exists.

The intention-based argument   The intention-based argument states that, because of its very nature, to desist from providing food and drink to individuals whose death is not imminent, seems to demonstrate an intention to bring about their death (Finnis 1993: 335) and that withdrawing artificial nutrition and hydration starves the patient. According to Meilander, we cannot:

> . . . when withdrawing food from the permanently unconscious person, properly claim that our intention is to cease useless treatment for a dying patient. These patients are not dying and we cease no treatment aimed at disease; . . . [since this is true] . . . [a]t what, other than death, could we be aiming?

> (Meilander 1986: 197)

The PVS is not a terminal illness. The only 'life-sustaining treatment' which PVS patients receive is food and drink, because they can breathe on their own. This, albeit medicalised, form of food and drink was quite literally keeping Anthony Bland alive. Categorically, therefore, when it was withdrawn there was no element of doubt at all that he would die. Thus, there could be no reliance on the 'doctrine of entitlement' (on the grounds that the doctor merely foresaw with virtual certainty, but did not intend the patient's death), nor on the principle of double effect (as the admitted primary intention was to bring about the patient's death). The *only* way in which the doctor could be absolved was therefore by virtue of the acts and omissions tactic.

The causation-based argument   The causation-based argument claims that the patient dies from the original illness or injury and not from any subsequent intervention by the doctor in disconnecting life-sustaining treatment. A medical condition which results in an inability to receive natural feeding so that artificial feeding and hydration becomes necessary conveniently provides the cause of death when the artificial means of feeding is withdrawn. Thus, while starvation may well be the 'but-for' cause (see next chapter), it is not the legal cause of death.

The problem with this argument is that PVS patients are not dying; they could survive for a number of years in that condition. (This is therefore more than *de minimis*, and is certainly more than the mere acceleration of death by minutes or hours referred to in *Adams* and *Sinclair*.)[43] In the case of patients in PVS, artificial nutrition and hydration sustains life; it is thus more than simply medical treatment and it is merely a semantic argument to suggest otherwise (Craig 1994: 140–1). Withdrawing nutrition and hydration cannot be seen as letting nature take its course because the patient would not have died then and at that time if the artificial nutrition and hydration had not been withdrawn. Death arises as a direct result of this. There can be no conclusion other than that the patient starves to death; stopping his sustenance is the cause of the patient's death when the treatment being withdrawn is artificial nutrition and hydration.

Concerns as to the categorisation of withdrawing artificial nutrition and hydration as medical treatment are evident in the fact that additional safeguards are required when it is withdrawn. Paragraph 81 of the General Medical Council[44] Guidance *Withholding and Withdrawing Life-prolonging Treatment: Good Practice and Decision Making* (2002) (the subject of the dispute in *Burke*, see below) states that where *a patient is not imminently dying* and withdrawal of artificial nutrition and hydration is being considered, the

---

43 See notes 11 and 38, chapter 2 above and the conclusion to chapter 4 below.
44 The General Medical Council is an independent body established under the 1858 Medical Act, and is designed to protect, promote and maintain the health and safety of the *public* by ensuring proper standards in the practice of medicine. It has the authority to remove the doctor from its register and remove his right to practice medicine. Information obtained directly from www.gmc-uk.org/about/role/index.asp (accessed 26 June 2006).

benefits of continuing the treatment must be balanced against the burdens and any suffering which would be caused to the patient in continuing the treatment.

In its original Guidance for decision-making, *Withholding and Withdrawing Life-prolonging Treatment*, the British Medical Association (BMA) set out the conditions to be taken into account in withdrawing treatment from PVS patients and the legal factors to consider. The Guidelines stated that decisions to withhold or withdraw artificial nutrition and hydration '*from patients whose imminent death is not inevitable*' (emphasis added) require additional safeguards and where the patient's death is believed to be inevitable, artificial nutrition and hydration may be withdrawn if it is not considered beneficial to the patient because it would prolong his life (BMA 2000: 56).[45] In such a situation, the patient would be expected to die of his condition before the effect of ceasing artificial nutrition and hydration was operative. The policy therefore effectively avoids the conclusion that withdrawing artificial nutrition and hydration is the cause of death.

Following Bland

As would be expected, the *Bland* case has been used as a precedent in a number of subsequent PVS cases and the approach has been approved as being compatible with the European Convention on Human Rights (*An NHS Trust v M* ([2001] 2 FLR 367); *An NHS Trust v H* ([2001] 2 FLR 501)).

The practice at present is that while there is no legal obligation to obtain a declaration from the court, where the legality of any proposed treatment is in doubt, 'good practice' should nonetheless require that one or other of the parties should do so (Lord Phillips in *Burke* (2): para 80). That this require- ment is not confined to PVS cases is right because that condition cannot always be identified or defined without ambiguity (especially when patients satisfy the criteria set out in some Guidelines but not in others).[46] Concern has been expressed, for example, that the precedent set in *Bland* has been

---

45 The Guidance is now in its 2nd edition (2001) and has also been updated following recent common law decisions such as *Glass* (1999 and 2000) and *Burke* (2004 and 2005).
See www.bma.org.uk/ap.nsf/Content/Endoflife (23 May 2006). Unlike the GMC, the British Medical Association is an independent trade union/a voluntary professional association of doctors which protects *doctors*' interests. The BMA does not have the authority to disci- pline doctors. Information obtained directly from http://www.bma.org.uk/ap.nsf/Content/ Hubaboutthebma (accessed 26 June 2006).

46 Butler-Sloss P preferred the Guidelines of the International Working Party on the Persistent Vegetative State to those of the GMC in *An NHS Trust v M* (2001) and *An NHS Trust v H* (2001). Under the former, the patient was in PVS, but under the latter she was not. These cases highlight the problems with diagnosis. See the report on Andrew Devine, who 'woke' from an allegedly persistent vegetative state, in *Guardian* 26 March 1997: 1.

extended to include patients who are in what has been described as a 'near persistent vegetative state' (Cusack *et al* 2000: 133). For example, in *Re D* ([1997] 5 Med LR 225) the patient did not fall within the guidelines proposed by the Royal College of Physician's (RCP) Working Group, and in the Irish case of *In the Matter of a Ward of Court* ([1995] 2 ILRM 401)[47] the patient, a 22-year-old woman who suffered brain damage from three cardiac arrests during surgery, without reference to any guidelines was simply said to be in a condition 'close' to PVS. In both cases, the patients had some 'minimal cognitive capacity', which placed them in an 'intermediate category between PVS and Locked-in syndrome' (Cusack *et al* 2000: 135)[48] and both authorised the withdrawal of artificial nutrition and hydration under *Bland* principles, even though they did not satisfy the criteria.

In both cases the usual statements were made as to best interests, the classification of artificial nutrition and hydration and the right of an incompetent patient to refuse treatment. The majority in *Ward of Court* also predictably held that the cause of death would be the injuries she sustained and not the withdrawal of artificial nutrition and hydration. It was, however, particularly controversial for Hamilton CJ to state that '. . . without the benefit of the nourishment provided by the treatment being afforded to her she would die within a short period of time and in this regard, she must be regarded as 'terminally ill', (*Ward of Court* at 428). If she was not going to die until the artificial nutrition and hydration had been withdrawn, how could she be terminally ill? (Mason and Laurie 1996: 271). Egan J, the only non-US judge to express a dissenting view, strongly disputed that she was dying (*Ward of Court* at 437), and agreed with Mason and Laurie that no matter how 'euphemistically it is worded', the patient was killed because the tube was removed; '. . . the proximate cause . . . [of her death] must . . . be the results of starvation because, otherwise, there was nothing to cause her death' (Mason and Laurie 1996: 280).

The courts nonetheless agreed to treatment withdrawal in all these cases even though doubt had been expressed as to whether or not the patients were all in PVS. In the more recent case of *W Healthcare NHS Trust v KH* ([2004] WL 2458658), however, the Court of Appeal for the first time had

---

47 The same could be said of *Re Representation Attorney General* ([1995] 3 Med LR 316), a case from Jersey where a child sustained brain damage following prolonged immersion in water; *Re H (Adult: Incompetent)* ((1998) 38 BMLR 11), where the patient suffered brain damage after a road accident (but did not satisfy the RCP's criteria); and *Frenchay Healthcare NHS Trust v S* ([1994] 2 All ER 403), where there was also some doubt as to the PVS diagnosis. The number of problems and/or misdiagnosis might be overcome if the courts used the same Guidelines in every case.

48 Locked-in Syndrome is where the patient is conscious but is unable to communicate. For a true account of a patient with the Syndrome, see Bauby (1997).

to consider withdrawing artificial nutrition and hydration from a patient who was most certainly not in PVS (she was in the final stages of Multiple Sclerosis). An appeal by the patient's family against a judgment ordering reinstatement of a PEG tube was dismissed, Brooke LJ holding firstly, that prior wishes expressed by the patient when she was competent were not 'of the quality and focus to constitute an advance directive' and secondly, that her expressed wishes did not cover the circumstances which would involve dying protractedly over a period of weeks from starvation (*W Healthcare NHS Trust v KH* at para 21). It is ironic that whereas in this case – where artificial nutrition and hydration withdrawal was refused – the court conceded that the patient would die of starvation, but that in the PVS cases where artificial nutrition and hydration withdrawal has been permitted they have always denied that this is the cause of the patient's death.

The competent patient in the US

It has been seen that the acts and omissions distinction plays a large part in judicial decisions where the patient is incompetent. It has less significance in the case of competent patients where the doctor's conduct does not have to be justified on the basis of whether he acted or omitted to act. Rather, the significance of the case lies in the autonomy of the competent patient and his right to reject even life-sustaining treatment. However, of major importance is, again, the intention of both the doctor and the patient in pursuing such a course, and what is categorised as the 'cause' of death in these cases.

As in the case of incompetent patients, the US courts have been dealing with requests for treatment withdrawal by competent patients certainly since the late 1970s, when the District Court of Appeal of Florida in *Satz v Perlmutter* (*Michael J. Satz, State Attorney for Broward County, Florida, Appellant v Abe Perlmutter, Appellee* 362 So. 2d 160; 1978 Fla. App. LEXIS 16354) held that the right of privacy of a competent terminally ill patient suffering from Motor Neurone Disease took precedence over the four state interests. A decision was made on the same basis in *Farrell (In the Matter of Kathleen Farrell* 108 N.J. 335; 529 A. 2d 404; 1987 N.J. LEXIS 328), where the court also confirmed that no liability, either criminal or civil, would attach to any person who withdrew life-sustaining treatment at the request of an informed and competent patient (*Farrell* at 415)[49]

US courts have also held that a non-terminal illness does not preclude a

---

49 The role of consent is significant here because, although it is not a defence to killing, this is precisely the effect it has in these cases. See *Burke* (2004 and 2005) below and the final chapter for more on this.

competent patient from exercising his right to refuse medical treatment.[50] The cases of *Bouvia* (*Elizabeth Bouvia v Superior Court* 179 Cal. App. 3d 1127 (1986)) and *McKay v Bergstedt* (106 Nev. 808; 801 P. 2d 617; 1990 Nev. LEXIS 156) are particularly significant in this regard. Elizabeth Bouvia was a 28-year-old cerebral palsy sufferer who at the time of the hearing was almost completely immobile and totally helpless. She requested that her nasogastric tube, inserted and maintained against her will, should be removed. The right to refuse medical treatment as a corollary of the right of privacy, and as described in *Conroy, Satz* and *Saikewicz*, was upheld, and the ruling in *Bartling*, that the patient did not have to be terminally ill, was also supported. The court, by implication, accepted that artificial nutrition and hydration was medical treatment when Beach J held that the number of years over which her life could have been maintained and the fact that removal of the tube would 'hasten or cause her death' were immaterial. In such circumstances, '[i]t is incongruous, if not monstrous, for medical practitioners to assert their right to preserve a life that someone else must live, or, more accurately, endure . . .' (*Bouvia* at 1144). The court confirmed that the aim and purpose of upholding treatment withdrawal decisions is to provide dignity, respect and comfort to the patient; '[t]his goal is not to hasten death, though its earlier arrival may be an unexpected and understood likelihood' (*Bouvia* at 1144; (foresight in our terms)).

In *McKay v Bergstedt*, the patient, Kenneth Bergstedt, had been a paraplegic for 23 years and was totally dependent on his respirator to survive. He was not terminally ill and was fully competent when he successfully requested withdrawal of the machine. The court confirmed that the right to refuse treatment was not absolute and balanced five state interests[51] against Kenneth's constitutional liberty interest and his common law right of self-determination. In his dissenting judgment, however, Springer J was critical of what he perceived as the court's approval of a 'killing act' which knowingly caused a human being's instant death (*McKay v Bergstedt* at 633).[52] His judgment, and others like it, highlight the continuing debate on the relevance of intention and causation in treatment refusal.

Both these key concepts were subsequently debated in *Quill v Vacco* and *Compassion in Dying v Washington* although, unlike the previous cases

---

50 In, for example, *Bartling* (*W.F. Bartling et al, Plaintiffs and Appellants v The Superior Court of Los Angeles County, Defendant and Respondent; Glendale Adventist Medical Center* 163 Cal. App. 3d 186; 1984 Cal. App. LEXIS 2892; 209 Cal. Rptr. 220).

51 In *McKay v Bergstedt* 1990: 621, the court recognised a fifth state interest – 'encouraging the charitable and humane care of those whose lives may be artificially extended under conditions which have the prospect of providing at least a modicum of quality living'.

52 Focusing on his belief that the patient committed suicide, for which see discussion in chapter 5, and especially *Thor v Superior Court* (5 Cal. 4th 725; 855 P. 2d 375; 1993 Cal. LEXIS 3430; Cal. Rptr. 2d 357).

discussed, the plaintiffs here were directly requesting that doctors be permitted to prescribe lethal medication with the aim of assisting their patients' suicides. In both Appeals Court cases, the judges saw no distinction between withdrawing treatment (an omission) and assisting suicide (an act) as the patients' deaths were deemed to be intended in both. In *Compassion in Dying*, Reinhardt CJ rejected the 'illusory line' between omission and commission as a 'distinction without a difference' (*Compassion in Dying* at 822).

As expected, the US Supreme Court reversed both decisions and confirmed that the distinction between treatment refusal and suicide was maintained and supported by state legislation and by the common law in decisions such as *Quinlan, McKay, Rasmussen* (*Mildred Rasmussen by Douglas P. Mitchell, her Guardian ad Litem, Appellant v Robert Fleming, Pima County Public Fiduciary, as Guardian for Mildred Rasmussen, Appellee* (157 Ariz. 207; 741 P. 2d 674; 1987 Ariz. LEXIS 180)), *Farrell, Bouvia, Bartling, Leach* and *Brophy*. In *Vacco v Quill*, Rehnquist CJ confirmed that causation and intention are the crucial distinguishing factors between the two contrasting practices. As to causation-based reasoning, he said that '. . . when a patient refuses life-sustaining medical treatment, he dies from an underlying fatal disease or pathology; but if a patient ingests lethal medication prescribed by a physician, he is killed by that medication' (*Vacco v Quill per* Rehnquist CJ at 13).

As to intention-based reasoning, Rehnquist CJ asserted that whereas in assisting suicide, the doctor 'must' intend the patient's death, in withdrawing treatment and administering pain-killing medication, his intent is to comply with his patient's wishes in the one and to kill pain in the other. Intent has been used for a long time to distinguish between two acts that may have the same result and, as in the principle of double effect, '. . . the law distinguishes actions taken "because of" a given end from actions taken "in spite of" their unintended but foreseen consequences' (*Vacco v Quill* at 15). In so saying, the Supreme Court followed the by now well-established law relating to treatment withdrawal from competent patients.

The competent patient in the UK

In the UK, treatment withdrawal from a competent patient first arose in the case of *Re AK (Medical Treatment: Consent)* ([2001] 1 FLR 129), where one of the youngest people to be diagnosed with Motor Neurone Disease, at 19, indicated by blinking (which was his only mode of communication) that his artificial ventilation be switched off two weeks after he lost the ability to communicate in this way. The case was unusual in so far as he was placed on artificial ventilation initially because the doctors were unsure as to the nature of his illness. The decision was firmly based on a competent patient's right to refuse medical treatment. Although he did not have to do so, Hughes J, quoting Lord Goff in *Bland*, confirmed that ceasing treatment was a lawful omission to continue with procedures to which the patient did not consent (*Re AK* at 135).

More recently and with substantially more publicity, Ms B, a tetraplegic, successfully made an application to the High Court for her ventilator to be removed in *B v An NHS Trust*. There is no mention of the acts/omissions distinction, as the decision is based totally on the supremacy of the competent patient's right of autonomy.

In contrast, *Annie Lindsell*[53] and *Dianne Pretty*,[54] both terminally ill with Motor Neurone Disease, asked for positive action to assist in their dying (as occurred in *Quill v Vacco* and *Compassion in Dying v Washington*). Annie Lindsell applied to the High Court for a ruling that her doctor could lawfully administer diamorphine to ease her mental and physical distress, even if this shortened her life, but dropped her case after being given assurances by the judge, the lawyers appointed by the Official Solicitor and by the Attorney General, that the principle of double effect applied to the mental distress allied with the disease as well as to the physical pain involved, even if this shortened the patient's life (Dyer 2001: 953). On this basis, the Dianne Pretty case could have been resolved in exactly the same way.

R (Burke) v General Medical Council et al [2004] WL 1640202 (HC) (1); R on the Application of Oliver Leslie Burke v the General Medical Council et al [2005] EWCA Civ 1003 (CA) (2)

Leslie Burke, suffering from spino-cerebellar ataxia, successfully brought an action for Judicial Review against the GMC claiming that their Guidance on *Withholding and Withdrawing Life-prolonging Treatment: Good Practice and Decision Making* (2002) was unlawful and incompatible with Articles 2, 3, 6, 8 and 14 of the European Convention on Human Rights (ECHR). The degenerative nature of the disease meant that, although he would retain his mental capacity virtually until his death, he would be unable to perform simple physical functions such as swallowing. He would require artificial nutrition and hydration and did not wish this to be withdrawn. He alleged that whereas the Guidance provided for the withdrawal of life-prolonging treatment, it did not provide for the opposite situation where a patient wished such treatment to be continued. In the High Court, Munby J gave a comprehensive judgment on a number of issues, including autonomy and self-determination, sanctity of life, dignity, duty of care, advance directives, competence and capacity, artificial nutrition and hydration, best interests, a patient's right to demand treatment, the duty to seek the court's approval in treatment withdrawal cases, and, of course, Convention implications. However, Lord Phillips MR in the Court of Appeal criticised the judgment

---

53 See, for example, *The Times* 15 October 1997, 29 October 1997 and 6 December 1997.
54 The case of *Dianne Pretty* is discussed in greater detail in the next two chapters.

for a number of reasons, and chose not to comment on those issues which he and the other judges in the Court of Appeal felt went '. . . far beyond the current concerns of Mr Burke . . . ' (*Burke* (2) at para 22). As a number of the issues are also beyond the specific focus of this book, and some have been covered already, analysis here will be limited to points pertinent to this chapter, namely best interests, artificial nutrition and hydration and withdrawing treatment from incompetent patients.

Best interests

Munby J (unusually, as best interests generally arise in the context of incompetent patients) examined the authorities at length and made three points. Firstly (and uncontroversially), that best interests was no longer confined to medical considerations, secondly, that *Bolam* was 'not determinative' (*Burke* (1) at para 90) and thirdly and more contentiously, that:

> . . . the decision as to what is in fact in the patient's best interests is not for the doctor . . . medical opinion . . . can never be determinative of what is in a patient's best interests. In the final analysis it is for the patient, if competent, to determine what is in his own best interests.
>
> (*Burke* (1) at paras 90–3)

Munby adopted Taylor LJ's formula in *Re J* (1990) (where he judged how 'intolerable' life would be for J if treatment were to be continued) and contentiously concluded that whereas '[t]he test is best interests . . . the touchstone of best interests in this context is intolerability' (*Burke* (1) at para 113).[55]

Saying that it is right for the competent patient to determine what is in his own best interests is correct, but only in so far as it is not contrary to the doctor's clinical judgment. In saying this though, it can be seen how Munby J made the leap into holding that a patient can demand treatment, because that proposition follows on logically from his first proposition (that it is for the competent patient to determine his own best interests).

In Lord Phillips's view, however, Munby's third point (above) '. . . equate[d] best interests with the wishes of the competent patient' (*Burke* (2) at para 27) and did not account for the fact that the patient and doctor's ideas as to what comprised best interests could conflict and that in the event of a conflict, the doctor's clinical judgment would prevail. As an objective test dependent on the context, Lord Phillips made it clear that it was impossible '. . . to attempt to define what is in the best interests of a patient by a single test, applicable in all the circumstances' (*Burke* (2) at para 63).

---

55 This was subsequently rejected by Hedley J in *Wyatt* (2005) (3); Butler-Sloss P in *Re L (Medical Treatment: Benefit)* (2004) and Holman J in *An NHS Trust v MB* (2006).

Artificial nutrition and hydration

In his judgment, Munby J clearly enunciates that artificial nutrition and hydration is medical treatment[56] and that where a patient such as Mr Burke is competent, its withdrawal before he lapsed into a coma would be a breach of Articles 3 (and 8) ECHR on the basis that *'he would be exposed to acute mental and physical suffering'* *(Burke* (1) at para 214).[57] In the Court of Appeal, however, Lord Phillips made a novel distinction between cases where artificial nutrition and hydration is sustaining life and where it is not. He said that a patient will eventually die, even if receiving artificial nutrition and hydration, and that in the final stages of a terminal illness, it does not prolong life in any event. Whereas artificial nutrition and hydration would sustain Mr Burke while he remained competent, in the very final stages of his disease it would no longer do so. Accordingly, Mr Burke would fall into that class of person for whom withdrawing artificial nutrition and hydration would not shorten his life because (a) the artificial nutrition and hydration was not prolonging it in the first place, and (b) the disease is what shortens his life *(Burke* (2) at paras 8–11). The distinction is not one that has been made before, and could initially be perceived as hair-splitting, but the clear explanation for this is that firstly, most of the previous cases involved PVS patients where artificial nutrition and hydration was evidently sustaining life; secondly on the facts of this case, the patient was competent and thirdly, the patient was asking for treatment not to be withdrawn (as opposed to asking that it be withdrawn).

Withdrawing treatment from incompetent patients

Because Munby J held that (a) to withdraw artificial nutrition and hydration from Mr Burke would be a breach of Articles 3 and 8 of the ECHR, and (b) it is for the patient to decide upon his own best interests, and (c) that he had made an advance declaration to that effect, logically, therefore, Munby J concluded that Burke's wish to continue with the artificial nutrition and hydration was 'determinative' *(Burke* (1) at para 214).

The Court of Appeal's judgment on this is somewhat contradictory as far as its practical effect on Mr Burke is concerned. Lord Phillips stated that:

---

56 And this is now covered by s 4 (10) Mental Capacity Act 2005 which states that ' "Life-sustaining treatment" means treatment which in the view of a person providing health care for the person concerned is necessary to sustain life.'

57 Two points can be made here – Munby J said that if the treatment was not severe enough to breach Article 3, it could alternatively breach Article 8 (para 130); secondly, that the patient himself did not have to be aware that the treatment was degrading in order for Article 3 to be breached. It was sufficient if witnesses to his treatment perceived it as degrading *(Burke* (1): para 149).

(a) Withdrawing artificial nutrition and hydration from a competent patient against his wishes would be murder (*Burke* (2) at para 34).
(b) There are no grounds for thinking that anyone caring for Mr Burke could withdraw his treatment (so suggesting that he is perfectly safe). However, Lord Phillips had to concede that it could only be inferred from paras 13, 16, 32 and 42 of the GMC Guidance that a doctor cannot discontinue artificial nutrition and hydration contrary to the wishes of a competent patient; the Guidance did not specifically say so (*Burke* (2) at para 64).
(c) However, Mr Burke could not demand treatment, and artificial nutrition and hydration could be withdrawn contrary to his wishes if clinically indicated, but '[t]his said, we consider in practice that the scenario we have just described is extremely unlikely to arise in practice' (*Burke* (2) at para 55).
(d) Paragraphs 32 and 42 of the GMC Guidance state that the patient's wishes should be respected unless this is 'clinically inappropriate'. Administering treatment that was necessary to keep a patient alive could not be described as 'clinically inappropriate', but the court had already held that, in Mr Burke's case, he came into that category of person where the artificial nutrition and hydration was not 'keeping him alive'. Logically, therefore, it would not be clinically inappropriate to withdraw his artificial nutrition and hydration, despite the court's continued reassurance that he need have no worries in this regard.

Also, the Court of Appeal's denial that Mr Burke had made an advance directive is hard to understand (*Burke* (2) at para 22), as bringing his request for a declaration to the High Court is no more or less than countless others have done when there is doubt as to the legality of proposed medical treatment. The reason for this denial may simply be because the 'advance directive' was in respect of a patient who wished treatment to be continued whereas Lord Phillips confirmed that an advance directive not to be kept alive should be respected. This is in line with the Court of Appeal's judgment that a patient cannot demand treatment now (or in the future). In fact, Lord Phillips said this would be contrary to s 26 Mental Capacity Act and would cause problems in the interaction between that section and s 4 of the Act (*Burke* (2) at para 57).

There was no mention of either intention or causation in the case and, as with other cases where the patient is competent, there was no need to bring in the acts/omissions distinction. The case is, however, important in so far as Lord Phillips did reiterate the long-standing common law principles of ascertaining a patient's best interests. He was correct to criticise Munby J's interpretation on this point, but it can be argued that Lord Phillips's criticism of other aspects of Munby J's detailed and thorough judgment was unduly harsh, especially as some aspects of Lord Phillips's judgment are equally open to criticism themselves.

Conclusion

The acts/omissions distinction is adhered to by the courts in order to absolve medical professionals from criminal liability. It helps to produce what the majority of people would consider to be the correct decision in medical cases and, as Meisel claims, it '. . . has served a useful political purpose: that of making passively hastening death acceptable to legislatures, to the medical profession, to the public and . . . to the courts themselves' (Meisel 2004: 284–5). However, the fact that the distinction is conceptually unclear and has no solid foundation upon which it can rest unchallenged, is problematic (President's Commission 1983: 61).

Firstly, the definition of what an act or an omission is does not actually explain what is acceptable and what is not. In fact, the definition of what an 'act' is, is unclear and there is no definition of omissions which explains it as a 'letting die'. Whether either activity is considered acceptable is not therefore based on the mere descriptive difference between acts and omissions, or killing and letting die. If it is agreed that a given act, or a course of conduct which is capable of being categorised as a non-act, is the proper/acceptable/ justifiable thing to do in the circumstances, it will be described as an omission (and thus as a letting die); if not, it will be categorised as a killing. In effect, the categorisation has already been made, and the conduct is subsequently fitted into that category.

In the case of the medical profession, categorising the withdrawal or withholding of treatment as an allowing to die leads to the corollary belief that doctors do not kill. This fits in nicely with the acts and omissions doctrine (Glover 1986: 99) and shows how easy it is to tailor the description of the event as an act or as an omission depending on the result sought to be obtained and the context of the enquiry. The law, acting as an instrument of public policy, interprets withdrawing life-sustaining treatment by a doctor as falling outside the general legal prohibition against deliberate active killing, but does not do likewise in the case of the interloper. This is evident in the cases analysed above, where it can be seen that only in very few cases have doctors been prosecuted where they have withdrawn life-sustaining treatment. Some of the judgments in those cases have questioned the validity of the acts/omissions distinction and some judges, such as in *Bland*, have unusually conceded that even though withdrawing treatment should be categorised as an omission, nonetheless the requisite intention to kill was present. This therefore leads to the second problem, which is that the decision as to whether an event is an act or an omission is not one based on intention and/or causation, because what the acts/omissions dichotomy effectively does is to rule out the significance of both intention and causation from those activities perceived to be omissions. Although in most cases the courts' stance is that the doctor's intention is not to kill the patient and that he does not cause the patient's death, this is in itself open to debate. To say that the patient's illness, rather than the withdrawal of life-sustaining treatment, 'causes' the patient's death simply means that a court will not hold the physician liable for the death (*Harvard LR* 1992: 2028–9). Causation is therefore the topic of the next chapter, which looks at the way in which causation, like intention, is manipulated according to the context and the identity of the actor.

Chapter 4

Causation

. . . no act is murder which does not cause death.
(*Per* Devlin J's summing-up in *Adams*, reproduced in
Easing the Passing (1986: 171)

Introduction

We already know that murder requires both *mens rea* and an *actus reus*. A person can be guilty of murder if he has the relevant state of mind to satisfy the *mens rea* element, and will satisfy the *actus reus* requirement if he has caused the death.[1] There must be a sufficiently direct link between a person's conduct and a particular consequence before that person can be said to have caused that consequence, so the absence of such a link or 'chain' of causation is an obvious check on unfettered liability.

Causation is particularly relevant in end-of-life situations because there are so many potential causes from which to choose *the* (legal) cause of the patient's death. In cases where, for example, there is one clear perpetrator who has undoubtedly intended to kill his victim, the cause of death is clear. However, in the principle of double effect and treatment withdrawal cases already examined and in the *novus actus interveniens* cases to be examined in this chapter, it has and will be shown that:

(a) Contrary to the doctrine of causation's assumption of a single cause, each case has more than one potential cause from which *the* cause has to be found, and that

(b) in administering pain-killing medication and in treatment withdrawal cases, the cause of death has been held to be the patient's pre-existing illness/disease, but that

---

1 As a 'result' crime, it requires a consequence and that consequence – the death of the victim – must have been caused by the accused's act or unlawful omission.

(c) in cases where there is an offender who has injured the victim, then he
     will be considered to be the blameworthy cause.[2]

As Brock explains:

> The inquiry into the cause of death is, roughly, something like this: We
> take all the factors which are 'but-for' causes, but for these factors the
> patient would not have died in that way and at that time. There will be a
> great many such factors, and we do not actually assemble them all, but
> rather restrict our selection of the cause from among them.
>
> (Brock 1989b: 128)

A 'but-for' (otherwise known as a 'factual') cause is the traditional distinction
the courts make between factual and legal causation. The effect of this distinction is that whereas a person may be the factual cause of a consequence,
he may not necessarily be its legal cause. This, like the absence of a direct causal
link, acts as a limit on liability, but there are also other limits developed by the
courts which will be analysed in this chapter.[3] One of these is where there has
been an intervening event (known as a *novus actus interveniens*) which can
break the chain of causation between the original event and the consequence.
An analysis of these cases (loosely divided into firstly, coherent principle and
secondly, withdrawal of treatment following injury by a perpetrator) will show
that, again, the doctor is invariably held not to be the cause of death in either.
Indeed, even more than this, the resulting picture will show that neither doctors (*R v Smith* ([1959] 2 QB 35) and *R v Cheshire* ((1991) 93 Cr App R 251)),
patients (*R v Blaue* ([1975] 1 WLR 1411)) nor the police (*R v Pagett* ((1983) 76
Cr App R 279)) will be held to have caused a death. In such circumstances,
blame has been firmly placed at the feet of the original culpable actor.
   Another possible limitation on liability relates to the relevance of foresight
(as opposed to intention) as the mental element and finally, the requirement
for a duty of care acts as a limiting factor in omissions cases as there can be
no liability without it. An analysis of court decisions relevant to each limiting
factor, taken together with an examination of the law as it relates to causation
and omissions (with continued use of the doctor/interloper distinction), will
illustrate how intention and causation are not, and cannot be the decisive
factors here. Rather, decisions are based on unstated criteria such as policy
and intuition which in themselves depend on full consideration of relevant
contextual factors.

---

2 The unusual way in which the Court of Appeal justified its decision in *R v Kennedy (No. 2)*
   ([2005] 2 Cr App R 23) is a good example of this.
3 There are so many limits on liability for consequences that Ashworth has been led to query
   what is the rule and which are the exceptions; Ashworth 2006: 127.

This is not a criticism; a decision by the courts that doctors are not responsible in these cases are decisions which not only reflect the notion of the doctor's role and his duty to his patients, but also support our instincts to find responsible the person we perceive as a wrongdoer deserving of blame. The criticism lies in the fact that courts have to manipulate established causal principles in order to achieve this.

Factual causation: the first limiting principle

The very basic factual, or 'but-for', test merely requires that there can be no factual cause unless the event or consequence would not have occurred but for the actor's act or unlawful omission; '. . . the act must be a *sine qua non* of the prohibited consequence . . .' (Ormerod 2005: 53).

This 'test' has been criticised as being too wide because in cases where, for example, a person has been wounded by another and is receiving treatment as a result, there will always be 'but-for' causation as the medical treatment would be unnecessary if the victim had not been injured by the defendant in the first place. In *Pagett*, Goff LJ said:

> . . . there are many acts which are *sine qua non* of a homicide and yet are not either in law, or in ordinary parlance, the cause of it. If I invite P to dinner and he is run over and killed on the way, my invitation may be a *sine qua non* of his death, but no one would say I killed him and I have not caused his death in law.
>
> (*Pagett per* Lord Goff at 287)

The 'but-for' test is insufficient by itself to attribute causal liability; certainly it is difficult to see how the *sine qua non* test of causation could assist in distinguishing between the doctor who switches off a life-support machine – whom the courts would find not guilty of causing the patient's death – and the interloper who does so. We would be disposed to find that the latter caused the death but that the doctor did not, but we would not find the answer to this conundrum in either intention or causation. The method by which one would be guilty of homicide and the other not is based on other considerations such as lawfulness, justification, consent and motive together with the use of the ploy devised by the courts in the form of the acts/omission distinction.

Novus actus interveniens: the second limiting principle

The lack of coherent principle

Pursuant to the requirement for a direct link between conduct and consequence, in criminal law causal responsibility normally rests with the person who carried out the last voluntary act. A *novus actus interveniens* would therefore be expected to negate the defendant's responsibility for the death of the victim. This principle was followed in the case of *R v Jordan* ((1956) 40 Cr App R 152), where the accused was given leave to appeal against his conviction for the murder of a man he had stabbed. It transpired that the direct and immediate cause of death was the abnormal medical treatment the victim had received and not the stab wound inflicted by the appellant, which had virtually healed.

However, the case, although it followed the authority of *R v Harding* (1936) 25 Cr App R 190) and *R v McGrath* ([1949] 2 All ER 495) on the limitations to be imposed in admitting new evidence, has itself been distinguished in subsequent cases, commencing (chronologically) with *R v Smith*, where the victim, in a catalogue of disasters, was stabbed twice by the defendant, and dropped twice while being carried to a medical facility where he was then, after some delay, given the wrong medical treatment. The intervening events – dropping the patient and administering the wrong treatment – could be expected to negate the defendant's liability for the death of the victim, but in establishing that the defendant was liable, and distinguishing *Jordan* as being 'a particular case depending upon its exact facts', Parker CJ emphasised that as long as the original wound was still an 'operating' and 'substantial' cause, then the death resulted from that wound, even if another cause of death was also operating at the same time (Parker CJ at 42–3).[4]

Some years later, in *R v Blaue* the victim, a young girl of 18, was stabbed by Blaue when she rejected his sexual advances. While the wound was not in itself fatal, as a Jehovah's Witness the girl refused the blood transfusion which was necessary to save her life. Lawton LJ held that her refusal did not break the chain of causation and that her death was accordingly caused by the stab wound inflicted by Blaue. He went on to say that '[i]t has long been the policy of the law that those who use violence on other people must take their victims as they find them' (Lawton LJ at 1415). *Jordan* was again distinguished and the 'operating and substantial cause' test from *Smith* applied.[5]

In the case of *Pagett*, a policeman shot and killed the 16-year-old pregnant girlfriend of a man who was using her as a shield. Goff LJ held that despite the fact that the shot which killed the girl was not fired by the defendant, he was nonetheless the cause of her death as his act 'contributed significantly' to it even if it was not '. . . the sole cause, or even the main cause . . .' (Goff LJ at 288). He went on to say that usually there was no need to give the jury a causation direction except in cases where '. . . a specific issue of

4 The principle was subsequently applied in *R v Watson* ([1989] Crim LR 733) and by the Court of Appeal in the case of *R v Dear* ([1996] Crim LR 595).
5 The same test was also applied in the Australian case of *R v Evans & Gardiner (No. 2)* ([1976] VR 523) where, as in *Cheshire* (1991), a stab wound had virtually healed before the victim died of a misdiagnosed bowel blockage which the court held was caused by the stabbing.

causation may arise' (Goff LJ at 280). Intervention by a third party was considered to be such an issue.

The 'test' set out by Goff LJ was that any intervening act had to be so independent of the accused's act 'that it should be regarded in law as the cause of the victim's death, to the exclusion of the act of the accused' (Goff LJ at 288). Relying on Hart and Honoré's treatise on *Causation in the Law*, Goff LJ held that, because the police officer was performing his duty, then he must have been acting involuntarily and was shooting back at the defendant for reasons of self-preservation. Therefore, his act was not independent of the wrongful act of the defendant and his activity did not absolve the latter from criminal responsibility (Goff LJ at 288–9).[6]

The same test of 'independence' arose in *R v Cheshire*, where the victim of a shooting died some months after the injury was inflicted. It was held that the defendant had killed the victim even though the evidence showed that the medical team had not recognised a respiratory complication. Where there was an intervention by doctors, the test laid down was that the treatment had to be so independent of the acts of the accused and was itself so potent in causing death, that the accused's contribution to the state of affairs could be totally discounted. Beldam LJ noted that the defendant's act was a significant cause of death even though the negligent treatment was the immediate cause; '[the] . . . complication was a direct consequence of the appellant's acts . . .' (Beldam LJ at 258). In *Cheshire* (and in *Pagett*) the court thus moved away from the *Smith* test (whether the original wound was still an operating and substantial cause) to whether the death was 'attributable' to the defendant's act (Allen 2005: 39); the wounds in *Cheshire* had healed, but as the complications arose as a direct consequence of the defendant's acts, these remained the cause of death.

Withdrawing treatment following injury

The second category of *novus actus interveniens* cases are those where the victim has been injured by a third party, but, unlike the previous category, is being kept alive by artificial means as a consequence of the injuries sustained. This series of cases, again chronologically, commences with an Australian case, *R v Kitching and Adams* ((1976) 6 WWR 697), where an inebriated victim was deliberately dropped onto the pavement by the two defendants who were removing him from the bar where he had been drinking. The victim was attached to a respirator which was turned off after ascertaining that brain death had occurred.[7] The defendants appealed against their conviction for

6 See also *R v McKechnie* ((1992) 94 Cr App R 51) and *R v Mellor* ([1996] 2 Cr App R 245).
7 In reality, the facts were slightly more complicated than this as his kidneys were removed after brain death, but before the respirator was turned off.

manslaughter on the ground that it was the doctors who had caused the victim's death when they removed his kidneys and turned off the respirator. In dismissing the appeals, except for a brief comment by O'Sullivan JA (to the effect that the defendants' conduct did not have to be a 'sole' or 'the effective' cause and that while there may well be more than one 'operative' cause, it would have to be shown that the doctors displaced the defendants as the operative cause in order for the doctors to be guilty), neither he nor Matas JA fully discussed the question of whether the doctors caused the death, except to say that it was not relevant for the jury to look at the doctors' conduct. The only question they had to decide was simply whether the accused had caused the death and not whether the doctors had acted properly or not.

Two years later the *novus actus interveniens* question arose again in *Finlayson v H.M. Advocate* ((1978) SLT (Notes) 60), a Scottish case. Here, the accused had injected the victim with large quantities of a noxious substance following which he fell ill, was taken to hospital and attached to life-sustaining machinery. When the machinery was disconnected, the appellant argued that the chain of causation had been broken. The court dismissed the appeal and in holding that 'the effects of the applicant's act were a substantial and operating and continuous cause of the death', Lord Justice-General Emslie concluded that disconnecting the machine could not be considered an extraneous or extrinsic act that would disturb the existing sequence of events. Whether the victim lived or died depended not just on the decision to remove life-sustaining treatment, but also on a number of other factors '. . . including whether any particular treatment was available and if it was available whether it was medically reasonable and justifiable to attempt it and to continue it' (Emslie LJ-G at 61).

Subsequently in *R v Malcherek, R v Steel* ((1981) 73 Cr App R 173), two victims had been attacked by two separate defendants and left dependent on ventilators which were later withdrawn. As in the two previous cases, the defendants claimed that treatment withdrawal was a *novus actus interveniens* and that the doctors had thus caused the respective deaths of the victims. The court dealt with the defendants' appeal and application for leave to appeal simultaneously as both appellants claimed that the trial judges had erred in withdrawing the question of causation from the jury. The Lord Chief Justice, Lord Lane, said that the medical treatment was only necessary because of the initial assault by the defendants. As such, and applying *Smith*, he held that the original wound was '. . . a continuing, operating and indeed substantial cause of . . . death . . .' (Lord Lane at 181). The doctor could not bear responsibility for disconnecting life-support if the victim would have died had the doctor not intervened in the first place. By trying to save the victim, the doctor did not thereby take the offender's place as the person who caused the victim's death simply because his treatment was not successful in saving the victim. This would be tantamount to punishing the doctor not only for treating the patient, but for that treatment being unsuccessful.

A more recent and interesting example of the complexities of causation and refusal of treatment arose in the US case of *Georgette Smith* (Vernaglia 1999: 12). In this case, Georgette Smith became a quadriplegic after her mother, Shirley Egan, shot her (after overhearing her daughter and son-in-law discussing putting her in a residential home). Egan was charged with attempted murder, but when Smith applied for and was granted permission to turn off the ventilator, the prosecution threatened to upgrade the charge to first degree murder. However, the charge was not upgraded and, following her daughter's death, Egan was tried for, but acquitted of attempted murder by an Orlando jury on 18 August 1999. The case raises a number of questions as to whether the shooting was a sufficient cause of death and at what point, if any, does medical treatment end the causative effect of an offence.[8] No case of its kind has arisen in the UK, but it can be surmised that, on the basis of the authority in *Blaue*, the murder charge would stand.

Analysis of cases

As one would expect, this series of cases has been the subject of much analysis and debate. To some extent – and mainly due to Hart and Honoré (see below) – this has centred around differing interpretations of normality and voluntariness together with the foreseeability of the responses of the participants in these various events. Such analyses simply highlight the difficulty in finding much consistency in the courts' reasoning in *novus actus interveniens* cases.

For example, Norrie found it hard to distinguish between the contrary decisions in *Jordan* and *Smith* (Norrie 2001). Firstly, in the former the treatment was 'palpably wrong' whereas in the latter it was 'thoroughly bad . . .' (surely a synonym for 'palpably wrong') and yet the decisions were different. He secondly claimed that, if *Jordan* was looked at in a broader context, it was possible to see that although the victim's wound was nearly healed in that case, it was nonetheless still the only reason why the victim had to be treated; as such, it '. . . remained an operative and substantial cause of the treatment' (Norrie 2001: 145). Thirdly, he noted that while in *Jordan* the court said that 'normal' treatment would not break a causal chain, no direct definition of abnormal is given. If the poor medical provisions available in the German barracks in the *Smith* case were the norm, how could they be termed abnormal? Relying on 'substantial cause' as the court did in *Smith* simply '[ducks] the question of the relevance of a new intervening abnormal act' (Norrie 2001: 146). Fourthly, in his analysis of *Cheshire*, Norrie (in claiming that it is another example of the courts' unwillingness to interpret defective medical treatment as a new intervening act) also saw that, in its timescale and factual detail, *Cheshire* was more like *Jordan* than *Smith* (Norrie 2001: 146).

8 www.cnn.com/US/9905/19/daughter.shot.03/ (accessed 27 June 2006).

In *Cheshire*, the court found against the appellant and yet did not use the 'test' set out in *Smith* and this may have been because of the nature of the appellant's grounds of appeal; his claim was that as the standard used by the trial judge to ascertain whether or not the chain had been broken by the doctor was recklessness (in the sense that somebody could not care less), the judge had effectively withdrawn the issue of causation from the jury because 'no juror would be likely to accept that a doctor treating a patient was reckless in the sense that he could not care less whether the patient lived or died' (*Cheshire* at 251). While Beldam LJ conceded that the direction was erroneous, he nonetheless held that the appellant had suffered no injustice because even if the patient's rare complication had been identified by more experienced doctors, '. . . the complication was a direct consequence of the appellant's acts . . .' (*Cheshire* at 258). Certainly by using recklessness/indifference by the doctor as the standard required to negate the appellant's liability, the latter's fate was sealed (Stannard 1992: 578).[9]

Blaue, of course, is different in the sense that the intervening act was a treatment refusal by the victim (and is thus comparable with other treatment refusal cases generally; see the next chapter). This can certainly be said to be a factual cause, but was held not to be the legal cause. However, simply saying that the chain was not broken because life-saving treatment was refused (on the basis that the defendant must take the victim as he finds her) does not really contribute anything new to the law (although it transposes a civil law concept into criminal law).[10] It might have been better to have said that the wound was still an operative and substantial cause.

Hart and Honoré took a different view and suggested that although the decision was correct, its reasoning was deficient because it wrongly assumed that a Jehovah's Witness could abandon her beliefs when, as a matter of conscience, she was not free to do so (Hart and Honoré 1985: 361). In their view, the victim's refusal of the blood transfusion was not an intervening act because it was not 'voluntary'. Interestingly, this was exactly the point made by Goff LJ in *Pagett*, that is, that the intervening act did not break the chain because acting in self-defence was an involuntary response. Beynon has suggested that perhaps it would have been better in *Pagett* simply to have recognised that firing back at a dangerous criminal was a 'normal' response (Beynon 1987: 551), but as was seen earlier, applying a standard of normality does not help to understand causation when it can be seen that 'normality' means different things to different people. In *Jordan*, for example, Hallet J described the treatment given in that case as 'not normal' and although he does not define normal, his judgment makes it clear that in the context of that case, not normal must have meant 'palpably wrong' (*Jordan* at 157). Stannard on the other hand, in his analysis of intervention cases, understands normal

9 See also Dennis 1993: 48.   10 Wrongly, according to Stannard 1993: 94.

to mean 'reasonably foreseeable' (Stannard 1993: 92) (see below) while Hart and Honoré define normal (mere) conditions as those which simply exist '. . . as part of the usual state or mode of operation . . .' (Hart and Honoré 1985: 35). As such they do not 'cause' events (because this function is reserved to abnormal events; see below for further analysis). In fact, Hart and Honoré's basic premise is that the courts use the concepts of a 'voluntary' intervention and 'abnormal' events to negate responsibility.

Despite inconsistent reasoning in the cases, and the resultant uncertainty in the law which arises from it, this has not detracted from the consistency in result which is that in all the cases (except *Jordan*) liability has been firmly placed with the original offender. This is equally evident in those cases where life-sustaining treatment has been withdrawn following infliction of an injury by a perpetrator. Perhaps the main criticisms of this category of cases are that firstly, no question was raised as to the propriety of the doctors' conduct[11] whereas today, doctors withdrawing treatment from a ventilator-dependent patient would be required to seek a declaration from the court as to the legality of the proposed course of action.[12] Secondly, the courts simply avoided discussing whether or not what the doctors did was an intervening act. In *Evans & Gardiner, R v Kitching and Adams*, and *Malcherek* and *Steel*, the judges emphasised that it was not the doctors who were on trial. By saying that, the courts 'sidestepped' the question (Mathews and Foreman 1993: 133) and offered an '. . . unconvincing rationalisation . . .' as to why '. . . the ordinary causal principle that a voluntary intervening act which accelerates death should relieve the original wrongdoer of liability for the result' was not applied (Ashworth 2006: 130).

Thus, despite allegations of some 'stretching' of established causation principles (Ashworth 2006: 124), the cases nonetheless support the proposition that on the one hand, permissible activities by doctors in carrying out their professional duties simply do not attract liability, and on the other, that the courts are seen to punish the person perceived to be blameworthy. This is particularly significant in light of Glanville Williams's interpretation of the *novus actus interveniens* doctrine. He claims that '. . . the doctrine is supported because it accords with our ideas of moral responsibility and just punishment, and serves social objectives' (Williams 1989: 392 and 405). He goes on to say that the courts are seen to excuse the 'venial intervener' (someone who

11 This point was made by Thomas J in *Auckland Area Health Board v AG* ([1993] 1 NZLR 235: 252). Another criticism is that both *Malcherek* (1981) and *Finlayson* (1978) show significant lack of clarity as to time of death. The Lord Chief Justice in *Malcherek*: 179, commented specifically that '[t]his is not the occasion for any decision as to what constitutes death'. This was subsequently remedied in *Bland* (1993), where the Lords accepted a brain death definition.

12 Indeed, these cases should now only be acknowledged subject to *Bland* and the present necessity to apply for a declaration before withdrawing treatment; the point is made by Salako 1998: 466.

acts 'semi-forgivably') in order to minimise harm. Logically therefore, '[a]n intervening *guilty* act shifts responsibility . . . from the initiator to the ultimate actor, whereas an intervening *innocent* act leaves responsibility with the initiator . . . ' (Williams 1989: 392 and 405). That this is correct can be seen not only in both categories of cases analysed above, but also in the so-called 'continuing act' cases where the defendant's *mens rea* and *actus reus* did not coincide. In *Le Brun* for example, the defendant had knocked his wife unconscious during an argument (when he had the requisite *mens rea*), but there was no *actus reus* until later when he dropped and killed her while dragging her along the pavement. The court said that dropping her could have been construed as a *novus actus interveniens* if he was trying to help her when he dropped her (as opposed to concealing what he had done). In that case, he would not be guilty of either murder or manslaughter (*Le Brun* at 107).

Foresight: the third limiting principle

We know that the wider definition of intention used by the courts includes foresight, but on a basic level it can be said that if an actor intended rather than foresaw a consequence, the evidence is stronger that he caused it. As Anscombe has made clear, '[i]f one can justly point to the prior existence of the intention as an influencing condition in an account of how the action was brought about, then it can indeed be called a cause' (Anscombe 1983: 185). Common sense therefore tells us that it may be more difficult to prove 'cause' where the agent simply foresaw the consequence and indeed, this is why foresight has been suggested as a possible limitation on liability in *novus actus interveniens* cases.

On the basis that a person is responsible for the reasonably foreseeable consequences of his action, is it right that he should be responsible for a consequence he does not foresee?[13] Stannard uses the 'classic body on the sea shore' scenario to explain what he calls the 'foreseeability principle'. In this scenario, if a victim is knocked unconscious by the defendant and left on the sea shore, the defendant would be held liable for the victim's death if the latter was drowned by the incoming tide, but not if he was struck by lightning or died in an earthquake, on the basis that drowning would be foreseeable but being struck by lightning would not. Using *Cheshire* as an example, Stannard applies the foreseeability principle to medical treatment cases, where he would expect to see that normal (in his interpretation – reasonably foreseeable) treatment would not break the causal chain (Stannard 1993: 91–2). This is in line with the decision in *R v Roberts* ((1971) 56 Cr App R 95), where a woman

13 See, for example, Law Com No. 177 (1989) Vol. 1, clause 17 (2) and the Law Commission's ongoing proposals to codify the general principles of criminal law, including external elements www.lawcom.gov.uk/criminal.htm (accessed 28 June 2006).

fearing what the driver of the car in which she was a passenger was about to do to her, jumped out of the car and was injured. It was held that the appellant had caused her injury because her reaction in jumping out of the car was reasonably foreseeable. The apparent irreconcilability of this with the decision in *Blaue* (where it could be said that it was not reasonably foreseeable that the victim was a Jehovah's Witness) has been explained by Herring on three possible bases: firstly, that refusal of the treatment in *Blaue* was an omission, whereas jumping out of a car was an act. Secondly, that *Blaue* could simply be a case on religious freedom. Finally, that the reasonable foreseeability test in *Roberts*, as amended subsequently in *R v Williams, R v Davis* ((1992) 95 Cr App R 1),[14] allowed for taking the victim's characteristics into account and '. . . it was reasonably foreseeable that a victim with the characteristic of being a Jehovah's Witness would refuse a blood transfusion' (Herring 2006: 117–18).[15] In *Williams* and *Davis*, the test applied was whether or not the victim's reaction was within an expected range of responses; '[i]f the reaction was "so daft as to make it [V]'s own voluntary act" the chain of causation is broken' (Ormerod 2005: 68). However, neither this, nor the foreseeability aspect are reconcilable with *R v Dear* where the foreseeability of the victim's conduct was regarded as 'immaterial' (Smith J.C. 1996: 596). As noted by Ormerod, the decision may be justifiable on the basis that the victim's (alleged) suicide arose as a direct result of the defendant's attack on him and not because of a totally unconnected reason (Ormerod 2005: 68).

The relevance of foresight and *novus actus interveniens* also arose in *Reeves v Commissioner of Police*, but the case is equally important for its emphasis on the relevance of duty in omissions cases.

The duty of care: a fourth limiting principle

In *Reeves*, the administratrix of a deceased prisoner brought a negligence claim against the Police Commissioner for failing to prevent the prisoner's suicide while he was in police custody. The Commissioner raised a number of defences, including *novus actus interveniens* on the basis that, as death was caused by the (competent) prisoner's own voluntary act, any link between the defendant's alleged negligence and the suicide was broken. The Court of Appeal held that the police authority, being aware that the prisoner was a suicide risk, owed him a duty of care which it had breached by failing to take reasonable steps to prevent the suicide. The *novus actus interveniens* defence failed because:

> . . . the suicide was not an *intervening* cause . . . or was not a *new* act:

---

14 Where a hitchhiker, fearing the defendants were going to rob him, jumped out of their moving car and was killed.
15 And upon which see generally at 115–18.

because foresight of its possible occurrence was part of the reason, indeed by far the most important part of the reason, for placing the defendants under their duty in the first place.

(*Reeves* (1) *per* Buxton LJ at 180)

The House of Lords (Lord Hobhouse dissenting) upheld the decision, the majority agreeing that there was no *actus* and no *interveniens* either, because '[t]he act by which the deceased killed himself was the very act which the commissioner was under a duty to prevent . . . [t]he chain of causation was not broken' (*Reeves* (2) *per* Lord Hope at 381).[16]

Although the court conceded that the duty (by a police authority to prevent the suicide of a person in their care) existed in 'unusual' circumstances in *Reeves*, it is arguable – and indeed has been argued in the context of treatment refusal – that a hospital authority, may 'by analogy . . . [be] in the same position as the police or a prison authority' (Wheat 2000: 182). Certainly, it is a well-established common law principle that a doctor owes his patients a duty of care, but the question must be asked, does that duty extend to preventing his patients from committing suicide? (On the assumption that refusing treatment in the sure knowledge of death equates to suicidal behaviour.) In *Burke*, Lord Phillips MR asserted that '[a] fundamental aspect' of the duty to care for a hospitalised patient '. . . is a duty to take steps as are reasonable to keep the patient alive' (*Burke* (2) at para 32). This can be said to support the view taken in *Reeves*, but, as will be seen in chapter 6, is totally contrary to the position where a competent patient refuses life-sustaining treatment, as not only must the doctor comply with the patient's (possibly suicidal) refusal, but also the question simply does not arise, as the patient's refusal is deemed not to be suicidal.

Moreover, a hospital authority is also distinguishable from a police authority for other reasons. Firstly, a patient goes into hospital voluntarily (unless sectioned under the Mental Health Act) whereas in cases such as *Reeves*, 'the person is (lawfully) held against his will . . .' (*Reeves* (1) *per* Morrit LJ at 190). Secondly, hospital authorities do not have the same element of 'control' over patients as the police and prison authorities have over prisoners. Thirdly, where a patient is competent and refuses life-sustaining treatment, the duty to care for that patient is negated.

Nonetheless, there is no doubt that the concept of duty has been extended in *Reeves* in the sense that the police authorities were required because of their relationship with the prisoner to prevent his suicide. There would be no equivalent (legal) duty on the part of, say, a passer-by to prevent a suicide as this would simply extend the principles of liability too extensively. This was

---

16 Although the judges in the House of Lords held that the deceased was 50 per cent contributorily negligent.

seen in the previous chapter, where a duty was defined as a device which narrows the sphere of liability. This is correct, but it has been and continues to be very difficult for the courts to decide how tightly duties should be confined and this is evident in the 'drugs' cases such as *Khan* and *R v Kennedy* ([1999] Crim LR 65 (1)). As in *Reeves*, duty and intervening events are intertwined in these cases also. For example in *Khan*, Swinton Thomas LJ proceeded on the basis of manslaughter by omission which might well have been successful if he had directed the jury on the requisite duty of care. He rejected the only possible alternative charge (of death resulting from the defendant's unlawful and dangerous act in supplying the drugs) on the authority of *R v Dalby* ((1982) 74 Cr App R 348), which had held that self-administration of a drug was a *novus actus interveniens* between the supply by the defendant and the death of the victim,[17] thus following the principle that responsibility rests with the last voluntary actor.

However, in *R v Kennedy (No. 2)*, this conclusion was very deliberately and cunningly avoided (and in the court's own words, this removed any '. . . difficulties relating to causation') (Lord Woolf CJ at 357). Again, this was a case where the deceased victim died after administering drugs supplied to him by the defendant, but the Court of Appeal (in case No. 1) held that preparing and handing over the filled syringe for immediate injection by the victim amounted to more than a mere supply. On the contrary, the court held that Kennedy was guilty of assisting or encouraging the victim to inject himself and as such, the case was distinguishable from *Dalby*. The defendant's active encouragement amounted to a 'significant cause of death' and the court went on to say '[w]hether one spoke of *novus actus interveniens* or simply in terms of causation, where an act causative of death was performed by the deceased, the critical question was whether the appellant was jointly responsible . . .' (*Kennedy* (1) at 66).

Following a reference by the Criminal Cases Review Commission, the case was re-heard in (a differently composed) Court of Appeal which nonetheless also held that the defendant and the victim were 'both engaged in the one activity of administering heroin.' As they were acting in concert, as far as the court was concerned, this satisfied the causation question, so there was no break in the chain of causation. Lord Woolf CJ said that the defendant's participation in the drug-taking by the victim satisfied s 23 Offences Against the Person Act 1861 whereby it was 'an offence to cause to be taken by

---

17 Although the Crown contended that *Dalby* was no longer good authority (following *Attorney General's Reference (No. 3 of 1994)*) ([1998] AC 245), the Court of Appeal held that as this was not before the judge at the time, and that as he had not left that question to the jury, then that avenue could not be pursued in the appeal, see *R v Khan* web.lexis-nexis.com: 5–6.

another person any . . . noxious thing thereby to endanger their life' (*Kennedy (No. 2)* at para 51).[18]

The only basis of the distinction between *Kennedy* and *Dalby* is that although in both cases the users had self-injected, in the former, Kennedy (complying with the deceased's wish) had given his client a fully primed syringe which the court found was sufficient for him to have 'encouraged and assisted' in the commission of the offence (Wilson 2002: 185–6). Can it rightly be said that this was sufficient to find a distinction between the two cases?[19]

The case is problematic for other reasons as well: it raises questions as to aiding and abetting and as to the extent of the participation (particularly in relation to 'causing' for which see the next chapter). More worryingly, one has to question Lord Woolf's (albeit *obiter*) view that:

> . . . intervening cases established that a person who caused their own death did not commit a crime, so it followed that a person who merely encouraged them to do so was not an accessory to manslaughter, as there is no principal to whom he is the accessory.
>
> (Phippen and Radlett 2005: 1054–5)

Why this should be confined to 'intervening cases' is unclear and this muddies the waters of any cases of aiding and abetting suicide, as committing suicide is not an offence (see chapter 6).

The previous section has highlighted the relevance of the duty of care and the implications of *novus actus interveniens* in omissions cases. It has also reinforced the complexity of the law relating to causation and the lack of any coherent principle and process by which the cause of a consequence is ascertained when there is more than one potential (legal) cause.

Finding 'the' cause: multiplicity and partial causes

In the same way that the law looks only to the presence of the intention required for a particular offence, so also it seeks to find a single cause amidst a multitude of possible 'but-for' causes.[20] Legal causation is the tool by which

---

18 In *Kennedy (No. 2)*: para 44, the court also held that the fact that the victim's self-administration of the drug was not an unlawful act did not mean that a person helping him (under s 23) did not commit an unlawful act.

19 See Smith's Commentary on *R v Wright* (2000b); Ormerod 2005: 60 (saying that the decision was made for policy reasons) and the Law Commission in LCCP 177 (2005): 204 (fn 10). All agree that the victim's voluntary act broke the chain of causation.

20 But see Beauchamp 1996: 6 where he says: '[t]o isolate a single event that causes death may not be possible, because our concepts of causation both in law and elsewhere are not sufficiently precise to allow us to isolate "the cause".' Compare Williams 1983: 398, where he says that '. . . in cases of multiple causation, it is unconvincing to select one cause as "the" cause.'

the law achieves this, but, as was seen in the *novus actus interveniens* cases, judges have not used consistent principles to find what they perceive to be the legal cause. The next part of this chapter will therefore examine two useful explanations of how causes can be determined. The first is the result of the empirical study by Sugarman mentioned earlier and the second is the famous work on causation by Hart and Honoré. In effect, the results of the former support the latter.

In Sugarman's study, the participants had to determine doctors' participation in euthanasia after reading vignettes which varied the doctor's actions and whether or not the patient requested death. The results indicated that those who took part in the study appreciated the presence of what they saw as two potential causes of the patient's death – the doctor's action and the patient's illness – because this meant that they could discount the doctor's contribution to the outcome, and decide that the patient's death was primarily a result of the deterioration in the patient's health. Significantly it was felt that, because neither cause necessarily produced death independently of the other cause, then the doctor's behaviour was not the only potential cause of the patient's death.[21] As Sugarman noted, it was important to measure the extent to which external causes played a part in any occurrence, because the greater their part, so the actor's part was correspondingly less (Sugarman 1986: 61). This theme is evident in the distinction Hart and Honoré make between causes and mere conditions.

In their theory of the plurality of causes, Hart and Honoré see that each individual event is surrounded by a vast number of circumstances or 'mere conditions' which, while they are required to produce an effect, may not actually be its 'cause'. Using the criteria of 'normality'[22] and 'voluntary actions'[23] to distinguish between a cause and a mere condition, a mere condition would be normal and thus defined by Hart and Honoré as:

> . . . factors we know of or assume the existence of, yet they are not the cause of the accident, although . . . without them the accident would not have occurred . . . normal conditions (mere conditions) are those present as part of the usual state or mode of operation.
>
> (Hart and Honoré 1985: 34–5)

Following doubt by critics as to how a cause and a mere condition can be distinguished, Hart and Honoré explain the difference by way of a story about a fire. A lawyer concerned with particulars would not say that the cause

---

21 Interviews with General Practitioner and Consultant Neurologist confirm.

22 On the basis that what is abnormal is '. . . what makes the difference between an accident and things going on as usual', Hart and Honoré 1985: 35.

23 A voluntary human action is one '. . . intended to bring about what in fact happens . . .' Hart and Honoré 1985: 42.

of a fire was the presence of oxygen; he would say perhaps that the cause was a lighted cigarette or lightning. The cause, however, according to Hart and Honoré, depends on the context and reason the question is asked, so that if a fire broke out in a manufacturing process where oxygen had to be excluded, oxygen would be the cause.[24] The conclusion they draw, therefore, is that not '. . . every factor necessary for the occurrence of an event is equally entitled to be called "the cause" ' (Hart and Honoré 1985: 12). In other words, some kinds of events or conditions are necessary or sufficient for others to occur and we know what kinds of events these are because generally they do occur and because our experiences and practices tell us that certain consequences will regularly follow if the conditions are right. Thus, some events are caused simply as a result of existing conditions rather than as a result of something specific that an actor has done or omitted to do. If, on the other hand, we do want to say that a person has caused an event, then Hart and Honoré's 'common sense' approach to causation is that such a person can only be the cause when he 'manipulates' an object in the environment or interrupts a course of events which would normally take place.

Their argument is persuasive because there are no doubt circumstances in our environment without the presence of which an event would not have the consequences it ultimately has, although these may not be its cause. However, even allowing for these 'mere conditions' or things that are part of the circumstances, the law still requires a cause to be found and how that cause is selected depends, as acknowledged by Hart and Honoré (and numerous others), on the context and on our particular interest or query. Often, we ask a question in a particular way because we want the answer to fit in with our perception of how something happened. We have already seen in the first chapter how easy it is to 'construct,' 'select' or 'rig' the way in which we can describe activities which are, according to Harris, '. . . infinitely expandable or contractable' (Harris 1985: 44).

Firth illustrates this with an example of a hunter who shoots himself and dies. He suggests we could say that his death was caused by any of the following: loss of blood, a severed artery, a bullet, a rifle, a defective lock and so on indefinitely. We could expand the example to speak of more general environmental conditions (for example, it might have been raining and he slipped causing the gun to go off accidentally) or to include the hunter's attitude or character traits as part of the equation (he may have been angry because he missed his prey and this made him careless). To take it further, but for the presence of the animal, he would not have gone hunting (Firth 1967: 376). In the same way we can say that an injured victim would not be on a ventilator 'but for' his injury and that he would not have died 'but for' the doctor switching off the ventilator. Similarly we can say that a cancer patient would not need

24 The example is used by Lord Hobhouse in *Reeves (No. 2)* at 391.

pain-killing medication 'but for' his illness and that he would not have died then and at that time, 'but for' the increase in the dosage (subject to the proviso that it is capable of causing death) and this is the crux of causation in the factual sense. If 'followed through', there would simply be a never-ending number of causes for every crime (Fletcher 1978: 589). The requirement of legal causation is thus necessary to limit the consequences for which persons are responsible, but ultimately depends on the need to find a blameworthy cause.

The way in which judges carry out this selection of blameworthy cause predominantly involves consideration of the actor's state of mind, that is, consideration of intention and foresight. However, focusing on a complex course of semantic and psychological hair-splitting over foresight or intention in an effort to find a purportedly rational juridical basis for deciding on blameable cause both clouds an already complicated issue and fails to grasp the real nettle. Focusing on the 'mental element' is tried and trusted – although frequently inconsistent – in the criminal law as the basic benchmark of liability. It is also the fetish used to help steer a way through the maze that is 'culpable cause' in cases including death. Yet a clearer solution would be found by acknowledging that neither intention nor foresight alone can provide proper solutions of good law.

The reality of causation decisions: unstated criteria and judicial manipulation

There is a widely held view that the concept of causation – like intention – is manipulated firstly, in order to avoid finding some persons who (a) play a causal role and (b) foresee a consequence, to be legally responsible for it (Skegg 1988: 137–8) and secondly, to satisfy the need to punish someone who is felt to be deserving of punishment for his unacceptable behaviour (Wilson 2002: 193).[25] In the *novus actus interveniens* cases, for example, judges have imposed standards which make it most unlikely that doctors will be the cause of their patients' deaths[26] and the same can be said of police officers, who also seem to enjoy a 'protecting mantle' in these cases. As Norrie confirms:

> There is a criminal, and the purpose of the causation rules is . . . to attribute responsibility to him. It is no answer to say that there is a supervening cause where that cause involves the police, the medical services, or physical or psychological characteristics of the victim.
>
> (Norrie 2001: 147 and 149)[27]

---

25 Wilson essentially says that causation holds to account those deserving of blame.

26 For example, witness the test laid down by Beldam LJ in *Cheshire* (1991) at 255–6.

27 Compare Skegg 1988: 181, who said that 'judges would . . . develop, modify, refine, or even fudge legal concepts, rather than direct the jury that the doctor was guilty of murder'.

That the law is stretched in order to ensure conviction of the perceived wrongdoer can also be seen in the continuous act cases such as *R v Thabo Meli* ([1954] 1 WLR 228), where the defendants were found guilty of manslaughter, even though they were not the actual cause of death.[28] Also in *Le Brun* (above, following *Church*) it was enough that the defendant had the *mens rea* of the crime at the beginning of the sequence of events, or alternatively, that there was no break in the chain of causation when he dropped his wife.

The same principle of punishing wrongdoing can be said to apply to the hypothetical distinction made between the doctor and the interloper who turn off life-support mechanisms. Upon what basis can we and do we claim that the doctor would not cause the patient's death, but that the interloper would? The intention (including foresight of virtual certainty) could be the same and the consequence is most certainly the same, so it cannot be said that these form the basis of any distinguishing factors.

Upon what considerations do the courts therefore base their decisions? The truth of the matter is that in ascribing cause, the courts arguably rely on grounds external to the analysis before a result can be obtained in a particular case. This very much reinforces the view that the reasons for a decision are not prepared until after the decision itself has been reached. Thus preconceptions have already been made which are based on policy, instinct and intuition, and on contextual factors – which include considerations such as the doctor's role, his motive and the patient's consent – in order to emphasise the importance of medical liberty and the necessity of not tying the doctor's hands.

Policy, instinct and intuition

The courts often make intuitive socio-political policy judgments (Norrie 2001: 144)[29] to achieve their goal of absolving doctors. Duff has said that intuitions are important; '. . . we "see" or feel immediately that this person is a murderer while that person is not, and we then look for rules and concepts to fit our intuitive judgment . . .' (Duff 1990: 36). Although Benjamin has claimed that '[w]e may not pick and choose which causal story we want to give in order to suit our prejudices' (Benjamin 1976: 16), this is exactly what we do; we exercise a value judgment[30] to determine what is killing and what is allowing to die. Having made that moral judgment, the conduct in question is examined to see if it fits into the category of killing or allowing to die. As

---

28 The defendants thought they had killed their victim when they rolled him over a cliff. He was, however, still alive, but subsequently died of exposure. The case was followed in *R v Church* ([1966] 1 QB 59). Again, the defendant thought his victim was dead when he threw her in the river, where she subsequently drowned. See also *R v Moore and Dorn* ([1975] Crim LR 229).
29 On policy generally see Wilson and Smith 1995: 406.
30 Beauchamp and Childress talk about this in the 4th edition of *Principles of Biomedical Ethics* 1994: 223, but subsequently published a 5th edition in 2001.

withholding or withdrawing treatment is not considered to be killing, any behaviour that falls within this category is condoned but contrarily, if we perceived withholding or withdrawing treatment to be unacceptable, we would interpret it as killing.

This is very much linked to our idea of what is right or wrong, or who is good or bad and nowhere is this better illustrated than in the distinction Lord Goff makes in *Bland* between a doctor and the malicious interloper who both disconnect life-sustaining treatment from a dependent patient. He said that the latter's conduct in actively preventing the doctor from prolonging the patient's life '. . . *cannot possibly* . . .' be interpreted as an omission (*Bland per* Lord Goff at 369 (emphasis added)). This categorical rejection of the interloper as omitting to act (even though he 'does' the same as the doctor) emphasises two closely linked conclusions. Firstly, the interloper's prohibited role in contrast to the doctor's permitted and justified role, and secondly, that in finding that blameworthiness equals culpability, the courts have to look to context and status. The common factor between the two points is that knowledge and consideration of context is imperative in finding both, because neither operate in a limbo. In order for behaviour to be considered justified (or not) all the circumstances surrounding it must be known. This is why decisions must be seen in the context of their social environment, especially the hospital environment where '. . . social arrangements and institutions, and . . . customs . . . result from living and working together' (Wilson and Hernstein 1986: 24).

The roles of context and status

In the first chapter, we saw how the context in which an event takes place has an impact upon the formulation of intention. It is equally relevant in ascertaining cause, especially in 'medical' cases, where it limits the liability of doctors. Where there are multiple causes, the way in which the cause is chosen will depend on the '. . . context and purpose for which . . . [the] . . . enquiry is made . . .' (Hart and Honoré 1985: 11). Hart and Honoré have adopted this view, although, ironically, they themselves have been criticised (by Norrie especially) for failing to take into account the 'broader context within which individuals operate'[31] (Norrie 1991: 692). Whereas we might well agree with Hart and Honoré's exposition on normality and voluntariness, their interpretation of what is normal, abnormal and voluntary is flawed by their discounting the broader social context which in itself affects what is voluntary, normal or abnormal, and what is not. How can a judgment as to any of these be made without considering the circumstances by which such standards are measured? To separate a decision from its surroundings is to ignore a vital element in ascribing cause. This is acknowledged by the courts when

31 See also Wilson 2005: 109.

exercising their choice as to blameworthy cause, because they would not have been able to develop the acts and omissions distinction or the principle of double effect as exclusive doctors' defences unless they had considered the context in which doctors carry out their functions. As has been argued by many (Tur 2002, Rhodes 1998, Stell 1998, and Otlowski 2000 included), their unique status and role protects them from liability (in the same way that the interloper's prohibited role does not; Brock 1989b: 128–9). This, together with their differing motives, operates as yet another distinction between them.

Motive as a distinguishing contextual factor

In the same way that motive was seen to be relevant in principle of double effect cases,[32] it also helps to explain why a doctor would not cause a patient's death when he withdraws treatment and why the interloper would, because in the same way that a doctor could say that his reason for administering pain-killing medication was to relieve suffering, so also can he use the same reason for withdrawing treatment.

There is much support for the idea of a motive providing an excuse or justification for a doctor's conduct and, indeed, some of the cases mentioned previously suggest a hidden motivational element. For example, in *Le Brun*, the trial judge said (and Lord Lane CJ agreed) that '. . . if the fatal injury happened in the course of well-intentioned efforts to help her he would not be guilty of murder or manslaughter' (*Le Brun* at 107) (because the chain of causation would have been broken), but if the defendant was trying to conceal what he had done to his wife, he would be guilty, because the chain would not be broken in those circumstances. The court has come perilously close to conceding the relevance of the offender's motive here; as Jefferson said of the case, '. . . if the accused had a good motive . . . he was not liable because he did not cause her death; if, however, he picked her up with a bad motive, such as concealing his attack on her, he was guilty for then he would have caused her death' (Jefferson 2006: 62). Put another way:

> . . . the *Thabo Meli* doctrine will apply only where the ongoing actions are still tainted by D's unlawful purpose. Had D dropped his wife while carrying her to hospital, his doing so would have been a separate incident, divisible from the earlier, unlawful transaction.
>
> (Simester and Sullivan 2004: 164)

The case emphasises the relevance of culpability in the ascription of liability by judges, but importantly it shows that judges do take hidden factors such

---

32 Jefferson 2006: 50, for example, advanced the idea that motive could possibly have provided Dr Adams with a defence.

as motive into account with a view to acknowledging and justifying the role of the medical professional.

Consent as a distinguishing factor[33]

We have already seen a number of differing interpretations which claim to explain the distinction between the doctor and the interloper,[34] but yet another important consideration is the impact of the patient's consent. This was certainly found to be crucial in the investigative study carried out by Sugarman referred to earlier in this chapter. One of the manipulated factors was whether the subjects of the study felt that doctors were less responsible for a death if the patient had requested it. The results showed that the doctor's responsibility was mitigated where he complied with a patient's request. To all intents and purposes then, the request from the patient justified – and mitigated – the doctor's responsibility (Sugarman 1986: 62).[35]

Consent was thus an important factor in people's perceptions of liability and responsibility, but as a person cannot consent to his own death,[36] this brings to light considerable inconsistencies which are particularly evident in the contradictory status and relevance (or irrelevance, depending on the circumstances) which consent has been given in the courts.

Firstly, if a competent patient specifically asks his doctor to hasten his death and the doctor complies, this would be murder (or assisted suicide). It would also be murder if the doctor (as long as he had the requisite *mens rea*)[37] withdrew treatment without a competent patient's consent (as, for example, the interloper would do) and the patient subsequently died. In *Burke*, for example, Lord Phillips said that where the patient plainly states that he wishes to be kept alive:

> [n]o authority lends the slightest countenance to the suggestion that the duty on the doctors to take reasonable steps to keep the patient alive in such circumstances may not persist. Indeed, it seems to us that for a doctor deliberately to interrupt life-prolonging treatment in the face of a competent patient's expressed wish to be kept alive, with the intention of

---

33 For a full history and review of consent see, for example, Callahan and White 1996: 26–32.

34 Justification; that the doctor acts lawfully; that the situation is not of the doctor's making; and that it is the differing motives that are relevant; see Beauchamp 1996: 9 on this generally.

35 Meisel 2004: 283, takes this a step further and argues that consent legitimates actively hastening death.

36 And neither can he waive his right to life; Williams 1983: 579; Lord Mustill in *Bland* (1993): 393; Kadish 1992: 858.

37 See Beauchamp's interesting 'thought experiment' 2004: 123.

thereby terminating the patient's life, would leave the doctor with no answer to a charge of murder.

(*Burke* (2) *per* Lord Phillips at para 34)

Thus in this situation, the consent of the competent patient is the only thing which would provide the doctor with a defence in such circumstances – and yet it is not a recognised defence.

Conversely (and based on the incontrovertible fact that a doctor can only treat a (competent) patient with his consent), a doctor incurs no liability for consensually withdrawing life-sustaining treatment, even if the patient knows that he will die as a result and is thus implicitly consenting to his own death. As Lord Browne-Wilkinson said in *Bland:*

> In the ordinary case of murder by positive act of commission, the consent of the victim is no defence. But where the charge is one of murder by omission to do an act and the act could only be done with the consent of the patient, refusal by the patient of consent to the doing of such act does, indirectly, provide a defence to the charge of murder.
>
> (*Bland per* Lord Browne-Wilkinson at 384)[38]

Moreover and again based on the authority contained in *Bland*, life-sustaining treatment can be withdrawn from incompetent patients without their consent, because the unconscious person is deemed to have released the doctor from his duty to care for the patient.[39] The consequence of these machinations is that while active killing with consent is penalised, both consensual and non-consensual treatment withdrawal which leads to death is not.

It is time for a more honest approach which acknowledges that the above considerations, and not just intention and causation alone, are the deciding factors in end-of-life decision-making.

---

38 It is interesting to speculate what the significance of this *obiter* statement would be in the absence of the acts and omissions distinction. It is not presumptuous to assume that such a statement would not have been made if the distinction did not exist, as this would then suggest that consent could be a defence to murder. Ironically, therefore, a patient can consent to an omission but not an act which causes death.

39 The Law Commission introduced a proposal to provide a person who performed medical treatment without consent with an exception from prosecution in LCCP 139 (1995) but this has not been implemented. In respect of a separate offence of killing with consent, see also the CLRC (1980), the HLSC (1993–4) and the Government's response, Cmnd. 2553 (1994). More recently, the Law Commission, in LCCP No. 177 (2005): Part 8, has bravely queried whether consent should operate as a double mitigation to reduce a murder charge to manslaughter where diminished responsibility also applies.

Conclusion

Causation is an additional, but inevitable, requirement for intention-based liability, but in order to find the 'legal' cause, judges have had to resort to manipulating the concept of causation so as to satisfy their perceptions of justice and to comply with society's expectations. This manipulation has led some to question the appropriateness of causation[40] in much the same way as the appropriateness of intention has been queried.

In the medical context, it has been seen that '[c]ausation is used as a device for denying liability for homicide' (Hughes 1958: 628). Certain factors, such as *novus actus interveniens*, lawfulness, foresight and duty have been and are used by the courts to limit the consequences for which a doctor is liable. However, while the above limiting factors may achieve the 'right' resolution, there is a need to acknowledge that doctors do play a causal role in their patients' deaths and continuing manipulation by the courts to avoid that conclusion does not hide the fact of its existence. It is true that a patient would not be dependent on a ventilator (or indeed require pain-killing medication) 'but for' his condition (thus factual causation is satisfied), but whenever a doctor decides to withdraw treatment on which a patient's life depends, his intervention, although described as permitting or allowing the patient to die (a) is a permitting or allowing *by the doctor*; and (b) even accounting for the argument that he is part of a course of events not of his own making, is still *a* (if not *the*) cause of death (although this does not necessarily mean that he is culpable) (Devettere 1990: 273) in the sense that the patient would not otherwise have died then and at that time. In allowing a death to occur *'at a particular time'* (Brock 1989b: 127) and earlier than it would otherwise have done, a doctor has unquestionably accelerated death. Although Hart and Honoré attempted to maintain a distinction between accelerating and causing death, in reality they are one and the same thing (because all of us are going to die anyway).[41] Devlin J himself equated the two in *Adams*, but, in holding that it was permissible to incidentally shorten life and conceding a defence for doctors who did accelerate death, he conveniently abandoned the 'orthodox proposition that shortening life involves causing death . . .' (Ashworth 2006: 126).

Undisputedly, the case provides doctors with a defence for causing death. It also suggests that an acceleration of death based on even minutes, hours, days or weeks would be sufficient. However, subsequent authority contradicts this in so far as it has been held that any acceleration of death must be more than *de minimis* in order to be a cause of death. The point was made in *R v Cato* ([1976] 1 WLR 110) and in *Sinclair* (one of the 'drugs' cases referred to earlier) where Rose LJ said:

---

40 See Honoré (2002/2004 reprint).
41 As was said in *Evans & Gardiner (No. 2)* (1976), '[d]eath is, of course, inevitable. Homicide is really the acceleration of the event.' See Jefferson 2006: 50.

For conduct accelerating death to be capable of being a substantial cause it would be necessary, in order to avoid the *de minimis* exception, for the prosecution to prove more than that death had been accelerated by mere hours or days in circumstances where intervening life would have been of no real quality.

(*Sinclair per* Rose LJ at 3)[42]

Whether this would apply to doctors treating their patients with pain-killing medication is another matter, but certainly this would not be a problem in PVS cases where a patient could potentially 'live' for another 30 years.[43]

Whichever view is taken, it is clear that the law relating to causation is confused and contradictory. This is evident in the cases examined throughout this book where neither the administration of pain-killing medication nor treatment withdrawal by doctors have been held to be the cause of the patient's death. In the latter cases, the courts have also held that treatment refusal by a patient, even with sure knowledge of death, cannot be construed as suicidal. With a view to analysing the courts' logic and in order to illustrate the ongoing problems associated with the concepts of intention and causation which have been highlighted here so far, the next two chapters will therefore look at whether or not it can be said that forgoing treatment is a way of committing suicide and following on from that, whether or not withdrawing treatment can accordingly be interpreted as assisting or aiding and abetting suicide.

42 It will be recalled that the appeal was allowed on the basis that a further direction should have been given as to whether acceleration of death was other than minimal.
43 See, for example, Beach J in *Bouvia* (1986): 305. This also assumes that 'life' has an absolute value, *per se*. Can it really be said that 30 years in a permanent vegetative state is 'life'? See, for example, Harris (1985).

Chapter 5

Does a patient who refuses treatment commit suicide?

> *The judgment of a . . . suicide is . . . [one that is made for the reason that] future life . . . is worse . . . than no . . . life at all. This seems to be in essence exactly the same judgment that some persons who decide to forego life-sustaining treatment make.*
>
> (Brock 1993: 166)

Introduction

Suicide, a former common law criminal offence, was decriminalised with the passing of the Suicide Act in 1961 when it was conceded that punishing the suicide's family (as the suicide himself was beyond reach) served no useful purpose. The Act, however, also introduced a new offence under s 2 of aiding, abetting, counselling or procuring the suicide of another.

There is no statutory definition of suicide, but in everyday language, to commit suicide means to take one's own life deliberately. Someone who commits suicide is commonly understood to be '. . . one who no longer wants to live and who takes definite, effective steps to end her life – whether by actively killing herself or by avoiding available ways of preventing her own death . . .' (Mathews 1987: 710). As indicated in the opening quotation above, this chapter considers whether a patient who refuses life-sustaining treatment in the sure knowledge that he will die, can arguably be committing suicide.[1] However, even though suicide is not illegal, the courts have interpreted treatment refusal in the majority of cases (especially those involving patients who are suffering from a non-terminal debilitating disease and/or terminally ill patients) as non-suicidal, because, by doing otherwise, they would by implication be endorsing suicide. In principle, this would mean that the many sick people all over the country who refuse life-sustaining treatment would be

---

1 There are many who agree that refusing treatment is, or can be, a form of suicide, for example, Otlowski 2000: 70; Stell (1998); and Frey 1998: 39.

committing suicide and that any doctor involved would be deemed to have assisted in their suicides.[2]

Unfortunately, though, the courts have not consistently held that treatment refusal is non-suicidal and this inconsistency is dependent to a large extent on the identity or status of the patient. In order to demonstrate this inconsistency, this chapter compares the distinguishing factors used to reach decisions in cases involving patients who are suffering from a non-terminal debilitating disease and/or terminally ill patients (for ease of reference only, referred to as 'terminally ill' patients), Jehovah's Witnesses who refuse life-saving blood transfusions and prisoners who refuse to eat and drink (that is, go on 'hunger strike'). If the patient is terminally ill, the finding will be that the treatment refusal is not suicidal, so the patient's treatment can be withdrawn. In contrast, if the patient is a Jehovah's Witness, there is (or certainly was) a tendency to impose treatment on a patient whose religion and decision are seen as irrational; the '. . . politically hapless' Jehovah's Witnesses (Hoover 1972: 581) present an ideal opportunity, both for non-believers to criticise what is seen as a totally unreasonable and irrational stance, and for healthcare providers to exercise their paternalistic tendencies.

In cases of prisoners who refuse sustenance, different considerations will apply. Elements of culpability and blame will often be reasons the court will rely on to hold that the treatment refusal is suicidal and should thus be stopped. In *Caulk* (*In re Joel Caulk* 125 N.H. 226; 480 A. 2d 93; 1984 N.H. LEXIS 364), for example, there was a punitive element in Batchelder J's judgment, which exemplified the feeling that the prisoner should not 'escape prosecution' for fear of frustrating the criminal justice system[3] (*Caulk* at 96).

The problematic, and yet singularly constant element in all of these cases is that the distinction between refusing life-sustaining treatment/sustenance and suicide is said to be dependent on intention and causation. This should in itself therefore lead to consistent decision-making. However, this has not been so, certainly as far as intention is concerned; in some cases the courts have simply concluded that refusal of treatment is not suicide by ignoring the patient's intention and assuming that it is non-suicidal. In other cases, the courts will look to the patient's reasons (i.e. motives) for choosing death when determining whether this choice is to be respected.

Thus, just as previous chapters have shown the supremacy of intention, its role in judicial reasoning is underlined again here, but it is once more shown to be both contradictory and inconsistent and subject to manipulation by judges in order to avoid the suicide label. In treatment refusal cases particularly, the courts still persist in denying the truth that technology which prolongs life, the growing importance of autonomy and self-determination,

---

2 For other policy reasons see, for example, Mathews 1987: 743.
3 The prisoner was serving a 10 to 20-year sentence for aggravated sexual assault.

increasing secularisation and indeed more tolerant social attitudes (Velasquez 1987: 40 and 42)[4] towards severe life problems such as protracted and/or painful diseases have led to the possibility of accepting suicide as a rational, voluntary and deliberate act, especially in the terminally ill.[5]

In the interests of justice, it is arguable that judges should acknowledge these changes and should be more open in their recognition of what they are doing by simply admitting motive-based decision-making as an explicit and therefore transparent, predictable and fair part of a law which has been unduly compromised by over-reliance on intention and causation. However, as these are the key elements both in the purported distinction between treatment refusal and suicide and in the meaning of suicide itself, this chapter will begin by looking at definitions and associated problems.

Problems with defining suicide

There is no doubt that the way in which suicide was stigmatised in the past has left some residual 'negative' attitudes (Battin and Lipman 1996: 3) towards what was previously a much reviled (certainly from a religious point of view) criminal offence. This has been compounded by the still existing practice of linking 'suicide' with the word 'committing'; as Barrington has said, '... most ... things committed are, as suicide once was, criminal offences' (Barrington 1986: 231).

These factors, together with the difficulty in determining the existence of intention, different interpretations of suicide, and prevailing attitudes which influence our willingness to classify some things as suicidal and others not, make it difficult to define suicide. Generally, applying suicide as a label involves making a moral judgment (Price 1996: 298); if an activity incurs disapproval it will be called suicide, and if not, it will be called something else. For example, an admirable or heroic act of self-destruction, such as a father running into a burning building to save his children, or a soldier sacrificing his life for his comrades (or the often-used example of Captain Oates), may be described in a way other than as a suicide (Rachels 1986: 82) because the objective here is to achieve something other than death (Mathews 1987: 710). Again, exactly as was seen in the killing/letting die distinction, we exercise a value judgment to see if a certain type of conduct fits into a particular category description, and such a judgment here also has more to do with the use of preconception and intuition of whoever is choosing the descriptive term than with the intention of the actor whose conduct is being described.

4 Much has been written about this. As another example, see Gostin 1993: 97.
5 The literature on this is vast, and there are many who agree that suicide can be rational. For examples see Battin (1982); Graber (1981) and Brandt (1976).

Some definitions of suicide

Certain requirements must exist before conduct can be called suicidal. The following definitions will enable an analysis of these components to be made:

1. A 'death resulting directly or indirectly from a positive or a negative act of the victim which he knows will produce the result.'[6]
2. 'Voluntarily to do an act for the purposes of destroying one's own life while one is conscious of what one is doing'[7] (*Stroud's Judicial Dictionary* 1953).
3. Suicide is '. . . a voluntary act by which a person intends and causes his or her own death and which may be by omission or commission' (O'Rourke 1991: 317).
4. 'Suicide is the act of bringing about a person's death, provided that: 1) death is brought about by that person's own acts or omissions, and 2) those acts or omissions are (a) intentionally carried out (b) for the purpose of bringing about death (c) by those concretely particular means that actually brought death about' (Velasquez 1987: 48).
5. 'A person commits suicide if that person intentionally brings about his . . . own death and . . . death is caused by conditions arranged by the person for the purpose of bringing about his . . . death' (Rachels 1986: 81, quoting Beauchamp).
6. 'Suicide requires that an individual 1) intend his . . . own death, 2) act in such a way as to bring it about' (Childress 1998: 121, quoting the Park Ridge Centre).
7. '. . . when the dying person commits an act that has the immediate intent of ending life and has no other purpose' (Dyck 1973: 105).
8. '[T]he deliberate taking of one's life in order simply to end it, not instrumentally for any ulterior purpose' (Velasquez 1987: 45, quoting Margolis).
9. 'A proper suicide is one where a person non-instrumentally intends his death . . . [that is] he kills himself for no other reason than to terminate his life' (O'Keefe 1984: 363).[8]

---

6 This definition is based on knowledge; Durkheim (1952).
7 In the 6th edition of *Stroud's Judicial Dictionary* (2002) London: Sweet & Maxwell, it is defined as: 'voluntarily to do an act (or, as is submitted, to refrain from taking bodily sustenance)'.
8 A suicide is non-instrumental if there is no objective other than to die. This can be compared with an instrumental suicide where it may be that the suicide has more than one intention; the intention to die being secondary to the primary intention. In the case of self-sacrifice, the death is not therefore an end in itself, but is instrumental in achieving other ends, objectives or goals, such as freedom from suffering. See Childress 1982: 158 on 'instrumental' and 'expressive' suicide.

From these definitions, it can be concluded that suicide requires:

(a) an intention to die (and by implication the competence to form that intention is a prerequisite);
(b) the suicide must have 'caused' his own death by initiating a course of events specifically for that purpose;
(c) an act *or* an omission will suffice (although some would question the latter).

These three requirements will be examined individually in the context of treatment refusal, commencing with the first of the above points. This section also includes a discussion of problems with intention, examines rationality and competence and compares the three categories of persons in order to demonstrate the distinguishing factors which are used to reach decisions in each case.

The individual must intend his own death

'Traditional' cases of suicide and numerous coroners' judgments such as *R v City of London Coroner ex p Barber* ([1975] 1 WLR 1310), *R v Cardiff City Coroner ex p Thomas* ([1970] 1 WLR 1475), *R v H M Coroner for the County of Devon ex p Glover* ((1985) 149 JP 208), *R v H M Coroner for Northamptonshire ex p Anne Walker* ((1989) JP 356), *R v Huntbach ex p Lockley* ([1944] KB 606) and *In re Davis deceased* ([1968] 1 QB 72), confirm that suicide can never be presumed; indeed the presumption is against suicide in so far as intention has to be proved. The problem facing coroners in particular is, of course, one that has been referred to already – the subjectivity of intention. It has been said that '[t]here is no difficulty in obtaining the appropriate evidence relating to the means whereby the cause of death arose. The difficulty is in establishing the deceased's intent at the time' (Chambers 1989: 181). To assist with this, Beck devised a 'suicide intent scale' in which he stated that:

> *Intent* is defined as the seriousness or intensity of the wish of a patient to terminate his life . . . [and] is assessed simply by the behaviour of individuals as reported by others and by self-reports . . . intent [consists] of several major elements: first, the balance between the intensity of the wish to die vs. life-protective wishes; secondly, the patient's subjective probability estimate that his suicidal plan or wish will result in death.
>
> Suicidal intent generally cannot be determined by any single factor . . . but must take into account a variety of rather disparate elements.
>
> (Beck *et al* 1974: 45)

It is precisely these other disparate elements which are problematic in ascertaining intention, the key component in suicide. The next part of this chapter will therefore examine the problems associated with intention and which go to both rationality and competence, before going on to consider the three 'treatment' refusal groups.

Problems with intention

The problems with intention set out in the first chapter are, of course, equally applicable here. The inherent problem of subjectivity remains and, of particular importance in the context of suicide, the duality of intention which arises as a consequence of the presence of two intentions – the doctor's and the patient's. In addition, there are a number of contextual factors which affect the formulation of intention by the patient.

Contextual factors which influence the formulation of intention

Much has been written about the way in which the patient's illness and other influences confuse and distort his autonomous decision-making capabilities.[9] Commencing with the wider view, the dying patient may be affected by social and cultural factors; sociologists claim that no decisions are ever made without considering the social implications and restraints imposed by society.[10] Narrowing those parameters, institutionalisation itself, the practices, customs, rules and procedures and the ethos of healthcare (and prison) institutions may affect the patient's decision-making ability.[11] Narrowing it still further, psychological factors can influence the patient's thought processes and may stem from a variety of sources, such as (a) doctors, by 'the way in which they present information' to the patient and by their own response to the patient and his illness; (b) nurses, because they have a 'rapport' with the patient; and (c) relatives, because in their vulnerable state patients are more susceptible to any loved one's suggestions. The effects of the illness itself, pain, drugs, fatigue, exhaustion and loss of control are also important factors.[12]

Psychologically, the patient will be disorientated and open to feelings of stress, anxiety, hopelessness and humiliation[13] and in the case of 'terminally ill' patients, depression may be an additional controlling factor.

---

9 As so much has been written on the various factors listed in this section, some useful references have all been placed in the footnotes below without duplication, rather than individually after each separate point, as they often overlap. This is but a small selection of the vast literature on this; others are referred to in later footnotes.
10 See, for example, Kelleher 1997: 78; Grassi 1997: 130.
11 For example, Owens 1995: 291; Presidents Commission 1983: 102.
12 Again, as an example, see Kelly and Varghese (1996); Miles (1994); Kamisar 1958: 977; Hamerly 1998: 546; Louisell 1973: 728; Wanzer *et al* (1984).
13 For instance, Foley 1991: 294; Beck *et al* 1975: 1147; Weir 1989: 361.

Depression

The effects depression has on patient decision-making are extensively documented[14] and evidence shows that nearly all suicidal individuals were suffering from depression or some other diagnosable psychiatric illness.[15] In the case of 'terminally ill' patients, however, retrospective studies indicate that only a very small minority of terminally ill patients actually commit suicide[16] (and generally they will do so because of poor quality of life (Valente and Trainor 1998)),[17] but there is some uncertainty about the correlation between the effects of terminal illness, suicide and depression in the sense that the wish to end life may be a symptom of depression and what is perceived as depression may just be a natural reaction to being diagnosed with a terminal illness.[18]

This does not necessarily mean that anyone who desires suicide is depressed, but conversely, the lack of depression or mental impairment does not imply rationality either. Faced with a deteriorating terminal illness, the patient may feel that dying is the completely rational thing to do, but obviously, the only person who can decide this is the person himself. It is a subjective decision which a competent patient has the right to make even if it is perceived by others as an irrational decision. However, as a person's rationality is judged on the basis of his competence, the line between the two is somewhat indistinct.

Rationality and competence as prerequisites of intention

WHO IS THE RATIONAL PATIENT?

There are various helpful and equally unhelpful definitions of rationality. Valente and Trainor define it as '. . . the capacity to deliberate, to communicate in relationships, and to reflect on and examine one's own values and purposes' (Valente and Trainor 1998: 257). This contains some of the features in the 'definition' of competence in *Re C (Adult: Refusal of Medical Treatment)* (1994) (see below) and while it has to be conceded that rationality requires competence on the part of the patient, they do not mean the same thing.

A better definition is one offered by Siegel and Tuckel who say that a rational person must be '. . . unimpaired by psychological illness or severe emotional distress', but more significantly, that '. . . the motivational basis of . . . [the individual's] decision would be understandable to the majority of

---

14 In, for example, Christensen and McCrary (1993).
15 For example, Robins *et al* (1959) where only three out of 134 patients were considered 'well'; Hendin and Klerman (1993) where the results showed that 95 per cent were suffering from a psychiatric illness, although depression itself was the most frequently diagnosed psychiatric condition in cases of suicide, Fowler *et al* 1979: 219.
16 Approximately two to five per cent according to Valente and Trainor 1998: 257.
17 This discounts treatment refusal cases because they are not perceived as suicide anyway.
18 For example, Engelhardt 1989: 252 and Clarke 1998: 158.

the members of his community or social group' (Siegel and Tuckel 1984–5: 263–4). This gets to the nub of rationality in the sense that firstly, it acknowledges that the decision is one for the individual to subjectively make, secondly, that in the person's specific circumstances, we may well be able to understand why he made that decision, but that thirdly, that does not mean that we have to agree with it. As Lord Donaldson MR said in *Re T (Adult: Refusal of Medical Treatment)* ([1992] 4 All ER 649):

> An adult patient . . . has an absolute right to choose whether to consent to medical treatment, to refuse it or to choose one rather than another of the treatments being offered . . . This right of choice is not limited to decisions which others might regard as sensible. It exists notwithstanding that the reasons for making the choice are rational, irrational, unknown or even non-existent.
>
> *(Re T (Adult: Refusal of Medical Treatment)*
> *per* Lord Donaldson MR at 652–3)

Care must therefore be taken to ensure that judges do not erroneously suggest that it is the decision and not the patient that has to be rational as Butler-Sloss LJ came close to doing in *Re MB* ([1997] 8 *Medical Law Reports* 217) when she defined an irrational decision as one which is '. . . so outrageous in its defiance of logic or of accepted moral standards that no sensible person who had applied his mind to the question to be decided could have arrived at it' (Butler-Sloss LJ at 224).

Nonetheless, it is true that this subjective decision-making process by the patient is measured against the objective values of the treating doctors[19] in order to ascertain whether the patient is rational enough to make a decision. Due to this, there are those who say that suicide can never be rational[20] because, epistemologically, it cannot be rational to prefer death to continued existence, as what happens after death is unknown (Smith, G.P. 1989: 317). In response, it can be argued that as long as the patient's choice to end his own life is voluntary – irrespective of his knowledge of what lies after death – it is arguably a rational suicide by definition if one considers the context and surroundings which are known and in which the decision was made. This would include the patient's pain and suffering, physical and emotional needs (Powell and Kornfeld 1993: 334), physical surroundings and whether he is fully informed and aware of all his options. As has been said, as to rationality, decisions may seem appropriate '. . . *once we determine the context in which . . . [they] are made*' (Lester 1996: 54).[21]

---

19 The potential for paternalism is therefore at its peak here – see, for example, Fairbairn (1991).
20 For example, Fawcett 1972: 1304, and Owens 1995: 326.
21 (Emphasis added.) See the example that Rachels uses of a severely burned man; Rachels 1986: 54.

In any event, it is now enshrined in legislation (not in force at the time of writing) that if a person makes what others believe to be an irrational decision, this does not mean that the decision-maker lacks competence or capacity; s 1(4) of the new Mental Capacity Act 2005 states that '[a] person is not to be treated as unable to make a decision merely because he makes an unwise decision.'[22]

WHO IS THE COMPETENT PATIENT?

The provisions   It is interesting to see that the new legislation uses the notion of capacity rather than competence. These are really two different things; capacity '. . . hinges on cognitive and volitional attributes' (Mason and Laurie 2006) (and is therefore important as a necessary component for competence),[23] while the latter is a 'legal determination' left to the courts (Marzen 1994: 824). Both are, however, used interchangeably and both are (like rationality and suicide itself) – and despite the provisions in the new Mental Capacity Act – subject to the prevailing views and opinions of society.

Until the new Act, the only existing 'test' for competence was that contained in *Re C (Adult: Refusal of Medical Treatment)* where Thorpe J said that the test is whether the patient can comprehend and retain information, whether he believes it, and whether he can weigh it in the balance to arrive at a choice (Thorpe J at 824). These criteria were approved in *Re MB, Re AK, B v An NHS Hospital* and by Munby J in *Burke* where he stated:

> An adult is competent who currently has both capacity *and* the ability to communicate (communicate, that is, either by the usual means, or, for example, by the use of a computer or by means of a coded system of nods, blinks or other bodily movements) . . . The test of capacity for this purpose is well-established and is to be found and set out in well-known authorities . . . [and is] essentially . . . dependent upon having the ability, whether or not one chooses to use it, to function rationally: having the ability to understand, retain, believe and evaluate (ie, process) and weigh the information which is relevant to the subject-matter.
>
> (*Burke* (1) at paras 41–2)

A number of points can be made here: Firstly, the interchangeability of capacity and competence; secondly, Munby J's reference to communication (which is also contained in the Mental Capacity Act); thirdly, his linking of

---

22 Para 20 of the Explanatory Notes to the Act states that '[t]his means that a person who has the necessary ability to make the decision has the right to make irrational or eccentric decisions that others might not judge to be in his best interests'.

23 Mason and Laurie 2006: 461, fn 104, referring to an unpublished paper by C. Heginbotham.

capacity with rationality; fourthly, that his understanding of rationality fulfils the requirements of competence; and fifthly, it is 'decision-specific' (also as in the new Act).

Part 1 of the Act deals with persons who lack capacity. It contains provisions defining 'persons who lack capacity' (ss 2 and 3); it 'contains a set of key principles'[24] (in s 1). Section 1(2) establishes a presumption of capacity unless proved otherwise and s 2(1) defines a person who '. . . lacks capacity in relation to a matter if at the material time he is unable to make a decision for himself in relation to the matter because of an impairment of, or a disturbance in the functioning of, the mind or brain.'

This is a decision-specific/'diagnostic' test, but the test for actually assessing whether a person has capacity (s 3) is a 'functional' test, which looks at the decision-making process itself (explanatory notes paras 22 and 26). This is essentially the criteria set out in *Re C* together with the requirement of communication added in s 3(1)(d) as a 'residual category' (to cover persons who cannot communicate normally because of their illness (and as explained in Munby J's judgment above)).

Questioning capacity/competence   A patient's capacity/competence is generally not queried if he agrees to continue with treatment suggested by a doctor. It is only if he disagrees or requests treatment withdrawal that the question of his competence will be pursued. It seems to be the case that competence will always be questioned if there is any indication of a decision which could potentially be interpreted as suicidal, such as in the case of treatment refusal. It has become very easy to use rationality and competence as techniques whereby a doctor can override a patient's decision[25] and this was acknowledged by Butler-Sloss P in *B v An NHS Hospital Trust*, a case which arose simply because doctors disputed the patient's capacity to request withdrawal of mechanical equipment that was keeping her alive. Butler-Sloss P went to great pains to reject the contention made by some of the doctors that various situational factors such as the patient's dependence on others, her relationship with her doctor and the Intensive Care Unit environment, had eroded her competence. She emphasised that just because the doctors did not agree with the patient's decision, this did not mean that the patient was incompetent. Butler-Sloss P also acknowledged that one of the dangers in a scenario, such as the one presented in this case, was that of 'benevolent paternalism'. She went on to say:

---

24 Information from the Explanatory Notes to the Act, para 7.
25 This is particularly true of anorexic patients who refuse nourishment. Anorexia Nervosa is a mental illness for which food can be given without consent under s 63 Mental Health Act 1983. Invocation of this provision thus ignores the fact that the anorexic patient may well be competent at times (and the provisions of the Mental Capacity Act allow for 'temporary' competence, as indeed occurred in *Re C* (1994)).

... it is most important that those considering the issue should not confuse the question of mental capacity with the nature of the decision made
by the patient ... [t]he view of the patient may reflect a difference in
values ... [t]he doctors must not allow their emotional reaction to or
strong disagreement with the decision of the patient to cloud their judgment in answering the primary question whether the patient has the
mental capacity to make the decision.

(B v An NHS Hospital Trust at 21 and 23)

More recently, the question of capacity arose in *R (On the Application of B)
v S and others* ([2006] EWCA Civ 28) where B was detained at a secure
hospital under the Mental Health Act 1983 following a rape conviction. He
was diagnosed as suffering from bipolar affective disorder but had not
received specific medication for that condition for three years. As his condition was deteriorating, his doctor wanted to treat him compulsorily under s
58 of the Act.[26] B unsuccessfully claimed that he had the necessary capacity
to refuse the treatment (and even the medical experts were divided as to this),
and although subject to Mental Health provisions and not a case of refusing
life-sustaining treatment, the court's comments on capacity are nonetheless
pertinent.

In recognising 'the significance of capacity', Lord Phillips CJ conceded
that it was 'by no means [a] straightforward concept under English law'. He
felt that s 58 did not go far enough in defining capacity and held that:

'[w]hatever the precise test of the capacity to consent to treatment, we
think that it is plain that a patient will lack that capacity if he is not able
to appreciate the likely effects of having or not having the treatment.'

(R (On the Application of B) v S per Lord Phillips CJ
at paras 33 and 34)

However, he then went on to say that when it came to administering treatment
without consent, capacity was not the 'critical factor'; the fact that the treatment was to be 'imposed by compulsion' (*R (On the Application of B) v S*:
paras 42 and 50) and the common law doctrine of necessity were more
significant than the refusal or grant of consent (Lord Phillips CJ at para 31).

The implications as to the irrelevance of consent in this case are worrying,
but as a case where the patient was compulsorily detained, the above *dictum* is
limited in its application. In contrast, in cases where patients (such as Ms B)
are not so detained, once they have been confirmed as being competent, they

26 Section 58(3) provides that a patient should not be treated unless (a) he has consented and it
has been certified that he is capable of understanding the nature, purpose and likely effects of
the treatment, or (b) there is written certification that he is not so capable or has not consented,
but that treatment should be given to alleviate or prevent deterioration of the condition.

have the right to refuse treatment and their refusal has to be complied with. This is certainly the position in the UK, where there is, however, a dearth of cases. The position in the US is more complicated, but there are more cases, as will be seen below.

The 'terminally ill' patient who refuses treatment

Unfortunately, in the limited number of cases in the UK, there is no real discussion of the reasoning behind the courts' conclusion that refusing treatment is not suicide. In the first case, *Re AK*, the word suicide was not mentioned in Hughes J's judgment, while in *B v An NHS Hospital Trust*, when Ms B was asked whether it was her wish to die, or not to remain alive in her present condition, she replied 'the latter' (para 47). This is very much like reversing the question in *Bland* and can be criticised for its pure sophistry.

Due to the lack of authority, it therefore again falls upon US cases to assist in any analysis. Judges in US cases weigh the state interests, including the state interest in preventing suicide, against the patient's personal rights of autonomy/self-determination. If the treatment refusal is deemed not to be suicidal, the competent patient has the right to refuse treatment and the state has no right to intervene by invoking the state interests.[27] Conversely, if it is held to be suicide, the state interests are invoked to prevent the treatment being withdrawn.

In making the decision whether or not a treatment refusal is suicidal, cases are measured against a traditional and formerly criminal 'definition' of suicide (Sandak 1978: 286) (such as those listed earlier) which require a specific intent to kill oneself by virtue of an act (or omission) which causes death. This preoccupation with satisfying those requirements means that where terminally ill patients request treatment withdrawal, the courts do not contemplate the possibility that the patient's intention may well be suicidal. As Quinn has said:

> In a brave new world where patients could now legally forgo life-sustaining treatment, courts scrambled for reasons to preserve as legitimate a state interest in preventing suicide and consistently adopted an uncomplicated strategy: insist that forgoing life support is *not* suicide . . . [this] tell[s] us nothing about the actual intent of the individuals . . . [r]ather this framework obscures an unavoidable possibility: when a terminally ill

---

27 It would still of course be necessary to ensure that the patient's refusal came outside the definition of suicide otherwise the state interest would be invoked in any event. The problem therefore lies with the definition of suicide, which would thus have to specifically exclude treatment refusal cases – see below.

individual requests withdrawal of life-sustaining treatment, her decision may be to die . . .

(Quinn 1997: 155 and 159)

This proposition will be examined by looking at the US courts' analysis (or rather its lack of analysis) of intention in some of the treatment refusal cases.

In *Quinlan*, although the case has been described as '. . . the seminal case for the right to refuse treatment and the right to die', the court simply did not address the definitional problem of suicidal intent and held that removing the patient's life-sustaining treatment was not the cause of death (Penrose 1993: 727). In *Satz, Farrell*, and *Conroy*, the courts, in a little more detail, said that because (a) the patients wanted to live, (albeit on their own terms), and (b) their afflictions were not self-induced, this meant that their treatment refusals could not be classed as a suicide. However, the court's conclusions on the patient's intention in *Conroy* and indeed in *Saicewicz* lacked clarity in so far as in the former, Schreiber J said that Conroy's intention was 'probably' based on 'a wish to be free of medical intervention rather than a specific intent to die' (Schreiber J at 4) and in *Saicewicz*, Liacos J, despite holding that both intent and causation distinguished suicide from treatment refusal, nonetheless conceded that there may well be cases where the patient does intend to commit suicide (Liacos J at 427). However, in neither case did the judges pursue any inquiry into the 'probability' that the intention was not suicidal.

Again, in *McKay v Bergstedt* a mentally competent quadriplegic, who had relied on a ventilator to breathe for 23 years, requested that it be removed so that he could die. The patient's petition asking for a declaration that he was not committing suicide was allowed, therefore withdrawing his treatment was held not to be assisted suicide and was not illegal. Springer J's dissenting judgment, however, was very much in favour of interpreting forgoing life-sustaining treatment as suicidal. He said that because Kenneth had used the ventilator to breathe for 23 years, it was more than simply medical treatment; it was an integral part of his survival without which life could not have gone on. 'Taking away the ventilator was taking away his life', and moreover, disconnecting the ventilator would be a 'death-inducing act' which would amount to the '. . . immediate and proximate cause of the death of a person who concededly is seeking to take his own life'. There was nothing at all natural about it. Like other suicides, his life had become unbearable. His 'explicit' and 'expressed intention' was therefore to die (Springer J at 633). Similarly in *Brophy*, Liacos, Nolan, Lynch and O'Connor dissenting (in part) said that the patient would die as a direct result of the withdrawal of food and drink, and that it was his intent to commit suicide. However, the majority held that the state interest in preventing suicide was inapplicable because the patient's death would result from natural causes rather than from a cause 'set in motion nor intended by the patient . . .' (Liacos J at 626).

Conversely, and in contrast to the previous cases where the issue has been one of forgoing treatment, in *Compassion in Dying v Washington, Quill v Vacco, Rodriguez* and *Pretty* (see next chapter) the patients requested that positive action be taken to assist in their suicides. The Appeal Court in *Compassion in Dying v Washington* was compelled to invoke the state interest in preventing suicide, but held that it was overridden in the same way as it would be in normal treatment refusal cases. Thus, controversially, the court found no difference between, on the one hand, the positive course of action envisaged in this case and, on the other, withdrawing treatment, because in both, the intention – the death of the patient – was the same. If there was a difference, it was only '. . . one of degree and not of kind' (Reinhardt J at 823). Quinn saw this as a devious line of reasoning because the court simply 'extended the argument for letting patients die to include patients seeking assistance in dying . . .' and by doing this, avoided 'getting to grips with' the patient's intention in forgoing treatment (Quinn 1997: 159).

The US Supreme Court in reversing the decisions in both cases, reinforced the intention and causation-based distinction between refusing treatment and suicide (although it has to be said that the court conceded the difficulties in holding the line) and thus prevented the patients from committing suicide with their physicians' assistance.

The same result was reached by the Canadian Supreme Court in *Rodriguez*, which rejected (although not unanimously) Sue Rodriguez's application for a declaration allowing a doctor to provide means whereby she could end her own life, on the basis that she was requesting assistance to commit suicide. Likewise, the High Court, House of Lords and the European Court of Human Rights rejected an application by Dianne Pretty that her husband should not be prosecuted for assisting in her suicide. As the patients in both these cases evinced a self-expressed intention to commit suicide and they were not cases of treatment withdrawal, they can be factually distinguished from those other cases where a patient has refused treatment.

The Jehovah's Witness patient who refuses treatment

UK cases

It is well known that, under the dictates of their religion, Jehovah's Witnesses are not permitted to accept blood or primary blood products in any circumstances.[28] The reason they refuse blood is twofold: firstly, receiving a blood transfusion 'is a serious sin' which they must live with for their rest of their

---

28 Use of blood and blood products violates the Bible's injunction against 'eating blood'. Deuteronomy 12: 23–25; Leviticus 7: 26; Genesis 9: 3–4.

lives (Ehrlich CJ in *Public Health Trust of Dade County v Wons* 541 So. 2d 96; 1989 Fla. LEXIS 171; 14 Fla. Law W.112 at 100), and secondly, it prevents them from attaining salvation or eternal life[29] (Johnson J in *Re S (A Minor: Consent to Medical Treatment)* ([1994] 2 FLR 1065 at 1068).[30]

As all but two of the cases involve minors whose parents were Jehovah's Witnesses (albeit some were nearing *Gillick* competence and were themselves followers of the faith), it is impossible to ascertain directly the patient's intention in those cases. Indeed, the courts' preoccupation was rather with ensuring that the child patient was completely aware of the significance of refusing a blood transfusion. Certainly, the standard of understanding required was set at a much higher level than it would be for adults facing the same situation[31] and it goes beyond that which can be reasonably expected. Grubb rightly suggested that the court's demand for such a high level of understanding was simply 'a device patently intended to justify a finding of incompetence' (Grubb 1999: 60).

Another clear aspect of the cases is that the courts have minimised the effects which receiving blood has on the lives of Jehovah's Witnesses. In *Devon CC v S* ([1992] 11 BMLR 105), for example, Thorpe J trivialised the 'spiritual' damage to a Jehovah's Witness who received blood products when he said that any inquiry as to the future consequences for a patient whose life had been saved by an ungodly act had 'little foundation in reality'. As the decision had been taken out of the parents' hands, it '. . . absolve[d] their conscience of responsibility' (Thorpe J at 109).

There is no doubt that this can operate as a 'loophole' through which Jehovah's Witnesses can be helped (Childress 1982: 168–9),[32] but as it is so central to the reason for rejecting the treatment in the first place, it should play an equally central role in the courts' decision. In fact, in *HE v A Hospital NHS Trust* ([2003] WL 21729346) (the most recent and one of the only two adult UK cases (other than *Blaue*)), Munby J did express his sensitivity to this (para 44), although he nonetheless ordered a blood transfusion to be given to the patient. However, the focus in the case was primarily the effect of an advance directive made by the patient after she became a Jehovah's Witness but prior to her reversion to the Muslim faith (as a

---

29 Many of the cases emphasise the choice a Jehovah's Witness has to make between corporeal and spiritual life, for example, Simons J in *Fosmire v Nicoleau* (75 N.Y. 2d 218; 551 N.E. 2d 77; 1990 N.Y. LEXIS 91; 551 N.Y.S. 2d 876: 233).

30 The same sentiment is expressed by him in *Re O (A Minor)* [1994] 19 BMLR 148: 149. See also *Malette v Shulman* [1990] 67 DLR (4th) 321, and *Wons* (1989).

31 Seen in *Re S (A Minor) (Consent to Medical Treatment)* (1994); *Re E (A Minor)* ([1993] 9 BMLR 1) and *Re L (Medical Treatment: Gillick Competency)* ([1998] 2 FLR 810).

32 See also how Childress distinguishes between 'acceptance' (which Jehovah's Witnesses cannot embrace) and 'reception' (which they can) as long as they have 'resisted' to the best of their ability in Childress 1985: 79.

condition of her marriage to a Muslim). Nothing is said about either intention or causation in the case, except in so far as Munby J (referring to dicta in *Re T (Adult) (Refusal of Medical Treatment)*) said *obiter* that, in his view, even the most committed Jehovah's Witness would not want to die and that this, together with her abandonment of the faith, invalidated her advance directive.

Re T (Adult) (Refusal of Medical Treatment) is the other and perhaps better known case, but it contains some unusual elements which make it difficult to extract any firm principles. Firstly, the patient was found to be incompetent, secondly it was held that her prior refusal did not cover the medical situation which transpired and thirdly, while T herself was not a Jehovah's Witness, her mother was, and the issue arose as to whether or not T had been unduly influenced by her mother.

Lord Donaldson MR declared *obiter* that a patient who refused life-sustaining treatment was not committing suicide, but as there was no specific consideration of intention in the case (the above considerations would have precluded the formulation of an intention anyway), this conclusion must have been reached, not from looking at the patient's intention but from a simple repetition of what would appear to be developing as some kind of a 'blanket' general principle. In addition, it can be suggested that the court scrabbled for reasons to override the patient's decision-making capacity simply because it did not agree with a decision it saw as irrational.

US cases

In US cases, despite the different considerations which arise, the legal and philosophical arguments raised by the courts are the same in respect of Jehovah's Witnesses as they are for other treatment refusal cases. Also, the courts' application of intention as marking the line between forgoing treatment and suicide is both erratic and inconsistent. For example, in *Heston* (*John F. Kennedy Memorial Hospital v Heston* 58 N.J. 576; 279 A. 2d 670; 1971 N.J. LEXIS 282), the court simply ignored the patient's expressed intention entirely. Miss Heston had said that she did not want to die, but the court took the view that despite this expressed intention, she must have known that death was inevitable. Effectively, by adopting 'knowledge' as the necessary test, the court 'unwittingly adopted' Durkeim's definition of suicide (Byrn 1975: 17) when it did not need to do so. For this reason, the court held that it was her intention to die, and as such, the state interest in preventing suicide should be invoked to prevent this.

The reasoning in the case has been criticised by both Sandak and Byrn on the grounds that the patient's statement that she did not wish to die was sufficient evidence that specific intention – an 'indispensable element of . . . suicide was lacking' (Byrn 1975: 18; Sandak 1978: 299 *et seq*). Evidently, the court was unwilling to accept the patient's intention, but if it had done so, it could have allowed her to refuse the treatment without risking conflict with their usual policy of not endorsing suicide.

In contrast, the court in *Erickson v Dilgard* (44 Misc. 2d 27; 252 N.Y.S. 2d 705; 1962 N.Y. Misc. LEXIS 2552) adopted a different form of reasoning when it denied the patient was committing suicide, by imposing a requirement of certainty. Rather than just saying that Dilgard did not have the necessary intention to commit suicide (his willingness to be operated on was evidence of this), the court instead made it a prerequisite of the intent component in the definition of suicide that the patient be certain of death and concluded that as death was not certain, then the patient was not suicidal (*Erickson v Dilgard*: 706; Sandak 1978: 297). By adding this element of certainty to the definition, the court made it easier for itself to state that the patient did not meet the suicide 'test' and was thus able to allow refusal of treatment without conflicting with policy.

Adopting totally different reasoning again, the judge in the District of Columbia Court of Appeals in *Georgetown College* (*Application of the President and Directors of Georgetown College* 118 U.S. App. D.C. 80; 331 F. 2d 1000; 1964 U.S. App. LEXIS 6510) said that any discussion about specific intent would merely amount to quibbling (Wright CJ at 1008) and this despite the fact that intention is said to be the key factor in these cases. Moreover, this case can be compared with the Canadian case of *Malette v Shulman*. In both, the patients had previously expressed their views (in the former, she had made it clear that she did not want to die, and in the latter, the patient carried a card which categorically confirmed that she was a Jehovah's Witness and was not to be given a blood transfusion under any circumstances). In both cases their prior refusal was disregarded once they became unconscious; both were declared incompetent (and can be distinguished on this ground from *Erickson v Dilgard*); and in both cases the court ordered the blood transfusion. However, in *Malette v Shulman*, the court confirmed that because there was no wish to die, then there was no suggestion of suicide or euthanasia and that, accordingly, the state interest in preventing suicide was inapplicable (and the other state interests were overridden as well). The patient was awarded substantial damages for the offence committed against her (Brahams 1989: 1407 and 1990: 586).

In contrast, in *Georgetown College*, the court invoked both its *parens patriae* jurisdiction and the state interest in preventing suicide, despite its acceptance that the patient had no suicidal intent.[33] Having ascertained that the patient's voluntary presence in hospital proved that she wanted to live, the court then went on to contradict itself on the importance of intention and:

---

33 The case was criticised on this aspect by Byrn 1975: 36; if the patient is acting voluntarily, is competent and fully informed, the state should not invoke the state interests particularly where there is no harm to society from the patient's action.

... went beyond the simplistic criterion of knowledge of consequences to examine underlying religious motivation. Yet in the same breath, it explicitly denied the significance of specific intent. In so stating, the court rejected as virtual irrelevancies the two primary components comprising the traditional definition of suicide – that the individual intends to cause his own death and that he initiates the act that leads to death. Thus, the *Georgetown College* court paradoxically expressed rejection of the very ground upon which it based its determination on the suicide issue – specific intent.

(Sandak 1978: 301)

Brooks Estate (*In re Estate of Brooks* 32 Ill. 2d 361; 205 N.E. 2d 435; 1965 Ill. LEXIS 34) and *US v George* (239 F. Supp. 752; 1965 U.S. Dist. LEXIS 7100) both of which followed a year later, distinguished *Georgetown College* (in *Brooks* because the patient had no children and in *George*, on the basis that the patient was competent). *Brooks Estate* placed the patient's religious beliefs over and above the state interests and the patient was allowed to refuse treatment. This is the most honest, and '[t]he most articulate statement for the position opposing interference with a patient's decision . . .' (Cantor 1973: 234). It shows that the court was prepared to support patient autonomy even in the face of what some would regard as an incomprehensible decision by a patient to refuse blood. However, both this and *Erickson v Dilgard* – the only two cases where the courts allowed patient autonomy to override the state interest in preventing suicide – were subsequently distinguished in *Heston*.

This examination of US cases has shown that although intention is the decisive factor in suicide, the courts either rely on assumptions of non-suicidal intent, or they use varied and different interpretations of the meaning of intention. They also invoke the state interest in preventing suicide even where it is totally inappropriate and unnecessary to do so. This lack of consistent principle together with the use of manipulative techniques has thus enabled the courts to permit enforced treatment on the majority of Jehovah's Witness patients.

The prisoner who refuses food and drink

UK cases

Dicta from UK cases regarding prisoners who refuse food and drink are unfortunately both confusing and contradictory. The question first arose in *Leigh v Gladstone* ((1909) 26 TLR 139), where Lord Alverstone CJ held that it was lawful to force feed prisoners if their health and lives were to be maintained. The case was, however, distinguished as a product of its time in *Home Secretary v Robb* ([1995] Fam 127) where a (competent) prisoner refused to eat and drink. Thorpe J held that there was no duty on either the Home

Secretary or prison staff to provide the prisoner with food or drink against his will and that it would thus be lawful to refrain from doing so. Thorpe J favoured the decision in the American case of *Thor v Superior Court* (5 Cal. 4th 725; 855 P. 2d 375: 1993 Cal. LEXIS 3430; 21 Cal. Rptr. 2d 357) together with the dissenting judgment of Douglas J in *Caulk*, both discussed below. What is unusual is that Thorpe J borrowed the US practice of balancing the prisoner's autonomy against countervailing state interests. As to the state interest in preventing suicide (and referring to *Bland*), Thorpe J noted that a patient who refuses life-prolonging treatment does not commit suicide because '. . . the refusal of nutrition and medical treatment in the exercise of the right of self-determination does not constitute an act of suicide.' Such a conclusion was reached without any query being raised as to Robb's intention, or as to his reasons for refusing nourishment. The court did, however, deem it significant that he had engaged in a hunger strike twice before, and that he was prone to certain 'manipulative tendencies' (Thorpe J at 128).

In his comment on the case, Kennedy agreed that Thorpe J was right to lay *Leigh v Gladstone* to rest, but nonetheless criticised the medical law approach adopted by Thorpe J, on the basis that food and drink are not treatment in a non-medical environment (Kennedy 1995: 190).[34] He noted, however, that this might have explained why Thorpe J chose to adopt the reasoning in the US case of *Thor* and why he chose to bring state interests into the equation. Moreover, as Kennedy points out, there was a significant difference between Robb and Thor as the latter was not only a prisoner, but was also a quadriplegic patient who was refusing medical treatment he was already receiving as opposed to an able prisoner going on a hunger strike. As such, the medical law framework and the invocation of the state interests was appropriate in his case.

Kennedy also questioned the 'permissiveness' of the declarations granted, which said that the prison authorities '. . . *may* abstain from providing food and water . . . [they do] . . . not say that they *must* abide by the prisoner's decision.' This leaves unanswered the question as to whether they have the 'power' to feed, even if they may not have a duty to do so (Kennedy 1995: 191).[35]

In a more recent and much publicised case, *Ashworth Hospital ex p Brady* (Smith Bernal Case No. CO/68/2000),[36] Brady went on hunger strike as a protest against the way in which he had been manhandled when he was being moved from one ward to another in the secure hospital in which he was being detained for his psychopathic disorder.

Some way into the hunger strike, the treating doctors commenced force feeding under s 63 of the Mental Health Act 1983 (whereby treatment can be

---

34 The same point is made by Williams J. 2001: 293.
35 See Williams, J. (2001) on the same point in his analysis of *Brady* below.
36 And see Foster (2000).

given to the patient 'for the mental disorder from which he is suffering' without his consent). Brady claimed that his refusal of food had nothing to do with his mental disorder and was, rather, a rational decision by a competent person (para 23). Kay J, however, agreed with the respondents that the hunger strike was 'a manifestation or symptom of the personality disorder' (para 44) and applying *B v Croydon Health Authority* ([1995] 1 All ER 683), held that artificial nutrition and hydration was medical treatment which was required to be given to him as treatment for the mental disorder under s 63.

Brady's motive and intention came under Kay J's scrutiny because whereas Brady's initial motive for his hunger strike was in response to the assault upon him and to the regime to which he was subjected (para 11), he sometime later formulated the intention to starve to death. As a result, psychiatrists instructed to appraise his competence found it hard to assess either his motive or his intention (para 47) and Kay J himself also said that it was impossible for him 'to arrive at a certain conclusion as to what the applicant's present intention is.' Nonetheless, he still felt able to say that there was very little evidence 'which would point to a clear, settled or unequivocal intention on the part of the applicant to starve himself to death.' Indeed, the evidence suggested that it was all manipulative, a protest, an intention 'to win a power struggle, but not to die . . .' (para 51). This was an important conclusion because, as Kay J himself conceded, force feeding under s 63 was unchallengeable if Brady's motive throughout the hunger strike was simply to protest and not to starve himself to death (para 46).

Although he did not have to adjudicate on it, the judge then turned to the respondent's alternative ground which was that, if s 63 had been held to be inapplicable, Brady lacked the capacity to consent in any event. Kay J agreed that he failed the third leg of the *Re C (Adult: Refusal of Medical Treatment)* test.

The next part of the judgment is interesting because Kay J (in response to the respondent's third possible ground if both the s 63 and incapacity argument had failed) debated whether or not a power or duty existed to prevent suicide, or indeed, whether a competent prisoner's right of self-determination outweighed any other 'public interests' such as the preservation of life, maintaining the integrity of the medical profession and, indeed, avoiding undermining institutional discipline if prisoners had the right, for example, to commit suicide (para 67). Kay J in effect distinguished *Robb* and followed *Reeves* (where it had been held that prison and police authorities had a duty of care to prevent a prisoner from committing suicide) and in respect of the latter said, *obiter*, that:

> [i]t would be somewhat odd if there was a duty to prevent suicide by an act . . . but not even a power to prevent self-destruction by starvation. I can see no moral justification for the law indulging its fascination with

the difference between acts and omissions in a context such as this and no logical need for it to do so.

(*Brady per* Kay at para 71)

Having said that, he was unprepared to make a finding on the issue (not least because it was not the respondent's primary ground and there was insufficient evidence on it), but he did comment that, in these circumstances, he would prefer to find in favour of the respondent hospital (i.e. that the state interests should override the patient's right of self-determination) (para 46).

Kay J's judgment in *Brady* was criticised by John Williams in his article on hunger strikes. He sets out five different categories of strike[37] but focuses particularly on category 1 (strikes relating to frustration) and notes that not all hunger strikes in this category are suicides (Williams J: 293). Secondly, he observes that Brady (on his own evidence) falls into both categories 1 and 4 (strikes with rational or irrational suicidal aims) (Williams J: 287), thirdly, that '[i]t is simplistic to categorise all hunger-strikers as suicidal' (Williams J: 286) and fourthly, that it is imperative to make an early determination of a hunger-striker's motive in order to decide how to deal with it.

His particular criticism was that Kay J's *obiter* statement (in the quotation above) failed to distinguish between a prison suicide (as occurred in *Reeves*) and hunger striking (as in *Robb*). The inherent danger here is that persons in categories 1 and 4 would be treated in the same way, when they are patently not the same. He thus concluded that conflating propositions from different situations and then applying them to a hunger-striking prisoner is questionable and leads to confusion (Williams J: 293).

That this is so has been highlighted in a more recent incident, following the death of Terry Rodgers by starvation while awaiting trial for his daughter's murder.[38] It seems that Rodgers had been the subject of four psychiatric assessments, and that his 'state of mind was going to play a major part in his trial.' An inquiry is to be held in light of his previous suicide attempt, but also because a decision was made to section him under the Mental Health Act (whereby feeding may have been compulsory) but which decision was later repealed.[39]

During his hunger strike, Rodgers said that he was 'determined to die' but

---

37 Williams, J. 2001: 287. The categories are: 1. Strikes relating to frustration. 2. Strikes intended to gain attention. 3. Strikes used as a bargaining tool. 4. Strikes with rational or irrational suicidal aims. 5. Nutrition refusal for medical reasons (although he concedes himself that the categories overlap and are open to criticism for a number of reasons).

38 Rodgers died in February 2006 while in custody for allegedly shooting Chanel Taylor, his newly married daughter, in July 2004. He fled after her killing, but was arrested in a forest near Hucknall after a four-day police manhunt.

39 Information obtained from www.hucknalltoday.co.uk/ (local newspaper) (accessed 14 March 2006).

his death raises a number of contentious questions. Firstly, and on the authority contained in *Robb*, as long as he was competent, one would presume that he had the right to starve himself to death. Secondly, however, we have already seen from *Reeves* that police and prison authorities have a duty of care to prevent a prisoner in their custody from committing suicide; as in *Reeves*, Rodgers had previously attempted suicide and the authorities were therefore aware of the suicide risk. Thirdly is the case distinguishable from *Reeves* (where the prisoner hanged himself) because refusing food and water is (a) an omission and/or (b) is not 'suicide'? If Kay J's *obiter* statement in *Brady*, above, holds, then there would be no distinction.

US cases

In *Robb*, it was seen that Thorpe J favoured Douglas J's dissenting judgment in *Caulk*. Here, the prisoner, facing a life sentence, said that he did not want to live if he could not live as a free man. He accordingly refused food and drink with the aim of 'allowing himself to die'. He made it categorically clear that he was not 'making any demands or asking for anything in return for his fast' (*Caulk* at 94). In pure and simple terms, he had only one purpose, and that was to die.

Batchelder J distinguished between this case and those cases where a terminally ill patient chooses to avoid life-prolonging treatment by saying that here '. . . the defendant has set the death-producing agent in motion with the specific intent of causing his own death' and, therefore, the state interest in preventing suicide prevailed. Batchelder J feared that giving into his behaviour would disrupt discipline and impact upon prison resources (*Caulk* at 96–7). The case has to be considered unique if only for the fact that an additional state interest in the proper administration of the criminal justice system seemed to have been invoked in order to justify a departure from established authority. This is directly contrary to the other established cases where a person refuses food and water, and it can only be assumed that Caulk was treated differently simply because of his status as a prisoner.

This was not, however, the conclusion reached by the Supreme Court of California in *Thor*. In this case the prisoner, Howard Andrews, refused to consent to a gastronomy which the prison doctor requested in order to feed the prisoner against his will. The significant distinguishing factor in the case, however, was that Andrews was also a quadriplegic following an incident in the prison some five months into his life sentence. Arabian J, expressing the unanimous judgment of the court, followed the well-established treatment refusal authorities (including the majority in *McKay v Bergstedt*) and held that in the case of a competent adult who is a victim of such an irreversible condition where life is totally dependent and sustained artificially, his right of self-determination to refuse treatment overrode all four state interests. The fact that he was a prisoner did not change this fundamental right, as, under the relevant Penal Code, there was no 'threat to institutional security or public safety', and furthermore, the court also held that prison officials had 'no affirmative duty' to administer the treatment (*Thor* at 3–4).[40] Arabian J dismissed the relevance of the decision in *Caulk* (although, admittedly, he was not bound by it) by saying that it was pertinent to look to the inmate's motive in refusing treatment and that as such:

> [u]nder the facts of this case, we have no occasion to address, and therefore do not decide, any related issues that might arise in the event of an otherwise healthy inmate with no underlying affliction engages in a course of conduct for nonmedical reasons, such as a hunger strike, that subsequently necessitates therapeutic intervention to prevent death.
>
> (*Thor per* Arabian J at 45; fn 16)

In view of the rejection of *Caulk* and the reasons for that which are indicated above, it is evident that in *Thor*, the patient's quadriplegia was a deciding factor; it is also significant that Arabian J distinguished between on the one hand, a healthy person who goes on hunger strike (which would require intervention), and on the other, a person with an incurable underlying affliction who refuses nourishment (as Williams did in his analysis of *Brady* above). The status of the prisoner, and not his intention, thus became the key issue, because, as Kennedy noted in his commentary on the *Thor* case, the court simply presumed that the patient/prisoner's intention was not to commit suicide and this was obviously enough to override the state interest in preventing it (Kennedy 1994: 222).

The suicidee must have caused his own death

The second prerequisite for satisfying the suicide definition is that the suicidee must have caused his own death. It has already been seen that judges have held that the cause of death in cases where patients refuse life-sustaining treatment is the underlying disease and not the patients' refusal of treatment. Logically, therefore, suicidal refusals cannot be the cause. However, from a purely factual point of view, a patient's refusal of treatment accelerates his own death, which would not have occurred at that time but for the patient's decision. This is certainly true where the medical treatment being refused is artificial nutrition and hydration; because of the absolute certainty of death, its refusal can be more readily perceived as being both the cause of death and as being a suicide (McCormack 1998: 63). As noted by Egan J in *Ward of Court*, a patient who is not dying will become a dying patient when food and drink are forgone. This was acknowledged by Balchelder J in

---

40 Compare the duty to care for prisoners found in the UK case of *Reeves* (1) and (2).

Caulk when he held that a prisoner's refusal of food and drink would cause his death, because, by his refusal, he was himself initiating the death-producing agent. That it was used in this case to prove suicidal intent is unusual as, generally, the concept is a key identifier of the non-categorisation of treatment refusal as suicidal by judges in the majority of US cases looked at here.[41] However, saying that a patient who requests treatment withdrawal will not satisfy this condition (because passively refusing treatment is not an initiation of an event which causes the patient's death), does not acknowledge the fact that suicide can be committed by omission as well as by commission.

Acts and omissions in suicide

Judges in the majority of cases presume that suicide can only occur by virtue of a positive act. This is clearly demonstrated in the differing conclusions reached by the courts in the two Canadian cases of *Rodriguez* and *Nancy B v Hotel-Dieu de Quebec* ((1992) 86 DLR (4th) 385). As Sue Rodriguez wanted positive assistance to die, her intention was held to be suicidal, but as Nancy B requested a withdrawal of treatment, her intention was deemed not to be suicidal. This charade has also been encouraged by US judges, for example, Beach J (in *Bouvia*: 306); Abrams J (in *Jane Doe*: 1270); and Steffen J (in *McKay v Bergstedt*), all of whom specifically held that suicide could only be carried out by way of 'affirmative measures'.[42]

Out of the nine definitions of suicide provided earlier, the first, third and fourth specifically confirm that suicide can be committed via an omission.[43] Advocates of the view that refusing treatment can be suicidal have said that whether one shoots oneself, takes poison, or disconnects a respirator, it is still suicide;[44] as Fletcher has said: '[i]f I decide not to eat or drink any more, knowing what the consequences will be, I have committed suicide as surely as if I had used a gas oven' (Fletcher 1973: 121).

This view has been endorsed by UK and US judges (although mainly in dissenting judgments or as *obiter dicta*) such as Kay J (in *Brady* at para 71); Lynch J (in *Brophy* at 642); Weintraub CJ (in *Heston* at 673); O'Connor (in *Jane Doe* at 1275); and Scalia J in his celebrated judgment in *Cruzan v Director, Missouri Department of Health* ((1990) 497 U.S. 261; 111 L. Ed. 2d

---

41 In UK cases, while not specifically discussed in that context, it is nonetheless a factor which has been used to distinguish between killing and letting die; see section on ***killing and letting die – a causation-based distinction?*** at page 67. It also links in with patient choice; it can be argued that patients who choose to reject treatment cause their own deaths. See, for example, Wilson 1995: 140.

42 See Graber's excellent chapter (1981).   43 See also Lanham 1990: 408.

44 See, for example, Harris 1985: 203; and Brock's chapter on 'Forgoing Life-Sustaining Food and Water: Is it Killing?' in Brock (1993).

224; 110 S. Ct. 2841) where he perceived what he called the 'action-inaction distinction' as 'irrelevant', saying:

> [i]t would not make much sense to say that one may not kill oneself by walking into the sea, but may sit on the beach until submerged by the incoming tide . . . Starving oneself to death is no different from putting a gun to one's temple as far as the common law definition of suicide is concerned; the cause of death in both cases is the suicide's conscious decision to 'pu[t] an end to his own existence.'
>
> (*Cruzan per* Scalia J at 296–7)[45]

Thus, the line the courts draw between suicide and supposedly dying from natural causes is artificial. The fact that it is a passive and not a positive action is irrelevant because the patient is intentionally submitting to a death which is both a known and certain consequence of his treatment refusal, when that death could be avoided.

Distinguishing the three categories

Three points can be drawn from the analysis of the three categories of cases:

(a) The courts *purport* to distinguish between treatment refusal and suicide by focusing mainly on intent (and causation follows on from that).
(b) In so doing, the courts actually focus on the status of the individual concerned.
(c) It would arguably assist them further if they were to consider the reason for the treatment refusal.

The fatal error – intention in suicide

Although intent (and causation) are the factors which are claimed to distinguish between treatment refusal and suicide, the answers cannot however be found there; we need only to look at *Washington v Glucksberg* and *Vacco v Quill*, the two US cases which reinforced the importance of both intention and causation in the distinction between forgoing treatment and suicide, to see how difficult the judges found it to distinguish the form of intention in each. In *Washington v Glucksberg*, Stevens J held that:

> There may be little distinction between the intent of a terminally-ill patient who decides to remove her life-support, and one who seeks the

---

45 Citing Blackstone and *Caulk*. See the interesting article by Kadish 1992: 865.

assistance of a doctor in ending her life; in both situations, the patient is seeking to hasten a certain, impending death.

(*Per* Stevens J at 80)

Similarly in *Vacco v Quill*, Rehnquist CJ asserted that '. . . a patient who commits suicide with a doctor's aid necessarily has the specific intent to end his or her own life, while a patient who refuses or discontinues treatment *might* not' (*Vacco v Quill* at 14, emphasis added). It can be seen here that the courts' loyalty to intention as a prerequisite of suicide has led to uncertainty as to its meaning and its application.

The courts have interpreted what is suicidal by adhering to a conventional criminal-type suicide definition, such as those seen at the beginning of this chapter. One consequence of this, in the US particularly, is that there has never been an adequate analysis of the state interest in preventing suicide (not least because it has for some reason been considered as some sort of adjunct to the state interest in preserving life).[46] If this dependence on criminal intention has to remain the benchmark, it might be an option to redefine the state interest in preventing suicide so that it can be properly balanced against the patient's right to refuse treatment.

Sandak suggests that a better alternative would be to adopt a new definition of suicide, which replaces intent with objective (Sandak 1978: 312),[47] so that if the patient says he does not want to die, it would not be suicide and vice versa. He looks at those cases which he claims exemplify the suicide-determinative approach to judicial decision-making by the courts, who use the traditional definition of suicide to determine the distinction between refusing treatment and suicide at the expense of taking other considerations, such as patient motivation, into account. This would certainly enhance patient autonomy and would entail a more thorough consideration of the context in which decisions are made.

Status of the 'patient'

To some extent, the courts are already considering contextual factors when they look to a person's status to ascertain what is suicidal and what is not. In the vast majority of the cases examined in previous chapters, 'terminally ill' patients are, with very few exceptions, considered to be making what are perceived to be rational decisions to cease treatment without any suicidal intent. In contrast, Jehovah's Witnesses, again with very few exceptions, are seen as making irrational, although not necessarily suicidal, decisions;

46 See, for example, Arabian J in *Thor* (1993) at 29.
47 The word 'objective' (a) avoids definitional problems; and (b) is distinct from intention/ purpose.

if anything, it is their supposed irrationality which has prompted compulsory blood transfusions rather than any perceived suicidal tendencies.[48] As to prisoners, also with few exceptions, force feeding has been imposed based on the prisoner's status.[49] We can see, for example, that whereas *Robb* was competent, *Brady* was not. Similarly, we can see that as a quadriplegic prisoner Andrews in *Thor* was permitted to refuse life-sustaining treatment, but that *Caulk*, 'just' a prisoner, was not. Moreover, there was a punitive element in ensuring that he could not avoid his prison sentence by committing suicide. Having said that, it is difficult to draw any clear conclusions in this category of cases because of conflicting reasoning, the different factual situations in each case and divided opinions as to motivation and intent.

Nothing supports such an arbitrary way of distinguishing between the three categories, but it can nonetheless be clearly seen in the results of the decisions. It is suggested, however, that what could more properly differentiate between the three categories is the reason (motive) why each person refuses the treatment.

The answer – motive as a distinguishing factor

In definitions 7–9 listed earlier in this chapter, it was contended that a suicide can only be a 'proper' suicide if it is non-instrumental, i.e. that the suicidee kills himself for no other reason than to terminate his life. However, treatment refusals by terminally ill patients can never truly be non-instrumental, because there are any number of reasons why they refuse treatment. For example, to 'forgo extraordinary measures' (in *Leach v Akron per* Spicer J at 814), to stop drawing out the dying process, to obtain relief from pain, or to avoid being a burden (financial or otherwise) (Pellegrino 1992: 96). This is precisely why it is so easy for the courts to select any one of those reasons (as long as it has nothing to do with intending death) in order to hold that patients are not committing suicide. The non-instrumental definitions will thus never be satisfied in these cases, but this does not mean that terminally ill patients do not intend to die.

It has also been seen from the prisoner cases that they express various reasons as to why they reject food and drink. Caulk, for example, alleged that he simply wanted to die, but he would only have made that decision for a particular reason and this was – as he himself said – that he did not want to live if he could not live as a free man. In contrast, Brady made his (initial) decision as a form of protest (notwithstanding that some element of doubt existed as to whether he did want to carry his hunger strike through to death at a later stage).

---

48 See Stauch's interesting distinction between irrational and non-rational grounds for decision-making; Jehovah's Witnesses would come into the latter category. Stauch (1995).

49 See, for example, Kadish 1992: 864, his fn 44.

In the Jehovah's Witnesses cases, however, there is one reason and one reason only why treatment is rejected. It is a very specific religiously motivated (and possibly involuntary)[50] reason which, together with their often expressed wish that they do not want to die[51] (a factor often lacking in the terminally ill category) precludes any suicidal intention (Cantor 1987: 47).[52] There is no better example of the importance of ascertaining reasons than that set out in the earlier quote by Lord Donaldson in *Re T (Adult: Refusal of Medical Treatment)*,[53] but in the US cases, we saw that only in two cases (which were themselves subsequently distinguished) did the Jehovah's Witnesses' religious motivation take precedence over the state interests. Ascertaining motive would tie in neatly with Sandak's earlier suggestion, as his notion of looking to the individual's objective – which is, after all, just another word for motive – is the same.

Conclusion

In cases of terminal or debilitating illness, the courts have refused to accept that the right to refuse life-sustaining medical treatment can be used to commit suicide. If we acknowledge that everyone who wishes to commit suicide does so in order to stop having to experience undergoing something unbearable in their lives, for example, a cancer patient forgoing chemotherapy, this is very much like a suicidal decision. However, no enquiry is made into the patient's state of mind, except where there is a dispute as to competence. There is simply an assumption that the patient did not intend to commit suicide. It could be conceded that reliance on such assumptions, presumptions and inferences are part and parcel of the inherent problems caused by a subjective concept such as intention, and yet, the only dividing factor between treatment refusal and suicide is this very dubious, suspect and questionable concept.

Although understandable (if judges did not assume the absence of suicidal intention, then any patient who rejected life-saving treatment would be deemed to be committing suicide), the compulsive need to satisfy such a stringent criminal-type intention requirement in treatment refusal cases has seen the courts analysing intention in a completely inconsistent manner. Having based their reasoning on intention in some cases, in others the courts have somewhat confusingly ignored it, have demanded an unattainable level

---

50 Remember Hart and Honoré's comment on *Blaue* in chapter 4 above, and see, for example, *Re R (A Minor) (Blood Transfusion)* ([1993] 2 FLR 757): 760; *Re E (A Minor)* (1993) at 8; and *Georgetown College* (1964) at 1009 for more on this very point.

51 See, for example *HE v A Hospital NHS Trust* (2003) at para 48; *Georgetown College* (1964) and see Childress 1985: 79.

52 For a contrary argument on ends and means see Price (1996).

53 In the section on WHO IS THE RATIONAL PATIENT? at page 120

of certainty and understanding, or have held that knowledge of consequences has entitled them to intervene to prevent suicide despite the patient's assertions that he is not committing suicide. In the US cases in particular, if refusing treatment has been categorised as a suicide, the courts automatically have a right to prevent it by invoking the state interests. Indeed, in some cases, even where the court has conceded that the conduct is not suicidal, it has nonetheless inappropriately done so (as in *Georgetown College*, for example). This, together with the tendency to find patients who wish to forgo life-sustaining treatment to be incompetent, allows both judges and doctors to give free rein to their paternalistic tendencies and demonstrates the court's reluctance to recognise treatment refusal as suicidal. The policy reasons for this have been noted, but perhaps the clearest of these is that, in principle, if a terminally ill patient is seen to have a suicidal intent, then any doctor assisting that patient will be seen to be assisting/aiding and abetting suicide. This, then, is the topic analysed in the next chapter.

Chapter 6

Does a doctor who withdraws treatment assist in a patient's suicide?

> *The doctor's intent might . . . be the same in prescribing lethal medication as it is in terminating life support. A doctor who fails to administer medical treatment to one who is dying from a disease could be doing so with an intent to harm or kill that patient.*
>
> (*Washington v Glucksberg per* Stevens J concurring at 81)

Introduction

The previous chapter has shown that, although some terminally ill patients who forgo life-sustaining treatment clearly do intend to die, the courts have simply decided that this has nothing to do with suicide. However, if it is accepted, as has been argued, that some treatment refusals are suicidal, must it also be the case that doctors who withdraw life-sustaining treatments are helping some patients to commit suicide? This conclusion is problematic because, ideally, one would not want it to be said – bearing in mind the essence of a doctor's role – that medical professionals are aiding and abetting/assisting their patients' suicides. Unfortunately, however, there would appear to be no real means by which this conclusion can be avoided or remedied. One could argue perhaps that a patient's consent negates any duty of care, but a patient cannot consent to his own death (or at least he cannot consent to his death by positive means). Similarly, saying that withdrawing treatment is an omission does not help because (a) withdrawing treatment can equally be described as an act and (b) even if it is an omission, suicide and, some would argue,[1] aiding, abetting and assisting suicide can be carried out by virtue of an omission. As such, treatment withdrawal by the doctor can be a cause or at least the part cause[2] of the patient's death. Similarly, claiming

---

1 See, for example, McLachlin J, dissenting in *Rodriguez* (1993) below at page 163 and Kay J in *Brady* (2000) chapter 5 above at pages 132–3.

2 See, for example, Frey's 'contributory theory of causation' by which he claims that 'S is a cause of P if it helps to produce or contributes to the occurrence of P'. i.e. a part cause would

the absence of intention cannot avoid the conclusion either because often, both the patient and the doctor's clear intent can be that the patient dies. In fact, the intention required for accessorial liability, as will be explained below, is both complex and confusing in so far as the intention required by the principal and the accessory are different. This chapter again therefore examines the role of intention and causation, but in the context of the accessorial role a doctor would play in aiding and abetting/assisting suicide.

Aiding and abetting suicide is a statutory offence created in s 2(1) Suicide Act 1961 at the same time that suicide itself was decriminalised; a patient who commits suicide thus 'commits' no offence. In relation to accessorial liability, this is problematic in itself when considered alongside the, usually derivative, liability which attaches to accessorial provisions. Furthermore, ascertaining intention, ascribing cause, and distinguishing between active and passive behaviour is just as problematic here as in the other aspects already considered. The cases analysed here show that in order to counteract these problems and in order to facilitate use of their 'avoidance tactics', judges do rely to a great extent on the compassionate motives or culpability of the assisting person. Once more, both pre-categorisation and context are taken into account to substantiate these.

This chapter will begin by contrasting the relevance of intention, causation, the acts/omissions distinction and motive within the context of both aiding and abetting suicide (UK) and assisting suicide (US). Although there are practical distinctions between aiding, abetting and assisting suicide on the one hand, and voluntary euthanasia on the other, it is not that easy to separate them. Traditionally, the distinction is based on who performed the last act; if the patient acted last, the activity is categorised as assisted suicide, but if the doctor acted last, it is seen as euthanasia. The cases are therefore analysed and examined according to that criterion. Analysis of active and passive conduct is also particularly important here, where it will be seen that there are differing levels of suicide assistance and that mere presence – where the accessory does nothing to prevent a suicide – may not suffice for legal responsibility. Finally, proposed reforms will be considered.

What is aiding and abetting?

Section 2(1) Suicide Act 1961 states that '[a] person who aids, abets, counsels or procures the suicide of another . . .' can be liable for up to 14 years in prison. The words 'aids, abets, counsels or procures' constitute the *actus reus* of the offence and are exactly the same as the words used to define any secondary participation in crime (as in, for example, s 8 Accessories and

---

be '. . . anything that helps to produce, that stands in a productive relationship to anything else.' All contributory, or part causes taken together, would thus be the cause. Frey 1996: 75.

Abettors Act 1861, as amended). They should be interpreted in the same way, but in the case of aiding and abetting suicide, they are used to define what is in itself the principal offence.

Essentially, the four accessorial words have individual meanings: 'aiding' is where the accomplice 'helps, supports and assists' the principal; 'abetting' is to incite, instigate or encourage; 'counselling' is to give advice, solicit or encourage. 'Procuring' traditionally means to 'produce by endeavour',[3] but has been more recently defined by Watkins LJ in *R v Beck* ((1985) 80 Cr App R 355) (a case brought under s 20(2) Theft Act 1968), as a causing or a bringing about. Of the four, only procuring really implies any causal connection between what is done and the commission of the offence,[4] although the position has been complicated somewhat by the dicta in *R v Bryce* ([2004] 2 Cr App R 35) where the Court of Appeal implied a more stringent causal link than that traditionally required in cases of simply 'aiding' (see below).

The *mens rea* element in accessorial liability is, however, significantly more complex not least because it is 'two-dimensional' (Ashworth 2006: 422) in so far as the accessory and the principal do not need to have the same mental element.

Intention in aiding and abetting suicide

The *mens rea* requirements are that firstly, 'the secondary party [D] must intend to assist or encourage the principal's [P] act, or in the case of procuring, to bring the offence about'. There are two elements to this first requirement: 'an intention to perform and an intention that the act will be of assistance'. This second element has been interpreted to mean that it is enough for D only to know that 'his acts would assist P'; it does not mean that it has to be 'proved that D acted in order to assist P.'

The second *mens rea* requirement is that 'the secondary party must have knowledge (or at least turn a blind eye) to the facts forming the essential elements of the principal's offence . . .'[5] As to the first part (knowledge), D cannot really know about events which have yet to happen, therefore knowledge has been interpreted as foresight by D of 'the likelihood of the essential matters.' He does not actually have to know that 'the essential elements of P's conduct constitute a crime'; it is enough that he knows of their existence. This would include knowing of the existence of P's *actus reus* and knowledge/foresight of P's *mens rea* (remembering that he does not have to have the same

---

3 *Attorney-General's Reference (No. 1 of 1975)* [1975] 2 All ER 684: 686. See Ormerod 2005: 171–4 and 494 for much of the preceding and following law on aiding and abetting.

4 Because procuring implies a greater level of assistance – see *R v Reed* ((1982) Crim LR 819).

5 Again, see Ormerod 2005: 179 and 183; there is no requirement that D actually intends that the crime be committed, although it must nonetheless be committed for secondary liability to arise.

mens rea as P) (Ormerod 2005: 185–6). The intention required by the accessory is thus much wider than that required by the principal in the sense that the former could be liable for what the latter *might* do.[6] As Ormerod says, the problems inherent in dealing with a situation where one person is required to have knowledge or awareness of someone else's intention to commit an offence are obvious (Ormerod 2005: 183).

As to the first requirement, assuming that a doctor does aid and abet a patient to commit suicide, the fact that he does not himself have to intend that the 'crime' be committed is irrelevant in the sense that it is sufficient for him, as the accessory, to know or be aware of the patient/principal's intention. Indeed, it is not incumbent upon the principal to have told the accessory about his intentions at all; the accessory can infer those intentions from the surrounding circumstances. According to Dennis's analysis of *Attorney-General v Able and Others* ([1984] 1 QB 795), it is enough that the supplier of a suicide instruction booklet '. . . realise[d] from the circumstances the likelihood that the recipient has the intention to commit suicide or is contemplating doing so' (Dennis 1987: 46–8).[7] Such a wide interpretation was justifiable in view of the fact that it was the only possible outcome envisaged in *Able*. Likewise, the case of *NCB v Gamble* ([1959] 1 QB 11) (a case involving the excess weight of a load on a lorry), effectively held that an accomplice did not have to act with the aim or purpose of assisting or encouraging the crime, but that mere knowledge of assistance was enough.

While this may seem to be an adequate explanation of the mental element required by the accomplice, it does not take *Gillick* into account. Bearing in mind that mere knowledge of assistance in *Gamble* was held to be enough, in *Gillick*, the doctor knew the contraceptive pill would assist the young girl's boyfriend, and yet he was found not to be an accomplice, seemingly because

---

6 It will be interesting to see if the new proposals on accessorial liability will remedy this. The Law Commission has been looking to reform accessorial provisions since Law Com No. 143 (1985); (and the same principles were re-stated in Law Com No. 177 (1989)). Subsequently, the Law Commission has introduced radical proposals to change the law relating to accessorial liability in LCCP No. 131 (1993), its Consultation Paper on *Assisting and encouraging crime*. It recommended abolishing s 8 Accessories and Abbettors Act (thus removing aiding, abetting, counselling and procuring) and creating two new inchoate offences of 'assisting' and 'encouraging' another to commit an offence, both of which would involve independent, as opposed to the usual derivative, liability and would exclude omissions. Part 5 LCCP No. 177 (2005) also examines complicity in first degree murder and indicates that the Law Commission intends to produce a consultative Report and draft Bill on secondary liability later in 2006. See www.lawcom.gov.uk/assisting_crime.htm (accessed 5 April 2006).

7 The case involved the distribution of a booklet by the Voluntary Euthanasia Society to its members containing information on ways to commit suicide. The Attorney General alleged this was an offence contrary to s 2(1) of the Suicide Act. This would answer any allegation by a doctor that he was, for example, prescribing medication to a patient on the pretence that the patient required them to sleep, but was in fact storing sufficient amounts to take all at once.

his intention was not '. . . to assist the boy but to protect the girl' (Ashworth 2006: 425). Thus, having just said that aim or purpose is not required, and that knowledge is sufficient, *Gillick* says the reverse. It is very easy to see how purpose and motive are confused here where it can just as easily be said that 'his motive was to protect the girl' and Lord Scarman acknowledged this when he said there can be no guilty mind as long as the doctor has exercised his clinical judgment as to what is best for his patient.

Causation in aiding and abetting suicide

General accessorial liability is derivative in the sense that the accessory's conduct is not enough by itself to violate the law (Fletcher 1978: 583). As Dennis puts it, derivative liability is '. . . founded on the wrongful act of another . . . [so that] liability may be attributed to persons who have not directly caused the harm involved' (Dennis 1987: 58). In aiding, abetting or counselling especially, the accessory does not 'cause' the offence, nor indeed does he have to be the cause of the offence, or of the principal's act;[8] if he were, he would effectively become the principal.

However, in aiding and abetting suicide, although the *actus reus* words must be interpreted in the same way as in any other complicity cases, liability is not derivative in the sense referred to above, because aiding and abetting suicide is itself the principal offence. The aider and abettor does not derive liability through the principal's act, because the principal is not committing an offence. Therefore, no liability attaches to the principal anyway.

Unfortunately, the two most recent cases of aiding and abetting suicide do little to clarify the causal position. In *R v Bryce*, the appellant had been convicted of aiding, abetting, counselling or procuring X to commit murder in that he had assisted X to kill by driving him to the victim's home to carry out the killing. The Court of Appeal said that while it may not necessarily be the case that there must be a clear causal link where an offence has been aided, abetted or counselled, nonetheless:

> . . . there must be some causal connection between the act of the second-ary party relied on and the commission of the offence by the perpetrator . . . and the assistance given by the appellant to facilitate the crime . . . [in driving X to shoot his victim] remained operative up to the time of the killing.
>
> (*Bryce per* Potter LJ at paras 73 and 93)

In *R v Wright* (*The Times* 17 May 2000), the appellant had been convicted of aiding and abetting the suicide of one and of murdering another of his

---

8 Although see the dicta in *Bryce* below. See Smith 1997: 458.

cellmates (in separate incidents) while they were in custody. The evidence suggested that both victims had expressed a desire to commit suicide by some means or other. Wright had assisted them to do so by using bedlinen as a noose with which they could hang themselves. The appeal was based largely on matters relating to the mental element, but in his commentary on the case, Smith stated that '. . . it is not . . . an offence to assist or encourage a responsible adult person fully voluntarily to take a serious risk of causing serious injury to, or even killing himself . . .' (Smith 2000b: 929). In his view, this was the approach that should have been adopted in *Kennedy*, but although such a voluntary act was held not to have broken the chain of causation in the drugs administration cases, the reasons for this can plausibly be explained on the (policy) need to punish drug offenders (Ormerod 2005: 60).[9] Moreover, if the same principle was upheld in aiding and abetting suicide, it would effectively mean that no one who assisted in a suicide would be liable under s 2(1). Conversely, if the same principle was applied in the treatment withdrawal cases (if they were held to be cases of suicide), the patient's voluntary act (if the patient was physically capable of performing the last act, and usually they are not) could be held to break the chain of causation. This would thus avoid liability on the part of the doctor, but would leave hospitals and courts in a position whereby they would be seen to be endorsing suicide.

Acts and omissions in aiding and abetting suicide

It is clear that aiding and abetting (and assisting) suicide can include a wide variety of activities ranging from, say, giving advice to more positive physical assistance. One would assume, however, that the aid has to be more than *de minimis* or that it is at least sufficient to satisfy the 'but-for' threshold. Does this therefore mean that omissions would not suffice?

Bearing in mind the requirement for a duty of care in omissions (i.e. treatment refusal) cases, a patient's possibly suicidal refusal would provide a doctor with a get-out clause from any charge of aiding and abetting suicide, because a voluntary refusal of treatment by a patient releases the doctor from his duty of care (albeit there is a duty to care *for* the patient until his death). Moreover, the most recent authority in a non-medical situation where a duty of care existed, suggests that failure to summon medical assistance during a suicide attempt would not suffice for a charge of aiding and abetting suicide. However, it would be sufficient for a charge of manslaughter by gross negligence. This very scenario arose in *R v Anderson* (*The Guardian* 28 April 2005), where a wife had failed to summon medical assistance for her husband (who had taken an overdose) until two hours after his death. She was tried and acquitted of manslaughter rather than aiding and abetting suicide on the

9 And see previous chapter.

basis that 'the Suicide Act . . . only applies to people who have actively assisted someone to die.'[10]

Although it was not queried whether or not Wright owed a duty of care towards his co-prisoners in *R v Wright*, Smith in his commentary on the case suggests that Wright did have a legal duty to intervene to prevent death, and that following the principle set out in *Miller*, Wright should have been guilty of murder as a result of his participation in the creation of the danger (Smith 2000b: 930).[11]

Where no duty of care exists, however, the straight accessorial provisions would apply and in the context of suicide in particular, the General Note following s 2 Suicide Act states that 'mere passive presence will not amount to complicity.' Moreover, despite the Law Commission's contrary view on the relevance of mere presence (LCCP No. 131: 22, para 2.25),[12] it is generally considered insufficient for the accomplice to stand by and watch without contributing in some way. Certainly, from a legal point of view, it would be relevant to make the distinction between passive assistance, such as a failure to prevent suicide and, say, supervising or directly aiding, as the former is unlikely to receive such a severe penalty, if it receives one at all.[13]

As no doctors in the UK have been prosecuted for aiding and abetting a patient's suicide (Jackson 2006: 915), an examination of further cases where lay individuals have been charged with the offence (*Bryce, Wright* and *Anderson* having already been analysed above) will show that both the amount of assistance and the means adopted to assist are important considerations in the ascription of liability. However, of more importance is that the cases also show that defendants, where they have shown a compassionate motive in assisting a 'victim' who has been suffering from a terminal or debilitating illness,[14] have either been discharged, or have received only a minimal sentence. Where a higher sentence has been imposed, it can be seen that the court has stereotyped the defendant where the motive has been less than exemplary, thus reflecting the view that blameworthiness depends to a

---

10 The decision follows that of *R v Downes* ((1875) 13 Cox C. C. 111) (albeit there was possibly a statutory duty there) but not that of *R v Lowe* ([1973] QB 702) where Phillimore LJ said that an omission did not suffice for constructive manslaughter. However, this did not mean that it would not suffice for gross negligence manslaughter. See Clarkson and Keating 2003: 659.

11 Interestingly, one of the three questions raised by the jury related to omissions liability. See also Potter LJ's *obiter dictum* in *Bryce* (2004): para 40, that aiding, abetting etc could 'possibly' be committed by an omission.

12 See the implications of s 5 Domestic Violence, Crime and Victim's Act 2004.

13 The illogicality of this was noted by Shaffer 1986: 363, when he compared two scenarios where on the one hand, a woman gives her sister a hose attached to a car exhaust and then leaves her in the garage, but on the other puts the hose in her sister's mouth. He asks whether there is a significant difference between the two.

14 Out of the 50 or so cases prosecuted since 1990, only one-fifth have led to a custodial sentence upon conviction; Samuels 2005: 536.

great extent on the judges' perception of culpability. The arguments already made as to the relevance of value judgments, context, and motive are equally applicable here, where judgments are being made as to which activities are condonable and which are not. The context of the offence, and whether or not the accessory's behaviour is seen as well intentioned, are equally valid albeit unadmitted factors which the courts have considered in these cases. The cases also show the inconsistent application of the 'last act' test.

R v Bowler (*Western Mail* 29 June 2001)

Anthony Bowler was charged with aiding and abetting a suicide for sitting with Elizabeth Gale while she killed herself. After originally being arrested on suspicion of murder, he was charged with the lesser offence, but the charges were subsequently dropped by the Crown Prosecution Service as there was no case to answer. The police confirmed there was no evidence that the death had been aided.

R v Chard (*The Guardian* 23 September 1993)

A teenager was cleared of helping a woman with multiple sclerosis to commit suicide. He had taken a bottle of paracetamol to her in hospital. Pownall J said there was no evidence to support the allegation that he had aided and abetted (although the cause of death was from an overdose of paracetamol) and the defendant had 'only provided her with an option of taking her own life'.

R v Pratten (*The Times* 26 and 27 October 2000)

A 63-year-old mother pleaded guilty to aiding and abetting her 42-year-old son's suicide. He was terminally ill with Huntington's Disease and had already told her he was going to commit suicide. While he was in a coma after a drugs overdose, she smothered him with a pillow. Boal J warned that the decision should not be misinterpreted and treated as a precedent. He gave her a conditional discharge to reflect his view that she had suffered enough already and because of the unusual circumstances of the case.

R v Jennison (*The Times* 30 June 1998)

The defendant confessed to aiding and abetting her mother's suicide by giving her an overdose of tablets at her request. When this did not work, she smothered her mother, who had chronic dementia and Alzheimer's, with a pillow. She received 12 months' probation. In the Crown Court, the judge said that it was only the exceptional circumstances of the case that had prevented her from facing a murder charge. He continued '. . . your culpability is very much at the lower end of the scale.'

R v Pitman ((1997) 4(9) Med L Monitor 2–3)

A son held the barrel of a rifle to his mother's head; being an arthritis sufferer, she could not do so herself, but she pressed the trigger. Mr Pitman was sentenced to nine months, suspended for two years. The court felt that they had no choice but to impose a custodial sentence, but bearing in mind that the maximum sentence is 14 years, he was treated with sympathy.

R v Lawson (*The Times* 9 June 2001)

A father received only a two-year suspended sentence for helping his daughter die. He had sat with her while she took 30 pills, then suffocated her with a pillow. She had been suffering from (untreated) depression and alcoholism for 10 years.

R v Hough ((1984) 6 Cr App R 406)

The appellant had offered to sit with the deceased, who had held a fixed intention to commit suicide for the last 12 months. She provided the deceased with sodium amytal tablets, and when the deceased was still breathing after two to four hours, the appellant put a plastic bag over her head and was charged and convicted of attempted murder. Although the court felt that what she had done fell within the scope of s 2(1) Suicide Act, Lord Lane CJ thought she '. . . was too ready to play an active part in the procuring or using the paraphernalia of death.' Whether it was called murder or assisted suicide, it was still a crime:

> In terms of gravity, it could vary from the borders of cold blooded murder down to the shadowy area of mercy killing or common humanity. The difficult problem was to decide where on that scale any particular case should be put.
>
> (*Hough per* Lord Lane CJ at 407)

Hough received a nine-month custodial sentence.

R v Wallis ((1983) 5 Cr App R (S) 342)

A man helped his 17-year-old drug addict girlfriend to commit suicide by obtaining various substances for her. He expressed the view that he did not feel it was his responsibility to dissuade her. He got the tablets, sat with her while she took them and did not call an ambulance until she was dead. His 12-month prison sentence was upheld on appeal.

R v David George Robey ((1979) 1 Cr App R (S) 127)

A woman, who had been severely scalded and had since then been suffering from severe depression, stabbed herself, but the appellant pushed the knife in further to end her suffering. He received a three-year sentence for 'actively assisting in the act which caused the death'.

R v McShane ((1978) 66 Cr App R 97)

A daughter was accused of assisting her mother's attempted suicide after secret video recordings were made of their conversations while the mother was in a convalescent home. Her appeal, that an attempt to counsel or pro-cure a suicide was not an offence, and that as a mere attempt, she did not have the necessary intention, failed. The court found also that her motive was a financial one and she received a four-year custodial sentence.

R v McGranaghan ((1987) 9 Cr App R (S) 447)

The appellant was sharing a prison cell with a disabled prisoner, whom he persuaded to commit suicide. He made a noose and helped his cellmate up on to a cupboard, and induced him to write a suicide note. The crime was considered by the court to be 'revolting' and fully deserved the eight-year sentence. It was conceded that the manner in which the offence had been committed in this case was particularly rare because it is the type of offence that is generally committed in the context of a mercy killing.

An analysis of the cases

If these cases are examined in light of the earlier definitions of aiding, abetting, counselling and procuring and the degree of activity or passivity, together with the accessory's motive and perceived culpability, then the inconsistencies in the courts' approach can be seen. It can also be seen that the traditional 'last act' test, which is said to distinguish between aiding and abetting suicide and voluntary euthanasia, does not hold here.

In *Bowler*, mere presence/non-prevention was insufficient to allow charges to be brought. In *Chard*, the principal did perform the last act, but the case is interesting in so far as Pownall J ignored the fact that by buying the para-cetamol, the defendant had contributed material aid without which the woman could not have committed suicide. In both *Pratten* and *Jennison*, the accessory performed the last act in smothering each principal, but *Pratten* was conditionally discharged in order to reflect her compassionate motive, while *Jennison* simply received a probationary sentence to show her minimal culpability. Yet both *Lawson* and *Hough* also performed the last act, but the former received a longer suspended sentence than *Pitman*, who nonetheless, like *Chard*, had provided his mother with the materials with which to commit the suicide. The only distinction between *Pitman* and *Chard* cases was the means by which the suicide was carried out. It must be assumed that providing a gun was considered to be 'worse' than providing medication (as would be the use of a knife perhaps). These cases all involved a person who was suffering from some recognisable disease or illness. Other than *Pitman*, these sentences do reflect and recognise the accessory's compassionate motive in the face of severe suffering.

In contrast, the more serious cases such as *Wallis, Robey, McShane* and *McGranaghan* reflect preconceived notions of blame and culpability commensurate with a far from praiseworthy motive. *Wallis's* girlfriend suffered from depression and yet, whereas he, like *Chard*, simply obtained medication for the suicide, he received a custodial sentence, perhaps to reflect criticism of his status as a drug addict. However, the distinction between *Wallis* and *Robey* is more evident, as in the former the principal performed the last act, but in *Robey* the accessory actively pushed in the knife. Again, the weapon is significant. In *McShane*, a daughter whose sole motive was to gain financially from her mother's death was given a four-year custodial sentence for procuring her suicide and in *McGranaghan*, the defendant received eight years for procuring his cellmate's suicide. *Wright* would also be classed as a case where the defendant's culpability was on the more severe end of the scale.

It can be seen from these cases, particularly *Hough* and *Jennison*, that there are levels of culpability which are reflected in the sentence and which depend upon the circumstances of the case and on the motive of the accessory. Indeed, the relevance of motive was explicitly acknowledged in *Hough* and in *Gamble* where Slade J conceded that the words 'assist' and 'encourage' automatically included motive (Slade J at 25).

This examination of aiding and abetting suicide demonstrates the complexities of intention, causation and active/passive behaviour in this area of the law and demonstrate that the last act is not a definitive test. Do the same considerations thus apply to assisted suicide?

What is assisted suicide?

The very specific statutory phrase 'aiding and abetting suicide', as contained in s 2(1) Suicide Act, has its more modern 'trendy' equivalent in the US, where the term 'assisted suicide' has been introduced by euthanasia supporters as a less serious alternative for assisted death than euthanasia. As Beezer J, dissenting, said in *Compassion in Dying v Washington*:

> . . . the issue of physician-assisted suicide as a plausible medical alternative is relatively new. Only since Dr. Kevorkian started assisting patients to commit suicide . . . has there been significant public and legal attention

to the possible differences between physician-assisted suicide and ordinary cases of aiding and abetting suicide.

(Compassion in Dying per Beezer J at 844)

It has been said that assisted suicide, as a 'morally intermediate act,'[15] '. . .
falls somewhere between termination of life support and active voluntary
euthanasia' (Kamisar 1995: 228), and its similarity to both is evident. For
example, when a doctor disconnects a ventilator from a competent patient at
that patient's request, is he withdrawing treatment or is he assisting suicide?
If a doctor is holding a potassium chloride syringe to the patient's arm
while the patient depresses the plunger, is that assisted suicide or euthanasia?
(Meyers and Mason 2000: 265–6). In view of the fact that the patient is
choosing to hasten his own death in all of these, can it be persuasively
claimed that there is a clear distinction between the three practices, and if so,
on what is the distinction based?

Assisted suicide and euthanasia: what are the distinguishing factors?

A significant number of authorities agree that voluntary euthanasia and
assisted suicide are one and the same.[16] For example, Gillon has stated that if
voluntary euthanasia is a request to die by an adult who wishes assistance in
doing so, it follows that it '. . . is essentially a form of suicide involving the
assistance of others' (Gillon 1969: 173). Aspects of intention have already
been analysed and it can be argued that the intention in both practices and
as between both parties can be the same (i.e. that the patient dies). As to
causation, however, this is reflected to some extent in a dubious distinction
based on who performed the last act that brought about the patient's death (if
the doctor acted last, he is the cause of death (euthanasia) but if the patient
acted last, he will have caused his own death, albeit with the assistance of
another). A hypothetical example, namely Kamisar's tablet scenario, will,
however, show that this 'test' does not offer a convincing distinction between
euthanasia and assisted suicide.

Briefly, the scenario involves a competent woman who has expressed a wish
to die. She swallows a lethal dose of medication, which the doctor has:

(a) placed under her pillow or by her bed;
(b) placed in her hand; or
(c) put in her mouth.

15 Angell 1998: 6.
16 To name just two, see Barrington 1986: 240 and Fairbairn 1991: 118.

One might argue that both (a) and (b) are assisted suicide because the patient still has to make the decision to pick up the medication, move her hand to her mouth and take it. It might, however, be argued that (c) is euthanasia because the doctor performs what appears to be the last act, *but*, even here the patient still has the choice whether to swallow or spit out the medication (Kamisar 1995: 231). Therefore, the ultimate choice whether to proceed or not still remains with the patient in all three, so the last act is not an effective distinguishing factor here.[17]

Perhaps, therefore, it can be alternatively suggested that the way in which each of the three choices in the table scenario is categorised depends to some extent on the level or 'degree' of participation involved.[18] For example, supplying information or means would be a lesser level of participation than, say, supervising which, in turn, would be a lower level of participation than directly aiding or causing. These 'levels' of participation were devised by Watts and Howell to distinguish between the potential consequences of each. In their view, the lowest level would be the '[p]rovision of information'; the second, the provision of 'means' (which they simply take to involve writing a prescription) and the most serious they categorise as the provision of 'direct assistance'. According to their criteria, (a), (b) *and* (c) would all amount to direct assistance (Watts and Howell 1992: 1043).[19]

Contrarily, however, Gostin argues that '. . . placing the lethal dose of medication in the patient's hand or mouth' would amount to active participation sufficient to cause death (Gostin 1993: 96) and therefore, in his view, both (b) and (c) above would be murder/euthanasia, and not assisted suicide. It can be seen, therefore, that these different levels of participation depend on how they are subjectively interpreted as events by other people. The relevance of this aspect, and indeed the irrelevance of the last act test, can be better demonstrated by looking at two cases where doctors who assisted in their patients' suicides were treated differently both by the courts and by their peers.

On the one hand Dr Jack Kevorkian[20] (*People v Kevorkian* No. 93–11482 Mich Cir. Ct, Wayne County December 13 1995) (who had already been acquitted of three previous charges of assisted suicide) used his suicide machine to assist Janet Adkins, an early-stage Alzheimer's sufferer, to commit suicide. He was found guilty of her murder (not of assisted suicide) and is presently serving a 10 to 25-year sentence. Unlike the patient in Quill's

---

17 It can also be claimed that it is discriminatory in that it ignores what is, perhaps, the most vital consideration – that assisted suicide usually takes place where a patient is physically unable to commit suicide by himself.

18 See Reinhardt CJ on the difference in degree between withdrawing treatment and assisted suicide in *Compassion in Dying* (1996) at 823. The New York Multi Society Task Force (1994) also recognised the difference in degree between assisted suicide and euthanasia.

19 Compare Kamisar 1995: his fn 38.

20 His name has become an eponym – to 'kevork' is to be put to death; Slovenko 1997: *vii*.

case below, Janet Adkins was not Kevorkian's patient and he had made no inquiries into either her condition or her capacity. Dr Timothy Quill, on the other hand, had been treating his leukaemia patient for some time, and knew her well (Quill 1991: 691). When she refused any further treatment, Quill discussed this fully with her on several occasions and she saw other specialists, but he accepted her decision. When she then said that she wanted to control the time of death, he directed her to the Hemlock Society. A week later, she contacted him for barbiturates. He saw her again because he knew they were recommended by the Hemlock Society as a suicide aid. He verified that she was not despondent; he made sure she knew the amount she needed to commit suicide, and he saw her once again before she took the medication.

Both are '. . . classic cases of physician-assisted suicide' (Brody 1993: 117); both satisfied the *actus reus* and *mens rea* elements of the offence; in both cases, the doctors provided some form of material aid and in both cases *the patient performed the last act*. Yet, the reaction was a unanimous rejection and condemnation of Kevorkian's method of 'assisting' his patient, but approval for Quill.[21] In what ways were they different? Can we say that Kevorkian's participation was more direct or active than that of Quill because the former used a suicide machine, while the latter wrote a prescription for barbiturates? Alternatively, can we distinguish the cases on the grounds that whereas Kevorkian was present at the death of his patient, Quill was not? No we cannot, because irrespective of his absence Quill knew of his patient's intention to commit suicide and had *already* assisted her by writing the prescription.

Using their different levels of participation, Watts and Howell's explanation of the distinction between the two is that the patient '. . . retain[s] [a] greater degree of control on choosing the time and mode of . . . death' where the doctor has only provided the (information or the) means. Accordingly, Quill in writing a prescription simply provided the means, whereas Kevorkian provided a more direct form of assistance. This is a plausible (causal) explanation of the distinction between the two, but it can also be argued that the way in which each of them carried out the process of assistance itself is based on the differing motivations of the two doctors; the one acted in what was – bearing in mind subsequent support of the one and criticism and imprisonment of the other – evidently a more acceptable and less culpable manner than the other. Certainly the distinction between them cannot be based on the last act (because in both cases the patients performed the last act) or on differing intentions. Similarly, it can be argued that intention is not necessarily the defining feature between assisted suicide and withdrawing treatment either, as can be seen in the two contentious cases analysed below.

21 Both cases are used to illustrate different kinds of assisted suicide by Watts and Howell 1992: 1043; Weir 1992: 118. For comparisons of the two cases, see also Miles 1994: 1787; Connelly 1997–8: 337 and the note in the *Harvard LR* 1992: 2036–7.

Assisted suicide and withdrawing treatment: the irrelevance of intention, causation and acts/omissions as distinguishing factors in Compassion in Dying v Washington, and Quill v Vacco

As has been seen, intention, together with causation and the distinction made between acts and omissions, have traditionally been used by the courts to explain the distinction between withdrawing treatment and assisted suicide. They were however rejected by the Washington and New York Appeal Courts in *Compassion in Dying v Washington*, and *Quill v Vacco*. In both cases, challenges were made to the constitutionality of federal legislation prohibiting assisted suicide. In the former, the challenge was made on the ground that a liberty interest (in suicide) was denied under the due process clause of the Fourteenth Amendment. In the latter, the challenge was that federal legislation breached the equal protection clause of the US Constitution, as terminally ill patients on life-support could hasten death by asking for that to be withdrawn, whereas patients not on life-supporting machinery did not have that option.

Both Appeal Courts controversially held that there was a violation of the relevant clauses of the Constitution and that, accordingly, doctors could prescribe drugs to be self-administered by competent terminally ill patients who wished to end their lives (*Quill v Vacco* at 727).

Compassion in Dying v Washington (United States Court of Appeal for the 9th Circuit)

Reinhardt J, delivering the court's (majority) opinion, held firstly that there was a constitutionally protected liberty interest in determining the time and manner of death, although he was careful to say that it was merely a right to 'hasten . . . a death that is already in progress' and not a right to suicide. As such, Reinhardt J doubted that the state interest in preventing suicide was 'even implicated' (Reinhardt J at 824). It was rather contradictory, therefore, for him to invoke it anyway, albeit holding that it was overridden in the same way as it would be in treatment refusal cases.

He held, secondly, that there was no distinction between withdrawing treatment and assisted suicide because in both the intention – the death of the patient – was the same; whether a doctor 'pull[s] the plug on a respirator' or 'prescrib[es] drugs' to allow a '. . . patient to end his own life . . . the death of the patient is the intended result as surely in one case as in the other' (Reinhardt J at 824). Today's society has not only erased the distinction between killing patients and allowing them to die, but it already condones a variety of 'death inducing practices'. Thus the social risks of allowing physician-assisted suicide would only differ in degree, not in kind, from risks already countenanced (Reinhardt J at 823). Reinhardt's opinion bears setting out in full:

The state responds by urging that physician-assisted suicide is different in kind, not degree, from the type of physician-life-ending conduct that is now authorized, for three separate reasons. [The state] argues that 'assisted suicide': 1) requires doctors to play an active role; 2) causes deaths that would not result from the patient's underlying disease; and 3) requires doctors to provide the causal agent of patients' deaths . . . The first distinction – the line between commission and omission – is a distinction without a difference now that patients are permitted not only to decline all medical treatment, but to instruct their doctors to terminate whatever treatment, artificial or otherwise, they are receiving. In disconnecting a respirator . . . a doctor is unquestionably committing an act; he is taking an active role in bringing about the patient's death. In fact, there can be no doubt that in such instances the doctor intends that, as a result of his action, the patient will die an earlier death than he otherwise would.

Similarly, drawing a distinction on the basis of whether the patient's death results from an underlying disease no longer has any legitimacy. While the distinction may once have seemed tenable . . . it was not based on a valid or practical legal foundation and was therefore quickly abandoned.

(*Compassion in Dying per* Reinhardt J at 822)

In just a few sentences Reinhardt J thus disposes of all the bases upon which a distinction has traditionally been made between withdrawing treatment and assisting suicide: intention, causation and acts/omissions.

Again, with reference to the relevance of intention, he further held that there was no distinction between using pain-killing medication to relieve pain and using it to administer death (i.e. by seeing no distinction between using pain-killing medication to relieve pain on the one hand, and to administer death on the other, he effectively rejected the principle of double effect as well).

Quill v Vacco (United States Court of Appeal for the 2nd Circuit)

The New York Appeals Court found there had been a breach of the equal protection clause, but interestingly, and unlike the Washington court, found no breach of the due process clause as there was nothing to suggest that there was an existing fundamental right to assisted suicide.

In a judgment as controversial and as criticised as that of Reinhardt J in *Compassion in Dying v Washington*, Miner CJ held firstly that there was no distinction between withdrawing treatment and assisted suicide. Noting 'the irrelevance of the action–inaction distinction', he held that 'the cause of death in [withdrawing treatment and self-administering drugs] is the suicide's conscious decision to put an end to his own existence.' He continued:

The withdrawal of nutrition brings on death by starvation, the withdrawal of hydration brings on death by dehydration, and the withdrawal of ventilation brings about respiratory failure . . . Withdrawal of life support . . . is nothing more or less than assisted suicide . . .

(Quill v Vacco per Miner CJ at 729)

He went on to say that none of these can be said to be as a result of the underlying illness or disease, and death in such circumstances is not a 'natural' progression of the patient's disease in any sense. Equally, he held that there was no distinction between those patients who were on life-support machinery and those who were not.

Calabresi CJ, concurring in the result and in a separate judgment, also rejected the distinction made between ' "active" assisted suicide and . . . what they call "passive" behaviour (actively removing life supports of feeding tubes, on demand, so that the patient may die)' (*Quill v Vacco* at 741).

The decision in *Quill v Vacco*, as in *Compassion in Dying*, thus rejected those aspects that have traditionally been considered to be fundamental to the distinction between withdrawing treatment and assisted suicide. It is unsurprising, therefore, that the US Supreme Court reversed both decisions and reverted to the more traditional jurisprudence in order to do so.

Assisted suicide and withdrawing treatment: the relevance of intention, causation, acts and omissions as distinguishing factors in Washington v Glucksberg and Vacco v Quill

Both cases were reversed by the US Supreme Court on the same day, the composition of the court being identical and near identical judgments being given in each case. In *Washington v Glucksberg* the Supreme Court held there was no violation of the due process clause because there was no liberty interest in assisted suicide and in *Vacco v Quill*, the court held that New York statutes prohibiting assisted suicide did not violate the equal protection clause. The statutes prohibiting assisted suicide and allowing treatment refusal respectively, did not distinguish between persons because everyone is entitled to refuse treatment and no one is permitted to assist suicide.[22]

Washington v Glucksberg (the US Supreme Court)

Rehnquist CJ delivered the Supreme Court's unanimous judgment in *Washington v Glucksberg*. After elaborating at length on the history of suicide and the due process clause and after citing vast authorities, he held that

---

22 Interestingly, this is also the basis of the House of Lords decision in respect of Article 14 of the ECHR in *Pretty* (2).

withdrawing treatment and assisted suicide are '. . . widely and reasonably regarded as quite distinct' (Rehnquist CJ at 40).

Souter J delivered a separate concurring judgment in which he emphasised the relevance of intention in the distinction, saying that:

> Where . . . a physician writes a prescription to equip a patient to end life, the prescription is written to serve an affirmative intent to die (even though the physician need not, and probably does not characteristically have an intent that the patient die but only that the patient be equipped to make the decision).
>
> (*Washington v Glucksberg per* Souter J at 138)

Stevens J also concurred in a separate judgment in which he looked at the relevance of *Cruzan*, examined the doctor's increasing role in 'making decisions that hasten the death of terminally ill patients' and elaborated on the role of intention. In upholding the acts/omissions distinction and the resulting cause of death, he nonetheless admitted that while there was a constitutional basis for saying that causation and intention were the kingpins of the distinction between permitting and causing death, they were not infallible or absolute. He was:

> . . . not persuaded that in all cases there will in fact be a significant difference between the intent of the physicians, the patients or the families in the two situations . . . [as with a patient, t]he doctor's intent might . . . be the same in prescribing lethal medication as it is in terminating life support . . .
>
> (*Washington v Glucksberg per* Stevens J at 80–1)

Vacco v Quill (the US Supreme Court)

The Supreme Court also reversed the New York Appeal Court's decision in *Quill v Vacco*, holding there was no violation of the equal protection clause on the grounds that, if everyone can refuse medical treatment and none can have assisted suicide, then no one is treated differently.

Rehnquist CJ again delivered the court's opinion and, citing 34 previous decisions (Annas 1998: 222), said that the well-established 'important, logical and rational' distinction between refusing treatment and suicide '. . . comports with fundamental legal principles of causation and intent.' As to the former, he said that when a patient refuses life-sustaining treatment, the disease is the cause of death, but that when he takes lethal medication, the medication causes his death (Rehnquist CJ at 13); as such, the court 'implicitly' recognised the distinction between letting and making a patient die.

On the relevance of intention in the distinction, Rehnquist CJ asserted that when a patient has a doctor's help to commit suicide, he inevitably has the specific intent to end his life, but a patient who forgoes life-sustaining treatment *might* not have that same intent (at 14; emphasis added). Moreover, a doctor who withdraws life-sustaining medical treatment 'purposefully intends, or may so intend, only to respect his patient's wishes'. In assisted suicide, however, the doctor 'must' intend the patient's death. Rehnquist went on to say that intent and purpose have been long been used to differentiate between two acts that may have the same result, but they are different and may be treated differently.

As in *Washington v Glucksberg*, separate concurring opinions were given by justices O'Connor, Stevens, Souter, Ginsberg and Breyer. Stevens J reiterated the uncertainty he had expressed in his judgment in *Vacco v Quill* as to the mental element involved in withdrawing treatment and assisting suicide (see above) and noted that, at least in some cases, the terminally ill patient who refuses treatment may in fact intend to die and that the doctor's intention may also be the same. He went on to say that '[t]he illusory character of any differences in intent or causation' between refusing treatment and assisted suicide may actually not apply to 'terminally ill patients and their doctors' (Stevens J at 48–52).

Comments

A great deal has been written about the judgments in the two cases.[23] The Appeals Courts judgments, in particular, have incurred much criticism, Arras for example saying that the two decisions made the '. . . various states within their . . . jurisdictions, the first governments in world history, excepting perhaps the Nazi regime in Germany, to officially sanction physician-assisted suicide' (Arras 1997: 363). It was hardly surprising that the Supreme Court reversed the Appeals Courts' decisions, if only on the basis of the policy implications if it had not done so, but it has to be said that the Supreme Court, while upholding intention as one of the key distinguishing factors between withdrawing treatment and assisted suicide, does show that the difference in the intention between the two practices is not as clear cut as it would have us believe. The arguments used by the majority remain as circular as in previous authorities (that a patient forgoing treatment does not intend to commit suicide, and that accordingly, the cause of death is the disease and not the patient's refusal). Stevens J was the only one to concede the difficulties of using intention and causation as distinguishing factors in withdrawing treatment and assisted suicide. Bearing in mind the problems already set out in this book, he was right to do so.

---

23 The Appeals Courts judgments have been particularly criticised, by, for example, Callahan and White 1996: 71; See also Bix (1995); Blake (1997); and Carolan (1997).

Upholding the acts/omissions distinction as a distinguishing factor: Rodriguez and Attorney-General of British Columbia

As in the two US cases above, Sue Rodriguez, a patient who was suffering from Lou Gehrig's Disease, also challenged the constitutionality of legislation (namely s 241(b) of the Canadian Criminal Code) which made it an offence to aid or abet a suicide. She claimed that (amongst other rights) the section violated her 'right to life, liberty and security of the person' under s 7 of the Canadian Charter of Rights and Freedoms and that she was entitled to assistance in dying as, by the time her disease had progressed, she would be physically unable to commit suicide by herself.

Sopinka J, speaking for the majority in the Canadian Supreme Court, upheld the validity of s 241(b) and, although he did not (as the judges did in the two US cases above) delve into the relevance of intention as a distinguishing factor between withdrawing treatment and assisted suicide,[24] he did nonetheless emphasise the importance of the acts/omissions distinction in holding that '. . . active participation by one individual in the death of another is both intrinsically and morally and legally wrong . . .' (Sopinka J at 401). Quoting both Lords Keith and Goff in *Bland* (as to the 'crucial distinction between active and passive euthanasia': 399), he held that:

> Regardless of one's personal views as to whether the distinctions drawn between withdrawal of treatment and palliative care, on the one hand, and assisted suicide on the other, are practically compelling, the fact remains that these distinctions are maintained and can be persuasively defended.
>
> (*Rodriguez per* Sopinka J at 406)

In looking at the rationales on which the distinction was based, he commented that once a patient has refused treatment '[t]he doctor is . . . not required to make a choice which will result in the patient's death as he would be if he chose to assist a suicide or perform active euthanasia' (Sopinka J at 405).[25]

In their dissenting judgments, both McLachlin and L'Heureux-Dube JJ

---

24 The only context in which Sopinka J emphasised the importance of intention was in the administration of drugs given for palliative reasons in the knowledge that death would be hastened. On this, he said that:

> While factually distinction[s based upon intent] may, at times, be difficult to draw, legally it is clear. The fact that in some cases, the third party will, under the guise of palliative care, commit euthanasia or assist in suicide and go unsanctioned due to the difficulty in proof, cannot be said to render the existence of the prohibition fundamentally unjust at 405–6.

25 The patient's consent thus operates as a 'defence' here again.

felt that s 241(b) did violate s 7 of the Charter, as it imposed an arbitrary limit on the patient's right to deal with her own person. McLachlin said that:

> If the justification for helping someone to end life is established, I cannot accept that it matters whether the act is 'passive' – the withdrawal of support necessary to sustain life – or 'active' – the provision of a means to permit a person of sound mind to choose to end his life with dignity.
>
> (*Rodriguez per* McLachlin J at 420)

In doing so, she not only rejected the acts/omissions distinction, but also conceded that, in some situations, it is justifiable to cause the death of another. Her second argument, in response to the view that the state had an absolute right to preserve life, was to note that Parliament had never acted consistently to 'criminalize acts which cause the death of another' and she used the example of causing death by omission, and death where a legal duty to provide the 'necessaries of life' has been removed by the patient's consent.

Meanwhile, Lamer CJC in his dissenting judgment said that the section discriminated against the patient's right of equality as her physical disability prevented her from committing suicide without aid, while healthy persons could do so (Lamer CJC at 358–9). He evaded the argument that the Code did not treat anyone differently (since no one can assist a suicide and everyone can refuse life-sustaining treatment) by saying:

> . . . although at first sight persons who cannot commit suicide and those who can are given identical treatment under s 241*(b)* of the *Criminal Code*, they are, nevertheless, treated unequally since by the *effect* of that provision, persons unable to commit suicide without assistance are deprived of any ability to commit suicide in a way which is not unlawful, whereas s 241*(b)* does not have that effect on those unable to end their lives without assistance.
>
> (*Rodriguez per* Lamer CJC at 364)

Comments

The majority adopted the traditional distinctions used to distinguish between withdrawing treatment and assisted suicide. The dissenting judges on the other hand, in rejecting such a distinction, concentrated on the effect of a patient's consent and a doctor's justification in assisting suicide. They also highlighted the problematic nature of the last act test which discriminated against a patient who was physically incapable of committing suicide by herself.

After the case, in which there was after all only a 5–4 majority, some commentators felt that Sue Rodriguez should not have been prevented from pursuing her chosen course;[26] certainly there was a perception, as McLachlin J suggested in her dissenting judgment, that Sue Rodriguez had been made into a scapegoat and was penalised because of the danger that any right granted to her would be abused by others (McLachlin J at 417).

Two subsequent events were particularly significant in demonstrating that perhaps, in her case, it would have been at the least morally permissible to have allowed her request. Firstly, that Sue Rodriguez did commit suicide in February 1994 with the assistance of an anonymous doctor who was not charged and secondly, that the dissenting judgments were endorsed by some of the members of the Special Senate Committee on Assisted Suicide and Euthanasia in their Report *Of Life and Death* in 1995.

Upholding the acts/omissions distinction as a distinguishing factor: Dianne Pretty v DPP

In this UK case, Dianne Pretty challenged firstly, the Director of Public Prosecution's refusal to undertake that he would not prosecute Mr Pretty for assisting in his wife's suicide. Secondly, that s 2(1) of the Suicide Act 1961 was incompatible with the European Convention on Human Rights (ECHR) and/or alternatively that applying s 2(1) of the Act was, in any event, a breach of Articles 2, 3, 8, 9, and 14 of the ECHR. The High Court (in *Dianne Pretty v DPP* [2001] WL 1171775 (1)), the House of Lords (in *Dianne Pretty* v DPP [2001] WL 1423045 (2)) and the European Court of Human Rights (*Pretty v The UK* (Application No. 2346/02 (3)) all dismissed the case.

The High Court and House of Lords decisions in brief

The first ground – the DPP's refusal to give an undertaking

Under s 2(4) of the Suicide Act, proceedings can only be instituted with the consent of the DPP. Liberty, which was acting on behalf of Dianne Pretty, wrote to the DPP asking him to undertake that he would not consent to a prosecution against Mr Pretty if he aided and abetted in her death. The DPP refused to give the undertaking, relying on s 3 Prosecution of Offences Act 1985 as the statutory provision which regulates his duties. The DPP's job is to institute and conduct criminal proceedings; he can only, therefore, function under s 2(4) when the offence has been committed. The judges in the High Court and House of Lords thus perceived the request by Mrs Pretty as requiring the DPP to grant a pardon or dispensation in advance. On this ground, therefore, they held that the DPP had no authority to grant it (*Pretty* (1) *per* Tuckey LJ at para 24; *Pretty* (2) *per* Lord Steyn at para 66).

---

26 See, for example, Martel 2001: 149.

The second ground – incompatibility of s 2(1) with the ECHR provisions

The second ground was that s 2 of the Suicide Act, which imposed a blanket ban on all assisted suicides, was incompatible with the ECHR and/or that the DPP, as a public authority which had refused to give the undertaking, had acted incompatibly with a convention right under s 6 Human Rights Act 1998. In both the High Court and the House of Lords, it was held that s 2 (1) of the Suicide Act was not incompatible with the relevant ECHR provisions and that for the same reasons given to dismiss the first ground, the DPP had not acted incompatibly under s 6(1) when he refused to give the undertaking.

In the High Court, Tuckey LJ said that in the conflict between the right to life and the right for an individual to do what she wants with her own body, the former takes priority. As a person cannot consent to her own death:

> [her] wishes are therefore not determinative of what can or must be done. The crucial distinction is between 'killing and letting die'. English law puts helping someone to take her own life on the wrong side of the line . . .
> (*Pretty* (1) at para 37)

In his analysis of Article 2 specifically, Tuckey LJ thought that there might be a way to support a distinction between assisted suicide and voluntary euthanasia,[27] because in the former, the suicidee is deprived of her life by her own act. The absolute prohibition against assisted suicide in s 2(1) could therefore be relaxed in some cases. However, he said that Mrs Pretty, in order to succeed in her claim, must have been able to show that the state had an obligation to relax the prohibition and she could not do this because the right to life protected in the article does not include the right to death. As he said:

> Article 2 is all in terms of protecting life, at the very least permitting life to take its course without active intervention to bring it to a premature end. There is nothing in the article to suggest that the state is obliged to allow someone to help another person bring their own life to a premature end. Indeed, if the article did have that effect it would . . . prohibit English law from allowing would-be suicides to be rescued . . . It

---

27 Although later in his judgment he expresses doubt as to whether a distinction should be drawn between them (*Pretty* (1) at para 62), this is evidently because of the lack of information about the proposed assistance. As Tuckey LJ noted, '[w]e are not being asked to approve physician assisted suicide in carefully defined circumstances with carefully defined safeguards. We are being asked to allow a family member to help a loved one die, in circumstances of which we know nothing, in a way of which we know nothing, and with no outside scrutiny by any outside person' (para 60). Lord Hope made the same point in the House of Lords (*Pretty* (2) at para 95).

is one thing to say that a person may passively accept death by refusing life saving or life prolonging treatment. It is another to say that we must stand idly by and let her take her own life.

(Pretty (1) per Tuckey LJ at paras 41–3)

In the House of Lords, both Lords Steyn (*Pretty* (2) at para 55) and Lord Bingham also emphasised the importance of the acts/omissions distinction, the latter saying that the distinction between ceasing '. . . life-saving or life-prolonging treatment on the one hand and the taking of action . . . intended solely to terminate life on the other' was a principle which was 'deeply embedded in English law' (*Pretty* (2) at para 9).

The alternative second ground – that s 2(1) breached Arts 2, 3, 8, 9, and 14 ECHR

Again, both courts held that s 2(1) did not breach Articles 2, 3, 8, 9, or 14 of the European Convention. In the House of Lords, Lord Bingham held that Article 2 was not infringed because it supported a right to life and not death (*Pretty* (2) at para 5); Article 3 because the DPP's refusal not to prosecute did not fall within the negative prohibition of the Article (para 14). Article 8 was not breached because it protects autonomy while an individual is living his life; it does not refer to the choice to shorten that life (*Pretty* (2) at para 23).[28] Similarly, there was no violation of Article 9 because Mrs Pretty's belief in the virtue of assisted suicide could not require that her husband be absolved from offending (*Pretty* (2) at para 31). As to Article 14, Lord Bingham held that it was not infringed because (a) Mrs Pretty's argument (that the Article was discriminatory because it prevented the disabled, but not the able-bodied, from exercising their right to commit suicide) relied on a misconception that the law confers a right to commit suicide, which it does not; (b) that Article 14 is not 'free-standing'; it has effect only in relation to other Convention rights, so if they are not breached, then neither is Article 14 (and there was extensive Strasbourg authority on this point); and (c) that s 2(1) Suicide Act does not treat people discriminatorily because it applies to all (*Pretty* (2) at paras 35 and 36).[29]

Lord Bingham also confirmed that the UK's policy on assisted suicide was exactly the same as in the rest of Europe (barring the Netherlands, but the

---

28   Whereas Tuckey LJ in the High Court found the judgments in *Rodriguez* useful (*Pretty* (1) at para 60), in his analysis of Article 8, Lord Bingham's views on *Rodriguez* were confusing; he appeared on the one hand to accept the majority judgment, but on the other, then seemed to distinguish the case on the basis of the dissimilarity of relevant legislative provisions (*Pretty* (2) at para 23).

29   See Pedain's contrary argument (2003).

circumstances of this case would not have qualified there either). Both he and Lord Hope emphasised that one of the aims of s 2(1) is to avoid abuse and to protect the weak and vulnerable, and while conceding that Mrs Pretty, as a competent adult, was not necessarily weak or vulnerable, nonetheless, a complete blanket ban on assisted suicide was the only way in which to achieve that aim.

Another aim of the section, and indeed of the Articles in the ECHR, was and is to preserve life. If the DPP allowed any exceptions to assisted suicide, this could open the gates to other such requests. It was therefore a proportionate response for Parliament to conclude that the public interest could only be met by a complete prohibition on assisted suicide (*Pretty* (2) at paras 96–7).

Pretty v UK – *the European Court of Human Rights' decision in brief*

The first ground – the DPP's refusal to give an undertaking

The European Court simply held that the DPP's refusal was not a disproportionate, arbitrary or unreasonable response bearing in mind the seriousness of what was proposed.

The second ground

The European Court, like the two UK courts, held that s 2(1) was not incompatible with and neither did it violate any of the challenged ECHR articles. Article 2 was not infringed because the right to life does not include a right to death (*Pretty* (3) at para 40); Article 3 because it imposed no positive obligation on the state to give the undertaking not to prosecute (*Pretty* (3) at para 56); Article 8 was not breached because the state's prevention of suicide was held to be 'necessary in a democratic society' for the protection of the rights of others under Article 8(2) (*Pretty* (3) at para 78). As to Article 9, again, this was not violated as Mrs Pretty's belief in assisted suicide did not come within those beliefs protected by the Article (*Pretty* (3) at para 82). Finally, her challenge under Article 14 failed because the court found there was sufficient justification for not distinguishing between those who could and those who could not physically commit suicide. The court felt that '[s]trong arguments based on the rule of law could be raised against any claim by the executive to exempt individuals or classes of individuals from the operation of the law'. It further stated that:

> [t]he borderline between the two categories would often be a very fine one and to seek to build into the law an exemption for those judged to be incapable of committing suicide would seriously undermine the

protection of life which the 1961 Act was intended to safeguard and greatly increase the risk of abuse.

(*Pretty* (3) at para 88)

The European Court of Human Rights thus effectively held that it would not approve of any individual exceptions to the Suicide Act and concluded that the UK's blanket ban on assisted suicide was a proportionate response with which to satisfy legitimate government interests.

Comments

Because the provisions on aiding and abetting suicide are analysed in light of the Articles in the ECHR, the judgments in *Pretty* have a different focus to pre-Human Rights Act cases. Nonetheless, in their analysis of Article 2, Tuckey LJ in the High Court and Lords Bingham and Steyn in the House of Lords all reiterated the importance of the distinction that has traditionally been made in the courts between killing and letting die, and this predictably formed one of the bases of the decision. Equally predictable, perhaps, was the courts' criticism of the lack of information given as to how it was proposed that Mr Pretty would assist his wife to commit suicide.[30] In the High Court, when Tuckey LJ asked for specifics, he was told by Mrs Pretty's counsel that the court had been told all that it needed to know. In the House of Lords, both Lords Hope and Hobhouse commented that even if he had been authorised to give the undertaking not to prosecute, the DPP possessed insufficient information or evidence about the proposed offence. Lord Hobhouse feared that further investigation would be necessary to ascertain whether in fact '. . . the death of the appellant had in truth been by suicide and what . . . had been the actual participation of Mr Pretty' (*Pretty* (2) at para 119).

Although this led the judges in both the High Court and the House of Lords to doubt the distinction between assisted suicide and euthanasia in this particular case (*Pretty* (2) *per* Lord Hope at para 95, and *Pretty* (1) *per* Tuckey LJ as above), the decision would not have been any different had they been given that information; as a direct challenge to assisted suicide legislation the result itself (as with the other cases above which have challenged assisted suicide legislation) was hardly unexpected. However, like *Rodriguez*, it is the type of case which can be readily cited in support of allowing positive assistance with death under carefully defined circumstances to 'qualifying'

---

30 Lord Hobhouse, *Pretty* (2) at para 123, also criticised the use of the judicial review procedure in this case as it sought to avoid and undermine 'the proper and fair management of our criminal justice system'.

individuals, although the idea of permitting any exceptions to legislation was specifically rejected in both cases.[31]

Distinguishing factors and the need for reform

Although distinctions based on intention, causation, acts/omissions (and the last act) may be tenuous, they are nonetheless widely accepted as the bases of the difference between withdrawing treatment and aiding and abetting/assisted suicide on the one hand and between aiding and abetting/assisted suicide and euthanasia on the other.

Although it has been conceded (in *Pretty*, for example) that there is no clear distinction between assisting suicide and voluntary euthanasia, there are nonetheless practical and psychological distinctions between them. The first is manifested in the different legal consequences for each offence (a mandatory life sentence as against a maximum of 14 years). The second is demonstrated in a number of surveys which show that whereas patients prefer doctors to perform euthanasia, doctors prefer to assist their patient's suicides.[32] Thirdly – and despite the previous point – the majority of proposals to change the law tend to focus on legalising assisted suicide rather than euthanasia (probably because it is seen as not quite such a 'drastic' option).[33] (Docker 1996: 140).

Advocates of legalisation of aiding and abetting/assisted suicide claim that the tide of public opinion seems to favour a change in the law (despite the House of Lords' argument to the contrary in *Pretty v DPP* and the doubts expressed by the HLSC (2005) (see below)). They also claim that arguments for permitting assisted suicide, certainly for compassionate reasons, are being more readily accepted. This has been demonstrated to some extent in the US where, for example, District Attorneys are unwilling to prosecute defendants where the case involves a terminally ill patient (Smith, G.P. 1989: 311), and in the UK courts, where leniency has been shown in cases exhibiting a compassionate motive.

It is obvious that something further will have to be done about the law relating to assisted dying if the exodus by UK citizens to the Dignitas clinic in Switzerland is to be stopped. Assisted suicide is not prosecuted in that

---

31 On the grounds that any benefits to the few were not sufficient justification to risk abuses to the many vulnerable people who would then be affected. See Kamisar (1995). Another argument is that allowing individual exceptions would diminish the force of the law – Cranford (1996). See Feinberg's criticism of this in Feinberg 1991: 133.

32 For evidence of this see, for example, Macdonald 1998: 73 and Dickinson *et al* 1997–98: 206.

33 Significantly, the BMA changed its policy of opposition to legislation to one of neutrality in October 2005; www.bma.org.uk/ap.nsf/content/AssistedDyingDebate (accessed 3 April 2006), but during its June 2006 Annual Representative Meeting in Belfast, it reverted to its previous policy of opposition to legalising either assisted suicide or euthanasia in the UK.

country if it is carried out by non-medical personnel for altruistic purposes and, as there is no residency requirement and the Dignitas membership payment is relatively low, it is an option which has been, up to January of 2006, exercised by 42 Britons.[34] Neither the UK courts nor local authorities have the power to prevent competent persons from leaving the country to pursue this course of action, as was held in *Re Z (An Adult: Capacity)*. Here, Hedley J removed an injunction granted to a local authority which prevented Mr Z from taking his wife out of the UK, holding that as Mrs Z was competent to make her own decisions, there was no legal basis for prohibiting her from going to Switzerland to commit suicide. The local authority's only obligation was to draw to the police's attention the fact that a criminal offence of aiding and abetting suicide might be involved.

The *Re Z* decision upholds s 2 of the Suicide Act; it does not change the law, although one commentator has argued that:

> ... *Re Z* takes a step ... towards limited judicial tolerance of assisted suicide for a physically disabled and chronically ill patient who has made a legally competent decision to go abroad for the purposes of an assisted suicide. It has done this by removing any legal obstacle which might have prevented that purpose being carried out.
>
> (De Cruz 2005: 266)

Hedley J did hint that it would not be in the public interest to prosecute Mr Z on his return to the UK (para 14) and it is significant that no other family members who have accompanied patients to the Dignitas clinic have been prosecuted under the Suicide Act either. Does this mean that a non-prosecution policy is being adopted? Or that there is a limited acceptance of assisted suicide (as long as it does not take place in the UK), or is it time to clarify these problematic categorisations and distinguishing factors by legalising aiding and abetting/assisted suicide?

Legalisation of/amendments to the Suicide Act?

There have been a number of proposals to amend the Suicide Act, for example:

(a) to make it a defence to any charge under s 2(1) that the accused acted on behalf of the suicidee and, in so doing, behaved reasonably, with compassion and in good faith (the Suicide Act (Amendment) Bill 1985);[35] alternatively:

---

34 *The Independent* 25 January 2006 in its report on Ann Turner. See also perhaps the most publicised case of Reginald Crewe for which see, for example (2003) 326 BMJ 271.
35 Introduced by Lord Jenkins. The Bill was unsuccessful. See Otlowski 1994: 176 for further discussion.

(b) that physician-assisted suicide should be removed from the statute book altogether; (Weir 1992: 125); alternatively again:
(c) that there should be a defence analogous to 'mercy' in circumstances where the motive is compassionate (Horder 1988: 309);[36] or
(d) to amend s 2 to exclude from its provisions '. . . a doctor who in good faith, accedes to a request made by a patient suffering from incurable physical illness, to be given assistance in terminating his life . . .' (Barrington 1986: 240–1).

This is similar to the option favoured in the most recent attempt at legalisation contained in the Assisted Dying for the Terminally Ill Bill 2005 (HL Bill 36) introduced as a Private Member's Bill into the House of Lords by Lord Joffe. According to the Long Title, the aim of the Bill is '[t]o enable an adult who has capacity and who is suffering unbearably as a result of terminal illness to receive medical assistance to die at his own considered and persistent request . . .' The Bill provides that a physician can prescribe medication (or provide the means of self-administration if the patient is physically unable to swallow) to assist a 'qualifying patient' to die. In order to qualify, the patient must be competent and have a terminal illness from which his unbearable suffering directly arises. The Bill also provides that s 2 of the Suicide Act should be amended to exclude from liability those who act under the provisions of the Bill.

The Bill has a protracted history in that it was first introduced as the Patient (Assisted Dying) Bill in 2003 (HL Bill 37). It did not progress, and was subsequently revised and re-introduced as the Assisted Dying for the Terminally Ill Bill in 2004. The Bill ran out of time, but was in the meantime the subject of a review conducted by a House of Lords Select Committee especially set up to consider it and to make recommendations for the future should the Bill be re-introduced (HL Paper 86-I (2005)). In a thorough review of the law both in the UK and abroad, and in a detailed examination of the proposals contained in the Bill, the Select Committee highlighted some of the problems and made a number of recommendations:

(a) The provisions did not clearly distinguish between assisted suicide and voluntary euthanasia.
(b) A clearer explanation of what the physician can and cannot do is required.
(c) The Select Committee was unhappy that the terminology used was not sufficiently clear or precise. For example, the term 'qualifying people' did not say who was included and who not (would it include prisoners?) and a more precise definition of 'terminal illness' is needed (the Select

---

36 And see Laing's response to what she calls his 'Complete Defence Thesis' in 'Assisting suicide' (1990).

Committee heard evidence on the problems in defining terminal illness, particularly in cases of degenerative diseases where the margin for error is greater and noted that in many cases, while unbearable suffering may well be present, it may not necessarily derive from the terminal illness, 'but simply exist alongside it' (para 130).

(d) 'Suffering unbearably' as a subjective qualification, should be replaced by 'unrelievable' or 'intractable' suffering, either of which would enable a more objective assessment to be made.

(e) The definition of competence 'should take into account the need to iden-tify applicants suffering from psychological or psychiatric disorder as well as a need for mental capacity'.[37]

Some of these recommendations have been addressed (but not all specifically as recommended) and the House of Lords, upon the re-introduction of the Bill, have delayed its second reading for six months, as from 12 May 2006.

Problems with legalisation

Perhaps the most common objection to legalisation is the danger of possible abuse inherent in the 'slippery slope'/thin end of the wedge argument. There is significant literature on this, but one wonders whether too much is made of it;[38] constant developments in the medical field and changing societal atti-tudes show how things move on. In the medical context, had we not moved along the slope (Landsman 1986: 145),[39] an increasing number of patients would still be suffering.

Secondly, and as noted by the HLSC, the wording of any legislation would have to be as clear as possible in order to keep ambiguities to a minimum. In Oregon, the first place in the world to legalise physician-assisted suicide for terminally ill patients, the Death with Dignity Act 1994, although said to be the 'most tightly drafted piece of physician-assisted death legislation' to come before the people of the USA (Smith C.K. 1996: 82), allows doctors to pre-scribe drugs to patients 'suffering from a terminal illness' who are 'experi-encing pain, suffering and/or distress' that is severe and 'unacceptable to the patient'.[40] It is restricted to patients in the last six months of life and it is this

---

37 These and other recommendations are in para 269 of the Report.
38 Keown's view of the position in the Netherlands is a classic example. Keown (1995). For a contrary view see van Delden *et al* 2004: 202, and for more on slippery slopes generally, see Smith (2005) and Orentlicher and Callahan (2004).
39 However, see Morgan 1992: 1448, who said: 'There is no slippery slope more perilous than that which is falsely supposed not to be slippery.'
40 Smith was a primary drafter of the Oregon Death with Dignity Act 1994 (which came into force in 1997 after various challenges) and which still faces attempts to repeal it. For a more up-to-date review, see, for example, Rothschild (2004).

restriction which has perhaps caused the greatest criticism of the Oregon legislation (Scofield 1995: 483);[41] it excludes patients who are suffering from a degenerative disease which is not 'terminal'[42] (the definition of terminal being itself problematic). If patients who are suffering from degenerative diseases are permitted to forgo life-sustaining treatments, they should not be prohibited from requesting physician-assisted suicide. Patients (like, for example, Sue Rodriguez and Dianne Pretty) should not be denied this right or liberty simply because they cannot perform the last death-causing act themselves (Kamisar 1995: 250–1).[43] Thirdly, legalisation of assisted suicide would not necessarily mean that doctors would obey that legislation any more than they do any other. Certainly, as a practice that tends to be carried out in private, it would be very difficult to regulate. Fourthly, a patient could still be subject to outside pressures whether physician-assisted suicide is legalised or not, and finally, the problems in ascertaining subjective conditions will persist even if assisted dying is legalised. How can a practice which depends on the individual patient's word that his pain is unbearable, or that he really wants to die, be objectively verified?[44]

Conclusion

The complexities of the law relating to aiding and abetting/assisting suicide are evident. The existence of technology and the availability of more sophisticated treatments which can prolong what can be a painful life have resulted in an increase in the number of people who choose to die earlier as a result of some terminal or long-term debilitating disease. That a number of these are physically unable to commit suicide and are often hospitalised means that doctors are, and will in the future, be asked more often to participate in events which result in their patients' deaths. Whether this is called assisted suicide or voluntary euthanasia really makes no difference, because at least both these 'labels' acknowledge that doctors are already involved in death-inducing activities. The distinction which is most problematic, however, is the one the courts constantly uphold and which blatantly denies any wrongdoing. That

---

41 It has also been criticised for encouraging secrecy and the lack of enforcement of reporting procedures by Hendin *et al* (1998). For up-to-date statistics see Tolle *et al* (2004).

42 Legislation which is limited to terminally ill patients is not wide enough for a number of other reasons as well. For example, it ignores the consequences of developing technology; it ignores demographic changes in so far as people are living longer lives while suffering from more chronic, degenerative diseases; see Weir 1992: 123. Including patients who are not 'terminally' ill would acknowledge that long-lasting debilitating illnesses, while not necessarily painful in themselves, nonetheless cause immense long-term suffering. It would also recognise the growing relevance of quality of life and would avoid the need to define the meaning of 'terminal'.

43 Compare Price 1996: 271.

44 These objections to legalisation are set out by Callahan and White 1996: 8–11.

distinction – between withdrawing treatment and assisting suicide – is said to be based on intention and causation, but these have been interpreted in so many conflicting, contradictory and circular ways that even the judges (as was seen in *Washington v Glucksberg* and *Vacco v Quill*) are hard pressed to 'hold the line' (Jennings 1991: 312).

It is time for all of us (but particularly judges) to admit that some cases of treatment refusal are suicides and that doctors do actively and compassionately assist in this. Over-reliance on traditional criminal definitions of intention, twisted notions of causation and denial of the significance of motive and context, provide judges with a screen behind which they can continue to pretend that assisted suicide and euthanasia are not already occurring in our hospitals every day. Why would doctors need to rely on the principle of double effect and the acts/omissions distinction if they were not already assisting in their patients' deaths?

Doctors are already exempted from the provisions of the criminal law by virtue of these informal 'defences', but they need to be formalised in a way which would explicitly consider motive and other situational factors as aids in ascertaining intention and in ascribing cause. Although these are said to be the key distinguishing factors in a variety of end-of-life practices, it has been seen that intention and causation are unable to stand alone.

Chapter 7

Reforms and the future

Intentions cannot be assessed in isolation from the other components of moral events. They must be related to the nature of the act in question, the circumstances under which it is performed and its consequences.

(Pellegrino 1996: 180)

Introduction

In the UK, no distinction is made between euthanasia and murder because, as a deliberate killing, it is put in the same class as murder irrespective of any distinctions between them. While it has to be conceded that both euthanasia and murder involve intentional killing, there are nonetheless very obvious differences between them which are manifested in the 'victim's' consent, the presence of compassionate motives, the context in which the death takes place and the circumstances of the person who dies. A just legal system should acknowledge these conceptual distinctions by formally treating differently those people who are affected by them (Murphy 1987: 7).[1]

Where the medical profession is concerned, a refusal to recognise these distinctions has led to the development of dubious ploys and informal 'defences' being applied to one specific profession. Where lay persons are involved, it has led to a circumvention of the law by judges who impose a minimal non-custodial sentence, and by juries who can exercise their right of 'nullification' (acquitting despite legal guilt) (Schopp 1998: chapter 7) by refusing to convict. These so called 'perverse' verdicts emerge where law and morality conflict, but, in reality, they are just a reflection of the irreconcil-ability of '. . . a legal system which ignores the underlying moral aspects of particular offences' (Norrie 2001: 45) and which has remained static in the face of technological developments, changes in societal values, and perceptions of what crime is.

---

1 A new 7th edition of *Philosophy and Law* was published in 2004, but the editors (Feinberg J. and Coleman J.) concede in the preface: *ix*, that it is an 'extensive and substantial revision' using new authors and selections.

Our understanding of what crime is changes with the passing of time (Croall 1998: 5);[2] as Jones has said, '. . . the content of the criminal law is not set in stone' (Jones 2006: 32). However, it appears to be so in the UK where the law has remained unchanged, despite evidence of shifting attitudes towards assisted suicide in particular (and, to a lesser extent, euthanasia) and challenges to the constitutionality and legality of laws which prohibit it.

It has been said that '. . . law is . . . an expression of society's feelings and needs' (Friedman 1971: 19), a '. . . codification of the will of the people . . .' (Davies 1995: 83). As such, there is an expectation that as society's values change, so the law should evolve in order to accord with those values.[3] This has been conceded even in the House of Lords where Lord Lowry said that '[i]t is important, particularly in the area of criminal law which governs conduct, that society's notion of what is the law, and what is right, should coincide' (*Bland* at 379–80).[4]

There is a growing recognition, however, that society and law are 'out of step' with each other (Watson 1977: 130–2) and this will continue while the relevance of consent and context, role and motive are persistently denied; ignoring these factors demonstrates how inappropriate it is to criminalise the behaviour of doctors in the performance of their duties. This chapter will therefore provide a recap of the present position, will consider various reform suggestions which have been advanced and will set out a tentative proposal for change which identifies key concerns.

The present position

'Principles need to precede practice, not to be reinterpreted to fit existing practices' (Docker 1996: 146)

As has already been argued, instinct and morally-based intuition play a large part in initially deciding whether conduct is acceptable or not. Once this has been done, the conduct is then fitted into a preconceived category which, ironically, has nothing whatsoever to do with the intention of the agent. As Ann Davies has said:

> . . . though we profess to be basing our assessments of other people's actions on our beliefs about their motives and intentions, it may, in fact, be our antecedent . . . views about what is and is not permissible that determine how we characterise agents' motives and intentions, and not vice versa.
>
> (Davies 1996: 119)

2 As White and Haines 2004: 7 say, '[c]rime is . . . an offence of the time' (and they use witchcraft as an example).
3 See, for example, Lord Keith in *R v R (Rape: Marital Exemption)* ([1992] 1 AC 599): 616D.
4 See also Lord Bingham in *R v G* ([2003] 4 All ER 765): para 33.

In other words, in such cases, judicial decision-making unacceptably involves a construction of justice rather than an objective assessment according to the precepts of the law. The courts will make a decision as to the result they desire before defining the law in whatever way happens to achieve that desired result, based on preconceived criteria and socio-political policy judgments, which in turn are usually founded on the need to punish a culpable person. The cases examined in this book indicate that there is a tendency to exculpate doctors (and the police, and indeed lay persons where they have shown a commendable motive of which the court approves) because they are perceived by judges and juries as being non-culpable. It has been seen already that judges stretch intention in doctor/murder cases so that they can ascribe liability only where behaviour is deemed to be blameworthy. Certainly, with increased media coverage of controversial cases involving doctors who have allegedly hastened their patients' deaths, it will become progressively more difficult for the courts to justify their reasons for applying the law so inconsistently. Statutorily acknowledging the uniqueness of the doctor's role in society would go a long way to achieving the uniformity which is lacking as a result of the present ad hoc judicial decision-making. It would also avoid a significant degree of judicial law-making in this area of the law where principles have been manipulated, and precedents have been created to fill the legislative gap.

Judicial practices and precedents

Sanctity v quality

As Parliament has made its intention not to intervene in these matters perfectly clear, judges have been left to make and develop law[5] where they consider it appropriate to do so. Whereas it may be considered trite to say that this is undemocratic, such practices can nonetheless provide solutions to new (particularly medical) questions where the legislature has not provided a resolution. Moreover, these are solutions which, depending upon the circumstances of the case, are deemed by most people[6] to be acceptable and right, although they do stretch existing legal principles excessively.

With the passing of time, and to counter the increasing legal problems raised by developing medical technology, judges have not only had to abandon traditional doctrines such as the supremacy of the sanctity of life,[7] but

---

5 And likewise with defences; Lord Mustill said in *R v Kingston* ([1994] 3 All ER 353): 370 that the court could recognise a new defence 'if practical and just' and if 'judicial decision rather than legislation is the proper medium'.

6 See, for example, the results of the survey carried out by Donnison and Bryson 1996/7: 175.

7 Which now has to give way to quality of life; see, for example, the cases listed in s 2(b) chapter 3 above at page 76 and *Re C (A Minor) (Medical Treatment – Refusal of Parental Consent)* ([1997] 8 Med LR 166): 170.

now also have to accept certain medical practices which were in the past considered to be abhorrent.

An examination of some of the relevant cases illustrates these two claims, beginning (chronologically) with *Re B (A Minor) (Wardship: Medical Treatment)* ([1981] 1 WLR 1421), where the parents of a Downs Syndrome baby refused consent to have an intestinal blockage removed. The baby was not terminally ill and was said to be capable of living a 'normal' life following surgery. The court allowed the appeal, Templeman J expressing his, by now, well-known *dicta* that:

> The decision . . . lies with . . . the court, to decide whether the life of this child is demonstrably going to be so awful that in effect the child must be condemned to die, or whether the life of this child is still so imponderable that it would be wrong for her to be condemned to die. Faced with a choice of either allowing the operation which may result in 20 or 30 years, or to terminate her life because she has an intestinal complaint, it is the court's duty to decide that the child must live.
>
> (*Re B per* Templeman J at 1424)

Some years later in *Re C (A Minor) (Wardship: Medical Treatment)* ([1989] 3 WLR 240), Lord Donaldson MR, in distinguishing *Re B*, considered that the quality of life of another baby, this time suffering from hydrocephalus, would be 'demonstrably awful and intolerable . . .' and balanced the short-term gain of treatment against the needless prolongation of suffering in ascertaining the baby's best interests (Lord Donaldson MR at 245–6).

Lord Donaldson subsequently considered both cases in *Re J (A Minor) (Wardship: Medical Treatment)* ([1990] 3 All ER 930), where he concluded that while *Re B* was on one end of a scale (where the baby was handicapped but had a reasonable expectation of life), *Re C* was at the other end of the scale (where the child was dying and continuation of treatment could only postpone that death). *Re J* came somewhere in the middle of that scale as the child was severely brain damaged, but was not dying.

Lord Donaldson, in approving *Re B*, said that the child's best interests should be ascertained by balancing the pain and suffering of continued treatment against the pain, suffering and quality of the child's life if it were to be prolonged. In basing the decision on what the child would do if he were able to make a decision, Lord Donaldson inappropriately advances the substituted judgment test. However, he must be praised for at least basing his reasoning on the perceived quality of life of a disabled person as opposed to one who was not disabled.[8]

---

8 Lord Donaldson quotes from McKenzie J's judgment in the Canadian case of *Re Superintendent of Family and Child Services and Dawson* ([1983] 145 DLR (3rd) 610): 620–1. See

In the same case, Taylor LJ stated that the criteria for decision-making '. . . must be a matter of degree'. At what point in the scale of disability and suffering ought the court to hold that the best interests of the child do not require further endurance to be imposed by positive treatment to prolong its life?' He answered the question by holding that:

> Where a ward of court suffered from physical disabilities so grave that his life would from his point of view be so intolerable if he were to continue living that he would choose to die if he were in a position to make a sound judgment, the court could direct that treatment without which death would ensue from natural causes need not be given to prolong his life, even though he was neither on the point of death or dying.
>
> (*Re J per* Taylor LJ at 931)

Essentially, these three cases formed the benchmark for the numerous cases which followed, such as for example, *Re C (A Baby)* ([1996] 2 FLR 43); *Re R (Adult) (Medical Treatment)* ([1996] 2 FLR 99), and *An NHS Trust v D and Others* ([2000] Lloyds Law Rep (Med) 411)[9] (to name but three) and which culminated most recently with the cases of *Winston-Jones; Re L (Medical Treatment: Benefit)* (both heard on the same day); *Wyatt* and *An NHS Trust v MB* (where, unusually, Holman J refused to grant a declaration to discontinue MB's ventilation). As with the earlier treatment withdrawal cases, the court continues to adopt the practice of weighing the benefits of continued life against the burdens of treatment (and this was especially evident in *An NHS Trust v MB*) in what is essentially a quality of life judgment.

'The "law" of Bioethical Entropy' (Ling 2002: 205)

Over the last 25 years or so, new technological developments and 'treatments' have seen the medical profession and the courts having to familiarise themselves with and decide upon end-of-life options which did not previously exist. Over time, and with constantly moving parameters, a consequence of this has been that practices which once would have been considered unacceptable are now condoned and accepted by the medical profession and by the courts. This is what Ling calls the law of bioethical entropy, the five stages of which he labels as: unthinkable, tolerated, permitted, expected and required (Ling 2002:

also Arabian J in *Thor* (1993): 28. Care has to be taken to ensure that disabled persons' lives are not devalued and that standards of non-disabled persons are not imposed upon them. To do so would leave the door open to the danger of disposing of 'burdensome' people (see Young and Ogden 1998: 23), or people whose lives are deemed worthless (and see Beezer CJ in *Compassion in Dying v Washington* (1996): 856 for simply 'utilitarian' reasons).

9 The latter distinguishing *R v Portsmouth Hospital NHS Trust ex p Glass* (1).

205). Essentially what this means is that people become accustomed to, or become comfortable with one particular step or stage of treatments before moving on and doing the same thing with the next stage. This 'psychological adjustment' to practices previously considered objectionable[10] (Clouser 1991: 307) become so habitual that any guilt formerly experienced simply disappears.[11]

The cases show clearly how these condoned stages have extended from withholding treatment to withdrawing treatment, to withholding non-extraordinary treatment (such as Do Not Resuscitate Orders and antibiotics) before moving on to withholding artificial nutrition and hydration. It is now acceptable not merely for a terminally ill patient to refuse treatment, but a patient who is not terminally ill or dying is also permitted to do so. It is also permissible for a patient to refuse life-sustaining food and water. Similarly in PVS cases, there have been instances where artificial nutrition and hydration has been withdrawn under *Bland* principles where definitional requirements were not satisfied and the patient was only in a 'near persistent vegetative state'. Thus, having moved up each step and approved of non-voluntary passive euthanasia (Docker 1996: 139), the only remaining hurdle would appear to be the legalisation of assisted suicide (see previous chapter) or of active euthanasia.

Reform suggestions

Legalising euthanasia

The only two countries which have passed euthanasia legislation are the Netherlands and Belgium. However, contrary to popular belief, the practice has not been legalised in either. Rather, both the Dutch Termination of Life on Request and Assisted Suicide (Review Procedures) Act 2001[12] and the Belgian Euthanasia Act 2002[13] create exceptions to their respective Criminal Codes where doctors have complied with the requisite procedures.

Legalising euthanasia is perhaps the most radical suggestion for reform, and in the UK, despite the introduction of numerous Bills into Parliament[14] (and it has to be said that the majority of these relate to assisted suicide, and

10 See Allman 1998: 21 and Cantor (2001) who lists how and which practices have become tolerated in the last 25 years.
11 The danger of this are set out by Gillet 1988: 66. See also Grossman 1995: 244.
12 For analyses of the legislation, see, for example, De Haan (2002) and Legemaate (2004).
13 For an analysis, see Adams and Nys (2003).
14 For example, the Voluntary Euthanasia Bill 1993 (no second reading), Doctor Assisted Suicide Bill 1997 (not introduced), Assisted Suicide Bill 1997 (also not introduced), Assisted Suicide Bill 1996 (never introduced into Parliament) and the 2005 Assisted Dying for the Terminally Ill Bill.

not euthanasia), they have all been, to date, unsuccessful. The same problems would apply to legalisation of euthanasia as were noted in relation to assisted suicide in the previous chapter, and although some studies have shown some support for legalisation (Donnison and Bryson 1996/7), there is also evidence which indicates that that support is far from unanimous. Otlowski, in her review of reform options, found that although people accepted the legitimacy of active voluntary euthanasia in some circumstances, there was nonetheless an opposition to its legalisation and a readiness to accept the 'existing discrepancies' and 'subterfuge'. Nonetheless, she concluded that the best option was to legalise active voluntary euthanasia, although she did identify inherent problems (Otlowski 1994: 202–3).[15] Certainly with the speed at which technology is developing, a more valid argument against legislation would be the practicalities attached to the requirement of constantly updating legislation to take account of constantly moving parameters.[16]

Other proposals

As well as the above legislative proposals, there have been a vast number of other more informal suggestions for reform. These include, for example:

(a) taking mercy killing out of the definition of murder (Lawton 1979: 461);
(b) taking euthanasia out of the scope of criminal law;[17]
(c) making it the object of a special defence (The Society of Labour Lawyers' evidence to the Royal Commission on Capital Punishment 1949–53: para 180);
(d) substituting murder and manslaughter with unlawful homicide (Lord Kilbrandon in *Hyam* at 98);[18]
(e) creating a new category of offence called 'killing with compassion' (Boothroyd 1988: 23);
(f) providing immunity from prosecution if the doctor follows certain procedures (Brazier 2003: 53);
(g) creating a Permanent Standing Advisory Committee to draw up a code of practice containing guidelines to review developments and form Working Parties (Kennedy 1983: 128–9);
(h) devising a set of regulations on assisting death with strict requirements of consent (Downie and Sherwin 1996: 324);

15 Otlowski 1994: 202–3. (Both the House of Lords in *Pretty* and the HLSC (2005) felt that there was significant opposition to legalisation.)
16 And that, put simply, we are not ready for such a radical step yet; Hendin and Klerman 1993: 145. Meyers and Mason 2000: 282 have likened the position to the abortion debate before the Abortion Act was passed in 1967.
17 See, for example, Sheldon and Thomson 1998: 281.
18 Compare Blom-Cooper and Morris 2004: 2.

(i) adopting a 'non-prosecution policy where there is no evidence of a "victim" ' (Brahams 1992: 2);
(j) creating a notification system of an intended assisted death to an independent body who would act on the patient's behalf (Eggleston 1994: 8); and
(k) redefining death to include PVS patients.[19]

As can be imagined, this last proposal has incurred significant criticism; a patient in PVS breathes on his own and his heart still beats on its own. On these criteria alone, the patient is still 'alive'.[20] As such, it would be impossible to bury or cremate such a 'person' (Brody 1988: 34).

Other proposals which have been more successfully debated, although not implemented, include creating a mercy killing defence, grading murder (both especially relevant in the light of the most recent 2005 Law Commission Consultation Paper on homicide (2005)), and the necessity 'defence' (also relevant following the cases of *Re A (Children)* and *HL v UK* ((Application No. 45508/99).

A mercy killing defence

A mercy killing defence was proposed by the Royal Commission on Capital Punishment as far back as the late 1940s–early 1950s (1949–53: paras 177–80) and the same proposal was subsequently made by the Criminal Law Revision Committee in 1976 (para 82).[21] As with recommendations to abolish the mandatory life sentence[22] (the aim of which was that judges could exercise discretion after taking into account all the circumstances, including motive and context), this proposal was not implemented, solely on the basis of the perceived difficulties in ascertaining motive. The taboo against motive and context has thus succeeded in denying a solution which may have given legal recognition to the relevance of these two very pertinent considerations.

While previous proposals all recommended a discrete mercy killing defence, the newest proposal from the Law Commission (LCCP No. 177 (2005)) propounds reformulating the diminished responsibility defence by abolishing the requirement in s 2 Homicide Act 1957 (that a person was 'substantially impaired by an abnormality of mental functioning arising from an underlying condition') and changing it to include 'an underlying or

---

19 That is by extending the definition of PVS to include 'neo-cortical' or 'cognitive' death. See, for example, Rumley 2001: 1670.
20 But it is debateable whether he is still a 'person'. A discourse as to 'personhood' is not within the remit of this book, but can be seen, for example, in Harris (1985) chapter 1.
21 Although the CLRC subsequently withdrew that proposal in its 14th Report (1980): para 115.
22 See, for example, the Report of the Advisory Council on the Penal System (1978): para 246 and the HLSC (1993–4): para 261.

pre-existing condition' which would include 'cases in which the origins of the condition itself lie in adverse circumstances with which the offender has had to cope'. As such, the abnormality would cover depression and would thus include, for example, 'a severely depressed husband who has finally given in to his wife's demands that he "put her out of her misery" ' (paras 6.54 and 6.4).

The proposal has much to commend it: firstly, it acknowledges honestly what is already happening under the existing s 2 provision and secondly, it would not entail changing the law drastically to accommodate the circumstances. It does, however, apply only to lay persons and early indications are that the proposal has met with opposition (on the grounds that even with the reformulated definition, it would still require a 'benign conspiracy' to accommodate it).[23] The Commissioners are thus rethinking this proposal.[24]

Grading murder

Another recommendation for reform is the grading of murder into categories which reflect the severity of the offence[25] (Fennell 1990: 337–8). Although rejected as a legislative option (again on the basis that it was considered too difficult to establish motive),[26] the criminal law already exercises a grading function in a number of ways; the different mental elements required for different offences enable grading of different levels of wrongdoing and thus of how severe or lenient the punishment should be (Robinson 1997: 125). Also, offences themselves are graded differently (for example, murder, manslaughter) in order to reflect the seriousness of the offence (Wilson 2002: 139).

Today, it is widely acknowledged that some murders are more heinous than others.[27] The distinction commonly made between the cold-blooded killer and the mercy killer is widely known in academic circles,[28] is recognised by formal bodies,[29] by judges in cases such as *Jennison, Hough* (Lord Lane CJ at 407) and *R v Howe* ([1987] 1 All ER 771 at 781), and by the public. In two

---

23 Law Commission Seminar 24 February 2006, and personal correspondence.
24 Note the relevance of s 269 and Sch 21 Criminal Justice Act 2003 here; one of the mitigating factors to be taken into account in sentencing is whether or not the murder 'was an act of mercy'. The Law Commission recommended that it 'ought to look hard at whether such a mitigating factor should take the crime outside the scope of murder . . . and into manslaughter instead' LCCP No. 177 (2005): para 1.114.
25 See also Duff 1990: 36 and the comments made by the HLSC (1988–9): paras 20–7 on this.
26 Having said that, ironically the aggravating and mitigating factors in Sch 21 Criminal Justice Act 2003 take variations of the gravity of murder into account.
27 See, for example, The Law Commission's Final Report on Partial Defences to Murder No. 290 (2004): para 2.35. The proposals contained in LCCP No. 177 (2005): paras 1.30–1.32 are based on a 'ladder' principle whereby offences are graded according to an ascending ladder of seriousness.
28 For example, Wasik 1982: 37 and Kenny 1978: 87.
29 Such as the Advisory Council on the Penal System (1978): para 244.

surveys carried out by Mitchell (1998: 453) and Pfeifer (Pfeifer *et al* 1996: 119) respectively, compassionate killings were categorised differently from the more terrible types of killing (as they were in the Sugarman study mentioned earlier).

While it has to be conceded that even a compassionate killer has the requisite intent to satisfy the murder definition, there is a clear difference between this kind of killer and the more evil kind, and whereas the law recognises this in sentencing (by virtue of s 12 Criminal Justice Act 2003), it is not acknowledged within the principles which underlie the criminal law such as fair labelling and correspondence, for example. The former '. . . requires that the description of the offence should match the wrong done' (Herring 2006: 19) and the latter '. . . requires a matching-up of D's *mens rea* with the harm for which he is held criminally liable . . .' (Mitchell 1999: 195).[30] In this respect, although euthanasia is carried out with the requisite intent for murder, it has already been seen that intention by itself is not sufficient to differentiate heinous from compassionate killings. As Ashworth notes, '[t]he law must resort to some kind of moral and social evaluation of conduct if it is to identify and separate out the gravest killings' (Ashworth 2006: 260–1). This involves making a value judgment about the defendant's conduct in light of the circumstances giving rise to the event.

Necessity

Another alternative is the common law 'defence' of necessity. This has been the subject of very chequered history of discussion by the Law Commission which in 1974 (Law Com No. 55) saw it as desirable but in 1977 (Law Com No. 83) called for its abolition. Neither of these totally opposing recommendations was implemented and, eight years later, the Law Commission proposed a compromise solution to the effect that necessity should remain a common law matter and that the courts should retain the power they had to develop and clarify the defence (Law Com No. 143 (1985)).

The necessity defence subsequently received judicial backing from the House of Lords in *Re F (Mental Patient: Sterilisation)* ([1990] 2 AC 1: 72–6)[31] and *R v Bournewood Community and Mental Health Trust, ex p L* ([1999] 1 AC 458). However, some doubt was cast on its status as a medical defence when the case progressed to the European Court of Human Rights (*HL v UK*), where it was held that the doctrine of necessity, while 'still developing', did not comply with the requirements of foresight, lawfulness or of avoiding arbitrariness. The Court thus found that Article 5(1) of the ECHR had been breached.

---

30 See also Herring 2006: 216–20, and the further reading indicated there.
31 Lord Keith of Kinkel approved *Re F* (1990) and the principle of necessity when a patient has become incompetent in *Bland* (1993): 361.

Since then, however, the status of the defence has been salvaged somewhat by the Court of Appeal in *Re F (Adult Patient: Jurisdiction)* ([2000] Lloyd's Law Rep (Med) 381) and in *Re A (Children)* where, by conceding that the operation to separate the conjoined twins was an act, the Court had to find some lawful excuse or justification to exonerate the doctors from a murder charge. In so doing, it distinguished *Dudley and Stephens* and *Howe* (the long-standing authorities that necessity was not a defence in murder cases)[32] and, as no other defence was applicable, held that the principle of necessity could be invoked where the doctors' conduct was not harmful because, when faced with a choice of two evils, the choice of avoiding the greater harm was justified.

More recently, necessity has also been endorsed again by the Court of Appeal in *R (On the Application of B) v S and Others* ([2006] EWCA Civ 28) where it was held that the defence was applicable (albeit in the context of the Mental Health Act). This is a justificatory defence which may well prove to be of further use in the future.[33]

The proposal: a special 'defence' or 'dispensation' based on justification?

It is evident that the legislature must take action to remedy the uncertainties and inconsistencies in the law which applies to end-of-life decision-making. In doing so, it is vital that it should consider certain concerns which are central to the success and effectiveness of any reform proposals it makes. At the core of these concerns is the inability of intention and causation, key criminal law principles, to properly maintain and uphold the essential characteristics of a system of law which, like any other, should be above reproach.

One way in which this concern could be addressed would be to ensure explicit consideration of motive, context, role and consent (even if by proxy) in any reform provisions. These would work with intention and causation as aids in the ascertainment of liability and in the ascription of cause. Statutory recognition of their importance would also enable the law to acknowledge that there are variations in culpability even in deliberate killing.

It is simply not feasible to continue pretending that doctors do not kill their patients when they withdraw life-sustaining treatment and increase pain-killing medication. However, this is a different kind of killing from the more terrible cold-blooded murder. 'Medical' killings are ones which occur in con-trolled circumstances, often with the patient's consent. As such, they should not as a matter of principle be labelled in the same way as heinous murders.

---

32 Doubt was also placed on the authority of *R v Dudley and Stephens* ((1884) 14 QBD 273) by the Supreme Court of Canada in *Latimer* (2001) where the necessity defence was nonetheless unsuccessful.
33 See, for example, Ost (2005) and Clarkson (2004).

Creating a new grade of homicide designed to cover such medical mercy killings would provide the basis for categorising these end-of-life events as something other than a murder and would go part of the way to providing doctors with some measure of protection in carrying out their role (provided that they have performed that role in an appropriate and proper manner).

This highlights another concern which is that although members of the medical profession are expected and required to carry out unique functions, they have not been given corresponding (statutory) safeguards,[34] although the number of doctors who have been exculpated from liability for 'killing' their patients has shown that special defences in the form of the principle of double effect and categorisation of acts as omissions are already being applied to absolve them.[35] Specifically incorporating these defences into legislation would answer a number of concerns: it would satisfy principle in so far as it would bring clarity to the law; it would also be explicit in its recognition that (provided certain qualifying conditions are complied with) in recognition of their role, exceptional defences for doctors can be clearly justified. It would satisfy practical aspects in that it would make the most of existing, albeit common law, defences; it would obviate the need to manipulate intention and causation; and it would counter the medical profession's reluctance to a major change in the law.[36]

Another important concern would be the status of such statutory defences. Much has been made of the distinction between justification and excuse in recent years. In strict definitional terms, a defence cannot be justificatory because '[a] justification negates the wrongfulness of the act and denies the element of wrongdoing . . .' (Fletcher 1978: 459).[37] Nonetheless, it would seem to be the more appropriate basis[38] for medical defences for a number of reasons. Firstly, a justification exempts whole 'categories of behaviour' rather than one individual person (Schopp 1998: 30). Secondly, justification can simply absorb intention into its agenda because it does not deny that the act is carried out with the requisite intention (if proved) to satisfy the offence definition. Thirdly, the merit of a justification is dependent on motive, context and

---

34 Reasons for this are given by, for example, Ost 2005: 158.
35 Certainly, it has been widely recognised that the principle of double effect is already operating as a defence; see chapter 2 above. Also, in LCCP No. 177 (2005): paras 4.72–4.91, the Law Commission conceded that doctors in prescribing medication 'have a defence to a charge of murder' and that 'recognition of the doctrine can be made . . . under "Defences" '.
36 Identified by the HLSC (2005).
37 Or, as has been alternatively explained, the conduct is seen as acceptable and right; Schopp 1998: 3 and 30 (although Herring 2006: 734, prefers to say that justifications are 'permissible'). For more on justification (and excuse), see Smith, J.C. 1989: chapter 1; Gardner 1996: 107–8.
38 On justification and culpability, see Clarkson (2004). On the link between motive, culpability and justification, see Sistare (1987) and on the relevance of motive to justification, see Husak (1989).

consent, consideration of which should be included for the reasons set out above. Fourthly, and bearing in mind that (a) a justification is founded on the law's preference for one course of action rather than another and (b) that healthcare professionals face treatment choices every day, a justificatory-based defence would at least acknowledge that the doctor selected the option which results in the least harm (Dressler 1982: 437).[39] Fifthly, therefore, a dispensation based on justification would acknowledge that society does not disapprove of (or at least tolerates) the doctor's conduct.[40] Finally, providing doctors with a legitimate justification can be said to satisfy the principles of correspondence and justice because, even if it was his intention to see his patient die, the doctor's compassionate motive and our perception of him as not being culpable distinguishes him from a cold-blooded murderer.

A new justifying proposal could thus ensure that in his role as a medical professional, a doctor who terminates the life of another should not be guilty of murder, but rather, that he should have a defence to medical mercy killing if he can show that his (compassionate) motive was to save his patient from physical and mental suffering,[41] and that the patient has consented to this course of action.[42]

Situational factors: consent, context and motive in the justificatory 'defence'

Previous chapters have already shown the relevance of consent and context to both justification and motive. That a patient's consent acts as a justification which mitigates a doctor's responsibility is a notion sustained by many.[43] Similarly, context is indispensable in ascertaining motive, as assessing the actor's reasons for acting cannot be ascertained in isolation.[44] The consequence of ignoring motive is the 'objectivisation' of criminal conduct. As Norrie has said (and he is not alone in this):

> . . . criminal responsibility . . . claims to be based upon individual justice

---

39 An essentially utilitarian view, which is debatable if you take the view that death causes the greatest harm, over and above the good of relieving unbearable pain and suffering. The Consultant Neurologist interviewed said: 'If someone doesn't want their life to continue, then I'm not harming them by acceding to their wishes.'

40 See, for example, Kugler 2004: 442.

41 This wording is based on the Society of Labour Lawyers' submission to the Royal Commission on Capital Punishment (1949–53): para 180.

42 As a matter of interest, compare the South Australia Act (Number 26) 1995 which permits life-shortening treatment with the intention of relieving pain and suffering if the patient has consented, if it is administered in good faith and in accordance with professional standards of palliative care.

43 See, for example, Sugarman 1986: 62; Brock 1993: 211; Devettere 1991: 124.

44 See Clarkson 2004: 18–21 on the relevance of context and role.

through the operation of a fault requirement, [yet] it completely ignores a normal mental element in human conduct in its attribution of fault . . . People act from motives and intentions and it is . . . 'childish' to imagine that culpability can be properly evaluated with reference to intention alone. Motive is crucial. . . .

(Norrie 2001: 36 and 44)[45]

Although motive is brought into account at the sentencing stage, the criminal law claims not to take it into account in ascribing liability. However, this is only 'partly true' because (a) there are some offences which specifically require a bad motive and (b) good motives can provide a defence in some instances.[46] This same ambivalence about the role which motive plays in ascribing liability is evident in the cases where some judges have dismissed its relevance,[47] while others have demonstrated its importance. For example, Viscount Maugham in *Crofter Hand Woven Harris Tweed Company Limited v Veitch* ([1942] AC 435 at 452) saw motive and intention as inseparable, and Lord Griffiths in *R v Court* ([1988] 2 All ER 221 at 224) said that '[i]f evidence of motive is available that throws light on the intent, it should be before the jury to assist them in their decision.'

Similarly, the relevance of motive was seen in the cases discussed in the previous chapter (such as *Pratten, Jennison, Lawson* and *Hough*) and in *Adams, Moor, Gillick* (Ashworth 2006: 425) and *Re (A Children)*, where the crucial feature was the doctor's motive. Even though the court showed disapproval of the defendant's motive in *Chandler v DPP* ([1964] AC 763) and *Le Brun*, it was nonetheless a deciding factor, in the same way that the defendant's good motive was a deciding factor in *Steane*. In fact, taking a defendant's good motive into account enables juries to exercise the foresight/intention get-out clause by holding that foresight of virtual certainty is not intention.

In view of the above, judges would have a difficult time defending their position that they do not take motive into account, but having said that, any reform proposals which entailed consideration of motive have all been summarily rejected mainly because of the perceived problems in assessing it. In response, it has to be said that if a jury can infer or find intention (a subjective mental state), they can do exactly the same with motive (also a subjective mental state) (Horder 1988: 313). Certainly, they should be able to recognise when a doctor's motive is both worthy and admirable[48] and whether he is acting for all the right reasons.

---

45 On the relevance of motive generally, see, for example, Gross 1979: 104; Sistare (1987) and Husak (1989).
46 For example, in duress and self-defence, Wilson 2002: 129.
47 See, for example, Farquharson J in *Arthur* (1981): 7 and Lord Mustill in *Bland* (1993): 394.
48 These good motives were identified in the interviews with the Accident and Emergency Consultant, the Consultant Neurologist and the General Practitioner.

Conclusion

It would be very easy simply to allow the present common law solutions to stand, and to maintain the 'middle ground,' as McCall Smith has persuasively argued. He has claimed that the existing practices of increasing pain-killing medication and withdrawing treatment reflect the flexible operation of a functional framework enabling doctors to intervene selectively in their patients' treatment regime. Doctors have recognised an understanding that it is not necessary to sustain life at all costs and they have incorporated this understanding into their everyday practice of medicine. He argues that this 'compromise' should thus be permitted to continue without any changes to the law (McCall Smith 1999).[49]

While it has to be conceded that flexibility to changing circumstances can be an advantage, developing defences for doctors on an ad hoc case-by-case basis creates uncertainty and unpredictability, and conflicts with fundamental principles of the rule of law. A better solution would be to build upon those traditional solutions – which have after all been seen to be an effective means of dispensing justice and of absolving liability in the appropriate case – as a foundation for formalising those methods of assisted dying which are already practised by the medical profession. Giving statutory recognition to the principle of double effect and the acts/omissions distinction would thus involve minimal disruption and would provide legislative support to the judiciary.

Incorporating the two defences into legislation would also statutorily recognise the special status of doctors in our society. They are, and should be, treated differently from everyone else because of the context in which they work. Their activities are deemed acceptable and justifiable to the extent that they (or the majority of them at least) act in a way that is medically and ethically appropriate. Provided they have acted in an appropriate manner, they should not be held responsible for consequences they cannot avoid, or for consequences '. . . demanded of . . . [them] . . . by the society which imposes responsibility' (Wilson and Smith 1995: 392). It is time, therefore, that the law desisted from considering a doctor's activities in criminal law terms[50] and from not punishing them on unclear grounds.

---

49 Weaker arguments are advanced by Brody 1996: 39, who, while acknowledging that allowing individual cases would both weaken the law and encourage abuses, nonetheless preferred to maintain the status quo because it kept the medical profession 'on their toes' and that this in itself was a better form of regulation than any legalisation would be. Contrast Singer 1994: 189.

50 See, for example, Biggs 1996a: 888.

Conclusion

> *In ... instances where doctors have faced the courts, legal fictions have frequently been used to circumvent the full rigour of the criminal law.*
>
> (Otlowski 1994: 169)

End-of-life decision-making has been sorely challenged during the last few years by changes in societal values[1] which have left the law, the judges and the medical profession trailing in their wake.[2] Increased individualisation and secularisation of daily life have led to a decline in paternalism and a corresponding rise in patients' rights to autonomy and self-determination (Latimer 1991: 487) expressed in particular through the right to refuse medical treatment and the growth in defensive/litigious behaviour.[3]

The problems facing the medical, and as a consequence the legal, profession have also been exacerbated by a change in the nature of disease. The prevalence now is for progressive neurological conditions of a degenerative, chronic nature (Weir 1992: 123), which account for 70 per cent of all US deaths (Kadish 1992: 858). Linked with this is the ability to maintain the lives of patients who suffer from those diseases for a longer period of time, which, in turn, means that a greater number of patients are dying in hospital.[4] This will have financial as well as medical implications and although mentioning the word 'resources' may lead to allegations of minimising the value of life, its future significance should not be underestimated; it is not inconceivable

---

1 There is much evidence of this, but see, for example, Logue (1996); Darvall (1993): Preface to and chapter 1; and Watson (1977).
2 As Sedley LJ said in *Re F* (2000), Parliament and the courts 'can find themselves left behind by time and tide'. Compare Martel 2001: 392: '[j]udges may be confronted with novel arguments – stemming from current conditions of existence – that find little or no resonance within pre-established . . . legal frameworks . . .'
3 This can perhaps be attributed to the present perception of the standing of the medical profession, following some loss of trust in doctors; Clark 1986: 200–1.
4 According to Kadish 1992: 858, 80 per cent in the US, and according to Biggs 1996b: 229, approximately 70 per cent in the UK.

that assisted suicide and euthanasia will be advanced for purely economic reasons (Marcus 1996: 174).[5]

In order to deal with these new developments, doctors have been forced to advocate a new ethos based on quality of life rather than sanctity of life (Ferguson and Bissett-Johnson 1996: 565) while the courts have been forced to advocate a rejection of fundamental principles by adopting 'legal fictions' (Otlowski 1994: 169)[6] such as the principle of double effect and the acts and omissions distinction in order to avoid liability on the part of health professionals. This has created anomalies, inequalities and inconsistencies which will continue for as long as end-of-life procedures remain confined within the narrow constraints imposed by intention and causation (Meisel 2004: 285).

The main aim of this book has therefore been to show how difficult it is to base end-of-life decision-making solely on these two concepts. Although they are the criteria upon which liability is based, they have both been manipulated and interpreted by judges in a variety of ways in order to satisfy their own perceptions of justice and to fit in with policy considerations. There is no doubt that in the absence of guidance from the legislature, the courts have had significant latitude to improvise and make do with the tools at their disposal. That this has been and continues to be problematic is due in no small part to their having to use criminal law principles which are inappropriate in medical end-of-life conditions. Surely it was never intended that a doctor's conduct should be regulated by the law relating to murder (Glantz 1987: 240) which, as the 'worst' crime, is disproportionate to the essence of ending life in such circumstances?[7] Furthermore, ascertaining the meaning and indeed the existence of intention in complex end-of-life situations is nigh on impossible.

As a subjective notion, intention is open to a variety of internal and extraneous influences. It is decontextualised and subject to constructibility and it is sometimes mistakenly confused with purpose and motive. Its legal 'definition', which includes foresight of virtual certainty, is best illustrated by the principle of double effect, and while this does provide doctors with a defence to criminal charges, it has to be conceded that the cases are not based on the standard tests of either intention or causation. If they were, it would have been more likely that doctors would have been held to have had the required mental element and to have caused their patients' deaths.

The courts have also claimed a distinction between an act which causes

---

5 See also Penrose 1993: 723. In contrast see the study by Emanuel and Battin 1998: 168, which showed that legalising physician-assisted suicide would save only 0.07 per cent of total US healthcare expenditures.

6 See also Berman 1980: *ix*.

7 It is also ineffective in the sense that it has no deterrent effect in the medical context; see Preston 1998: 1389.

death and an omission which does not on the basis that the former is intended whereas the latter is not. The fact that omissions can be both intended and can cause death has been ignored where behaviour (such as withdrawing life-sustaining treatment) has been so categorised, since the cause of death has been held to be the original illness or injury and not the treatment withdrawal. This is so even though it can be persuasively argued that the patient's treatment refusal and/or the doctor's compliance with the patient's wishes have broken the chain of causation. Certainly it can be said that the doctor is a cause, or at least the part cause, of his patient's death in the sense that it was accelerated by him.

In the same way, it can also be argued that the general principles applicable to *novus actus interveniens* cases have been adjusted in order to account for the difference between what is perceived to be either an innocent or guilty intervening act. Treatment refusals by terminally ill patients, for example, have been held not to break the chain of causation, nor to cause death and have not been considered to be suicidal either. In fact, although intention is a key concept in both suicide and assisted suicide, adherence to traditional criminal definitions of suicide together with assumptions of non-suicidal intent have prevailed as a means of denying that withdrawing treatment is an activity carried out with an intention to die or to be assisted in dying.

Manipulation of and over-reliance on intention and causation at the expense of ignoring real-life circumstances and complex real-life factors reveals a problem with the common law's classic pursuit of individual justice. This is why it has been argued that it is so vital that future discussions on possible reform should explicitly account for the doctor's role and motive and the patient's consent as part of the context in which medical 'killing' is carried out. This would ensure that blameworthiness and culpability can be *properly* apportioned. Incorporating existing Common Law defences into legislation would also achieve a number of objectives: it would show confidence in the judges by validating practices which they have been following and developing for many years. Officially sanctioning these practices would enhance their authority and would remove a major source of uncertainty and inconsistency from the law.[8] Furthermore, creating a new medically-orientated category of homicide would avoid burdening doctors with the murder label and would meet with the underlying principles and aims of the law.

It is time, therefore, that the 'mental gymnastics' (Freeman 2002: 251) and the 'fancy footwork' (Scofield 1995: 481) engaged in by judges in order to

---

8 The Law Commission has expressed its intention to revisit Part 1 of the Draft Criminal Code of 1989. This will involve publishing consultations on external elements of offences (especially causation, fault and defences) in 2006/7 www.lawcom.gov.uk/criminal.htm (accessed 19 June 2006).

satisfy fundamental principles[9] of the criminal law in inappropriate conditions was brought to an end; as Ashworth rightly argues:

> The courts should abandon the piecemeal and disruptive approach of reinterpreting basic concepts such as intention so as to accommodate . . . the distinction between doctors and other actors . . .
>
> (Ashworth 1996: 185)[10]

9 And in some instances, statutory requirements as well.
10 As the Consultant Neurologist said in his interview: 'I just think this intention business is quite silly. It's the consequences that matter. The consequences of what we are proposing to do and take responsibility for those consequences and make sure that's what the person wanted and that there are no bad side-effects for society.'

Bibliography

Adams, M. and Nys, H. (2003) 'Comparative reflections on the Belgian Euthanasia Act 2002' 11 (3) *Med LR* 353.

Allen, M.J. (2005) *Textbook on Criminal Law*, 8th edn, Oxford: Oxford University Press.

Allman, R.L. (1998) 'Euthanasia and physician-assisted suicide: A non-consensus reformed reflection' 52 (1) *J Pastoral Care* 19.

Anderson, N. (1978) *Issues of Life and Death*, London: Hodder & Stoughton.

Andrews, K. (1995) Letter to the Editor 'Tortuous arguments evade the issue' 311 *BMJ* 1437.

Angell, M. (1998) 'Helping desperately ill people to die' in L.L. Emanuel (ed.) *Regulating How We Die: Ethical, Medical and Legal Issues Surrounding Physician-Assisted Suicide*, Cambridge, Mass: Harvard University Press.

Annas, G.J. (1998) 'The bell tolls for a right to suicide' in L.L. Emanuel (ed.) *Regulating How We Die: Ethical, Medical and Legal Issues Surrounding Physician-Assisted Suicide*, Cambridge, Mass: Harvard University Press.

Anscombe, G.E.M. (1976) *Intention*, reprinted 2nd edn, Oxford: Basil Blackwell.

—— (1983) 'The causation of action' in G. Ginet and S. Shoemaker (eds) *Knowledge and Mind: Philosophical Essays*, Oxford: Oxford University Press.

Appleton International Conference on Non-Treatment Decisions (1992) 'Developing guidelines for decisions to forego life-prolonging medical treatment' 18 *J Med Ethics* (Supp) 3.

Arlidge, A. (2000) 'The trial of Dr David Moor' *Crim LR* 31.

Arras, J.D. (1997) 'Physician-assisted suicide: A tragic view' 13 J *Contemp Health Law and Policy* 361.

Ashworth, A. (1989) 'The scope of criminal liability for omissions' 105 *LQR* 424.

—— (1996) 'Criminal liability in a medical context: The treatment of good intentions' in A.P. Simester and A.T.H. Smith (eds) *Harm and Culpability*, Oxford: Clarendon Press.

—— (2000) 'Is the criminal law a lost cause?' 116 *LQR* 225.

—— (2006) *Principles of Criminal Law*, 5th edn, Oxford: Oxford University Press.

Barrington, M.R. (1986) 'The case for rational suicide' in A.B. Downing and B. Smoker (eds) *Voluntary Euthanasia. Experts Debate the Right to Die*, London: Peter Owen.

Battin, M.P. (1982) *Ethical Issues In Suicide*, Englewood Cliffs, New Jersey: Prentice Hall.

—— (1998) 'Is a physician ever obligated to help a patient die?' in L.L. Emanuel (ed.) *Regulating How We Die: Ethical, Medical and Legal Issues Surrounding Physician-Assisted Suicide*, Cambridge, Mass: Harvard University Press.

—— and Lipman, G. (1996) 'Introduction: The need to objectively examine issues in assisted suicide and euthanasia' in Battin and Lipman (eds) *Drug Use in Assisted Suicide and Euthanasia*, Binghampton, New York: Pharmaceutical Products Press.

Bauby, J-D. (1997) *The Diving Bell and the Butterfly*, London: Fourth Estate.

Beauchamp, T.L. (1996) 'Introduction' to T.L. Beauchamp (ed.) *Intending Death: The Ethics of Assisted Suicide and Euthanasia*, Englewood Cliffs, New Jersey: Prentice Hall.

—— (2004) 'When hastened death is neither killing nor letting die' in T.E. Quill and M.P. Battin (eds) *Physician-Assisted Dying. The Case for Palliative Care and Patient Choice*, Baltimore, Maryland: The Johns Hopkins University Press.

—— and Childress, J.F.. (1994) *Principles of Biomedical Ethics*, 4th edn, New York: Oxford University Press.

—— (2001) *Principles of Biomedical Ethics*, 5th edn, Oxford: Oxford University Press.

Beck, A.T. *et al* (1974) 'Development of suicidal intent scales' in Beck *et al* (eds) *The Prediction of Suicide*, Bowie, Maryland: The Charles Press.

—— (1975) 'Hopelessness and suicidal behaviour' 234 *JAMA* 1146.

Begley, A-M. (1998) 'Acts, omissions, intentions and motives: A philosophical examination of the moral distinction between killing and letting die' 28 (4) *J Advanced Nursing* 865.

Benjamin, M. (1976) 'Death, where is thy cause?' 6(3) *Hastings Center Report* 15.

Berman, H.J. (1980) 'Introduction' to C. Perelman *Justice, Law and Argument*, Dordrecht: D. Reidel Pub. Co.

Beynon, H. (1987) 'Causation, omissions and complicity' *Crim LR* 539.

Biggs, H. (1996a) 'Euthanasia and death with dignity: Still poised on the fulcrum of homicide' *Crim LR* 878.

—— (1996b) 'Decisions and responsibilities at the end of life: Euthanasia and clinically assisted death' 2(3) *Med L Int* 229.

—— (2001) *Euthanasia, Death with Dignity and the Law*, Oxford: Hart Publishing.

—— (2005) 'The Assisted Dying for the Terminally Ill Bill 2004: Will English law soon allow patients the choice to die?' 12(1) *EJHL* 43.

Bix, B. (1995) 'Physician-assisted suicide and the United States Constitution' 58(3) *MLR* 404.

Blake, M. (1997) 'Physician-assisted suicide: A criminal offence or a patient's right?' 5(3) *Med LR* 294.

Blom-Cooper, L.J. and Morris, T. (2004) *With Malice Aforethought. A Study of the Crime and Punishment For Homicide*, Oxford: Hart Publishing.

Boothroyd, J. (1988) 'Killing for compassion: The last legal taboo' *Law Magazine* 18 March, 23.

Boyle, J.M. (1980) 'Toward understanding the principle of double effect' 90 *Ethics* 527.

Brahams, D. (1989) 'Jehovah's Witness transfused without consent: A Canadian case' 11 *The Lancet* 1407.

—— (1990) 'The reluctant survivor' 140 *NLJ* 586.

—— (1992) 'Criminality and compassion' 89 (35) *LSG* 2.

Brand, M. (1984) *Intending and Acting: Towards a Naturalized Action Theory*, Cambridge, Mass: MIT Press.

Brandt, R. (1976) 'The morality and rationality of suicide' in E.S. Schneidman (ed.) *Suicidology: Contemporary Developments*, New York: Grune & Stratton.

Bratman, M.E. (2006) 'What is the accordion effect?' 10(1) *Journal of Ethics* 5.

Brazier, M. (2003) *Medicine, Patients and the Law*, 3rd edn, London: Penguin Books.

British Medical Association (1993) *Medical Ethics Today: Its Practice and Philosophy*, London: BMJ Publishing Group.

—— (2000 and 2001) *Withholding and Withdrawing Life-prolonging Treatment: Good Practice and Decision Making*, London: BMJ Books.

Brock, D.W. (1989a) 'Death and dying' in R. Veatch (ed.) *Medical Ethics*, Boston, Mass: Jones & Bartlett.

—— (1989b) 'Forgoing life-sustaining food and water: Is it killing?' in J. Lynn (ed.) *By No Extraordinary Means. The Choice to Forgo Life-Sustaining Food and Water*, Bloomington, Indiana: Indiana University Press.

—— (1992) 'Voluntary Active Euthanasia' 22 (2) *Hastings Center Report* 10.

—— (1993) *Life and Death. Philosophical Essays in Biomedical Ethics*, Cambridge: Cambridge University Press.

—— (2004) 'Physician assisted suicide as a last-resort option at the end of life' in T.E. Quill and M.P. Battin (eds) *Physician-Assisted Dying. The Case for Palliative Care and Patient Choice*, Baltimore, Maryland: The Johns Hopkins University Press.

Brody, B.A. (1988) 'Ethical questions raised by the Persistent Vegetative State patient' 18 (1) *Hastings Center Report* 33.

Brody, H. (1992) *The Healer's Power*, New Haven, Conn: Yale University Press.

—— (1993) 'Causing, intending and assisting death' 4 *J Clin Ethics* 112.

—— (1996) 'Commentary of Billings and Block's "Slow Euthanasia" ' 12 (4) *J Pall Care* 38.

Brownstein, E.G. (2001) 'Pain relief and causation of death in the context of palliative care' 8(4) *J of Law and Med* 433.

Buchanan, A. (1996) 'Intending death: The structure of the problem and proposed solutions' in T.L. Beauchamp (ed.) *Intending Death: The ethics of Assisted Suicide and Euthanasia*, Englewood Cliffs. New Jersey: Prentice Hall.

Buxton, R. (1988) 'Some simple thoughts on intention' *Crim LR* 484.

Byrn, R.M. (1975) 'Compulsory lifesaving treatment for the competent adult' 44 *Fordham LR* 1.

Callahan, D. and White, M. (1996) 'The legalization of physician-assisted suicide: Creating a regulatory Potemkin Village' 30 *University of Richmond LR* 1.

Cambridge Dictionary of Philosophy (1995) Cambridge: Cambridge University Press.

Campbell, R. and Collinson, D. (1988) *Ending Lives*, Oxford: Basil Blackwell.

Cantor, N.L. (1973) 'A patient's decision to decline life-saving medical treatment: Bodily integrity versus the preservation of life' 26 *Rutgers LR* 228.

—— (1987) *Legal Frontiers of Death and Dying*, Bloomington, Indiana: Indiana University Press.

—— (2001) 'Twenty-five years after *Quinlan*: A review of the jurisprudence of death and dying' 29(2) *J Law, Medicine and Ethics* 182.

Card, R. (ed.) (2006) *Card, Cross & Jones Criminal Law*, 17th edn, Oxford: Oxford University Press.

Carolan, B. (1997) 'U.S. Supreme Court rules: No Constitutional right to physician-assisted suicide' 3 (2) *MLJI* 43.

Carse, A.L. (1996) 'Causal responsibility and moral culpability' in T.L. Beauchamp (ed.) *Intending Death: The Ethics of Assisted Suicide and Euthanasia*, Englewood Cliffs, New Jersey: Prentice Hall.

Carson, D. (1995) 'Criminal Responsibility' in Bull, R. and Carson, D. (eds) *Handbook of Psychology in Legal Contexts*, Chichester: John Wiley and Sons.

—— and Bull, R. (2003) *Handbook of Psychology in Legal Contexts*, 2nd edn, Chichester: John Wiley and Sons.

Chambers' Twenty First Century Dictionary (1999/2005 reprint) Edinburgh: Chambers Harrap.

Chambers, D.R. (1989) 'The Coroner, the Inquest and the verdict of suicide' 29 (3) *Med Sci Law* 181.

Childress, J.F. (1982) *Who Should Decide? Paternalism in Health Care*, Oxford: Oxford University Press.

—— (1985) 'Civil disobedience, conscientious objection, and evasive non-compliance: A framework for the analysis and assessment of illegal actions in health care' 10 *J Med and Philosophy* 63.

—— (1998) 'Religious Viewpoints' in L.L. Emanuel (ed.) *Regulating How We Die. The Ethical, Medical and Legal Issues Surrounding Physician-Assisted Suicide*, Cambridge, Mass: Harvard University Press.

Christensen, R.C. and McCrary, S.V. (1993) 'Decisions to refuse treatment by depressed, medically ill patients' 4 *J Clin Ethics* 335.

Clark, D.H. (1986) 'The doctor's dilemma today' in A.B. Downing and B. Smoker (eds) *Voluntary Euthanasia*, London: Peter Owen.

Clarke, D.C. (1998) ' "Rational" suicide and people with terminal conditions or disabilities' 8 *Issues in Law and Medicine* 147.

Clarke, M. (1997) 'What is the doctrine of double effect?' 93 (31) *Nursing Times* 15.

Clarkson, C.M.V. (2004) 'Necessary action: A new defence' *Crim LR* (50th Anniversary edn) 13.

—— and Keating, H.M. (2003) *Criminal Law Text and Materials*, 5th edn, London: Sweet & Maxwell.

Clouser, K.D. (1991) 'The challenge for future debate on euthanasia' 6 (5) *J Pain and Symptom Management* 306.

Connelly, R.J. (1997–8) 'The medicalization of dying: A positive turn on a new path' 36 (4) *OMEGA* 331.

Cooper, S. (2000) 'Summing up intention' 150 *NLJ* 1258.

Council on Ethical and Judicial Affairs of the American Medical Association (1992) 'Decisions near the end of life' 267 (16) *JAMA* 2229.

—— (1994) 'Physician-assisted suicide' 10 (1) *Issues in Law and Medicine* 91.

Craig, G.M. (1994) 'Withholding nutrition and hydration in the terminally ill: Has palliative medicine gone too far? 20 (3) *J Med Ethics* 139.

Crane, D. (1975) 'Decisions to treat critically ill patients: A comparison of social versus medical considerations' *Milbank Memorial Fund Quarterly/Health and Soc* 1.

Cranford, R.E. (1996) 'The physician's role in killing and the intentional withdrawal of treatment' in T.L. Beauchamp (ed.) *Intending Death: The Ethics of Assisted Suicide and Euthanasia*, Englewood Cliffs, New Jersey: Prentice Hall.

Crewe, R. article in (2003) 326 *BMJ* 271.

Croall, H. (1998) *Crime and Society in Britain*, Harlow: Addison Wesley Longman.

Cusack, D.A. *et al* (2000) ' "Near PVS": A new medico-legal syndrome?' 40 (2) *Med Sci Law* 133.

Darvall, L. (1993) *Medicine, Law and Social Change*, Aldershot: Dartmouth Pub. Co.

Davies, A.N. (1996) 'The right to refuse treatment' in T.L. Beauchamp (ed.) *Intending Death: The Ethics of Assisted Suicide and Euthanasia*, Englewood Cliffs, New Jersey: Prentice Hall.

Davies, J. (1995) 'The case for legalising voluntary euthanasia' in Keown, J. (ed.) *Euthanasia Examined. Ethical, Legal and Clinical Perspectives*, Cambridge: Cambridge University Press.

Davis, L.H. (1979) *Theory of Action*, Englewood Cliffs, New Jersey: Prentice Hall.

De Cruz, P. (2005) 'Commentary . . . *Re Z (an adult: capacity)*' 13 (2) *Med LR* 257.

De Haan, J. (2002) 'The new Dutch law on euthanasia' 10(1) *Med LR* 57.

Dennis, I.H. (1987) 'The mental element for accessories' in P. Smith (ed.) *Criminal Law. Essays in Honour of J.C. Smith*, London: Butterworths.

—— (1993) 'Criminal causation' 46(1) *CLP* 42.

Devettere, R.J. (1990) 'The imprecise language of euthanasia and causing death' 1(4) *J Clin Ethics* 268.

—— (1991) 'Sedation before ventilator withdrawal: Can it be justified by double effect and called "Allowing a patient to die?" ' 2(2) *J Clin Ethics* 122.

Devine, A. article in the *Guardian*, 26 March 1997.

Devlin, P. (1985/1986 reissue) *Easing the Passing. The trial of John Bodkin Adams*, London: Bodley Head.

Dickinson, G.E. *et al* (1997–8) 'Attitudes towards assisted suicide and euthanasia among physicians in South Carolina and Washington' 36 (3) *OMEGA* 201.

Docker, C. (1996) in 'The way forward?' in McLean, S. (ed.) *Death, Dying and the Law*, Aldershot: Dartmouth Pub. Co.

Donnison, D. and Bryson, C. (1996/7) 'Matters of life and death: Attitudes to euthanasia' in Jowell, R, *et al* (eds) *British Social Attitudes The 13th Report*, Aldershot: Dartmouth Pub. Co.

Downie, J. and Sherwin, S. (1996) 'A Feminist exploration of issues around assisted death' 15 (2) *St Louis Uni Public LR* 303.

Dressler, J. (1982) 'Rethinking heat of passion: A defense in search of a rationale' 73 (2) *J Crim Law and Criminology* 421.

Duff, R.A. (1989) 'Intentions, legal and philosophical' *OJLS* 76.

—— (1990) *Intention, Agency and Criminal Liability. Philosophy of Action and the Criminal Law*, Oxford: Basil Blackwell.

—— (1995) 'Acting, trying, and criminal liability' in S. Shute, J. Gardner and J. Horder (eds) *Action and Value in Criminal Law*, Oxford: Clarendon Press.

Durkheim, E. (1952) *Suicide: A study in Sociology*, London: Routledge & Kegan Paul.

Dworkin, R.M. (1995) *Life's Dominion. An Argument About Abortion, Euthanasia and Individual Freedom*, New York: Knopf.

Dyck, A.J. (1973) 'An alternative to the ethic of euthanasia' in R.H. Williams (ed.) *To Live and to Die: When, Why and How*, New York: Springer-Verlag.

Dyer, C. (2001) 'High Court throws out "Suicide Aid" case' 323 *BMJ* 953.

Edwards, M.J. and Tolle, S.W. (1992) 'Disconnecting a ventilator at the request of a patient who knows he will then die: The doctor's anguish' 117 (3) *Annals of Internal Medicine* 254.

Eggleston, S. (1994) 'Whither Euthanasia?' 47 *Crim Lawyer* 6.

Elkington, J.R. (1968) 'The dying patient, the doctor and the law' 13 *Villanova LR* 740.

Emanuel, E.J. and Battin, M.P. (1998) 'What are the potential cost savings from legalizing physician-assisted suicide?' 339 (3) *NEJM* 167.

Engelhardt, H.T., Jr (1989) 'Death by free choice: Modern variations on an antique theme' in B. Brody (ed.) *Suicide and Euthanasia*, Dordrecht: Kluwer.

Fairbairn, G. (1991) 'Suicide and justified paternalism' in M. Brazier and M. Lobjoit (eds) *Protecting the Vulnerable. Autonomy and Consent in Health Care*, London: Routledge.

Farrington, D.P. (1995) 'The Psychology of crime: Influences and constraints in offending' in Bull, R. and Carson, D. (eds) *Handbook of Psychology in Legal Contexts*, Chichester: John Wiley and Sons.

Fawcett, J. (1972) 'Suicide, depression and physical illness' 219 *JAMA* 1303.

Feinberg, J. (1991) 'Overlooking the merits of the individual case. An unpromising approach to the right to die' 4 (20) *Ratio Juris* 131.

—— and Coleman, J. (eds) (2004) *Philosophy and law*, 7th edn, Belmont CA, USA: Wadsworth/Thomson.

Fenigsen, R. (2004) 'Dutch euthanasia: The new Government ordered study' 20 (1) *Issues in Law and Medicine* 73.

Fennell, C. (1990) 'Intention in murder: Chaos, confusion and complexity' 41 (4) *NILQ* 325.

Ferguson, P.R. (1997) 'Causing death or allowing to die? Developments in the law' 23 (6) *JME* 368.

—— and Bissett-Johnson, A. (1996) 'The withdrawal and withholding of medical treatment' *Fam Law* 563.

Fincham, F.D. and Jaspars, J.M. (1980) 'Attribution of responsibility' in L. Berkowicz (ed.) *Advances in Experimental Social Psychology*, New York: Academic Press.

Finnis, J. (1991) 'Intention and side effects' in R.G. Frey and C.W. Morris (eds) *Liability and Responsibility. Essays in Law and Morals*, Cambridge: Cambridge University Press.

—— (1993) '*Bland*: Crossing the Rubicon?' 109 *LQR* 329.

Firth, R. (1967) 'The men themselves: Or the role of causation in our concept of seeing' in H-N Castaneda (ed.) *Intentionality, Minds and Perception: Discussions on Contemporary Philosophy*, Detroit, Mich: Wayne State University Press.

Fletcher, G.P. (1969) 'Prolonging life: Some legal considerations' in A.B. Downing (ed.) *Euthanasia and the Right to Death*, London: Peter Owen.

—— (1978) *Rethinking Criminal Law*, Boston, Mass: Little, Brown and Co.

Fletcher, J. (1969) 'The patient's right to die' in A.B. Downing (ed.) *Euthanasia and the Right to Death*, London: Peter Owen.

—— (1973) 'Ethics and Euthanasia' in R.H. Williams (ed.) *To Live and to Die: When, Why and How?* New York: Springer-Verlag.

Foley, K.M. (1991) 'The relationship of pain and symptom management to patient requests for physician-assisted suicide' 6 (5) *J Pain and Symptom Management* 289.

Foot, P. (1978/2002 reissue) *Virtues and Vices and other Essays in Moral Philosophy*, Oxford: Clarendon Press.

Foster, S. (2000) 'Force feeding, self-determination and the right to die' 150 *NLJ* 857.

Fowler, R.C. *et al* (1979) 'Communication of suicidal intent and suicide in Unipolar Depression' 1 *J Affect Disorders* 219.

Freeman, M. (2002) 'Denying death its dominion: Thoughts on the Dianne Pretty case' 10(3) *Med LR* 245.

Frey, R.G. (1996) 'Intention, foresight and killing' in T.L. Beauchamp (ed.) *Intending Death. The Ethics of Assisted Suicide and Euthanasia*, Englewood Cliffs, New Jersey: Prentice Hall.

—— (1998) 'Distinctions in death' in G. Dworkin *et al* (eds) *Euthanasia and Physician-Assisted Suicide: For and Against*, Cambridge: Cambridge University Press.

Fried, T.R. *et al* (1993) 'Limits of patient autonomy: Physician attitudes and practices regarding life-sustaining treatments and euthanasia' 153 (6) *Archives of Internal Medicine* 722.

Friedman, L.M. (1971) 'General theory of law and social change' in J.S. Zeigel (ed.) *Law and Social Change*, Toronto: Osgoode Hall Law School, York University.

Gardner, J. (1996) 'Justifications and reasons' in A.P. Simester and A.T.H. Smith (eds) *Harm and Culpability*, Oxford: Clarendon Press.

—— (1998) 'The gist of excuses' 1(2) *Buffalo Crim LR* 575.

General Medical Council (2002) Guidance on *Withholding and Withdrawing Life-prolonging Treatment: Good Practice and Decision Making*.

Gillet, G. (1988) 'Euthanasia, letting die and the pause' 14 *JME* 61.

Gillon, R. (1969) 'Suicide and Voluntary Euthanasia. A historical perspective in euthanasia and the right to death' in A.B. Downing (ed.) *Euthanasia and the Right to Death*, London: Peter Owen.

Glantz, L.H. (1987) 'Withholding and withdrawing treatment: The role of the criminal law' 15 (4) *Law, Med and Health Care* 231.

Glover, J. (1977/1986 Reprint) *Causing Death and Saving Lives*, Harmondsworth: Penguin Books.

Gormally, L. (1994a) *Euthanasia, Clinical Practice and The Law*, London: The Lineacre Centre.

—— (1994b) 'Against Voluntary Euthanasia' in R. Gillon and A. Lloyd (eds) *Principles of Health Care Ethics*, Chichester: John Wiley and Sons.

Gostin L.O. (1993) 'Drawing a line between killing and letting die: The law, and law reform, on medically-assisted dying' 21 (1) *The Journal of Law, Medicine and Ethics* 94.

Graber, G.C. (1981) 'The rationality of suicide' in S.E. Wallace and A. Eser (eds) *Suicide and Euthanasia: The Rights of Personhood*, Knoxville: University of Tennessee Press.

Grassi, L. (1997) 'Psychiatric implications of euthanasia and assisted suicide in terminally ill patients' 13 (2) *New Trends in Experimental and Clinical Psychiatry* 127.

Griew, E. (1987) 'States of mind, presumptions and inferences' in P. Smith (ed.) *Criminal Law Essays in Honour of J.C. Smith*, London: Butterworths.

Griffiths, J. (1994) 'The regulation of euthanasia and related medical procedures that shorten life in the Netherlands' 1 *Medical Law International* 137.

Gross, H. (1979) *A Theory of Criminal Justice*, New York: Oxford University Press.

Grossman, D. (1995) *On Killing. The Psychological Cost of Learning to Kill in War and Society*, Boston: Little, Brown and Co.

Grubb, A. (1993) 'Attempted murder of terminally ill patient. Commentary on *R v Cox*' 1(2) *Med LR* 232.

—— (1993) 'Withdrawal of Artificial Hydration and Nutrition: Incompetent Adult *Airedale NHS Trust v Bland*' 1(3) *Med LR* 359.

—— (1999) 'Commentary on *Re L (Medical Treatment: Gillick Competency)*' 7(1) *Med LR* 58.

Hamerly, J.P. (1998) 'Views on assisted suicide. Perspectives of the American Medical Association and the National Health Organisation' 55 *Am J Health-Syst Pharm* 543.

Harris, J. (1985) *The Value of Life*, London: Routledge & Kegan Paul.

Hart, H.L.A. (1968) *Punishment and Responsibility. Essays in the Philosophy of Law*, Oxford: Oxford University Press.

—— and Honoré, T. (1985) *Causation in the Law*, 2nd edn, Oxford: Oxford University Press.

Harvard LR (1992) 'Physician-assisted suicide and the right to die with assistance' 2021.

Hendin, H. and Klerman, G. (1993) 'Physician-assisted suicide: The dangers of legalization' (1993) 50 *Am J Psychiatry* 143.

—— *et al* (1998) 'Physician-assisted suicide: Reflections on Oregon's first case 14 (3) *Issues in Law and Medicine* 243.

Herring, J. (2006) *Criminal Law Text, Cases and Materials*, 2nd edn, Oxford: Oxford University Press.

Hinkka, H. *et al* (2002) 'Factors affecting physicians' decisions to forgo life-sustaining treatments in terminal care' 28 (2) *JME* 109.

Honoré, A. (2002/2004 reprint) 'Principles and values underlying the concept of causation in law' in I. Freckleton and D. Mendelson (eds) *Causation in Law and Medicine*, Hampshire: Dartmouth Pub. Co.

Hooper, J. (2000) 'Mercy killing in the new Millennium' 40 (3) *Med Sci Law* 189.

Hoover, J.F. (1972) 'An adult's right to resist blood transfusions: A view through *John F. Kennedy Memorial Hospital v Heston*' 47 *Notre Dame Lawyer* 571.

Horder, J. (1988) 'Mercy killings – some reflections on *Beecham's Case*' 52 (3) *JCL* 309.

—— (1995) 'Intention in the criminal law: A rejoinder' 58 (5) *MLR* 678.

—— (2000) 'On the irrelevance of motive in criminal law' in J. Horder (ed.) *Oxford Essays in Jurisprudence* (4th Series), Oxford: Oxford University Press.

—— (2004) *Excusing Crime*, Oxford: Oxford University Press.

Hornsby, J. (1980) *Actions*, London: Routledge & Kegan Paul.

Hughes, G. (1958) 'Criminal omissions' 67 *Yale LJ* 590.

Hunt, R. (1999) 'Taking responsibility for affecting the time of death' 13 *Pall Med* 439.

Husak, D.N. (1989) 'Motive and criminal liability' *Criminal Justice Ethics* 3.

Huxtable, R. Letter to *The Times* 18 May 1999.

Institute of Medical Ethics Working Party (1991) 'Withdrawal of life support from patients in a Persistent Vegetative State after acute brain damage' (1991) 337 *The Lancet* 96.

Jacob, J.M. (1988) *Doctors and Rules. A Sociology of Professional Values*, London: Routledge.

Jackson, E. (2006) *Medical Law Text, Cases and Materials*, Oxford: Oxford University Press.

Jefferson, M. (2006) *Criminal Law*, 7th edn, London: Pearson Longman.

Jennings, B. (1991) 'Active Euthanasia and foregoing life-sustaining treatment: Can we hold the line?' 6 (5) *J Pain and Symptom Management* 312.

Jones, S. (2006) *Criminology*, 3rd edn, Oxford: Oxford University Press.

Jonsen, A.R. (1996) 'Criteria that make intentional killing unjustified: Morally unjustified acts of killing that have been sometimes declared justified' in T.L. Beauchamp (ed.) *Intending Death: The Ethics of Assisted Suicide and Euthanasia*, Englewood Cliffs, New Jersey: Prentice Hall.

Kadish, H. (1992) 'Letting patients die: Legal and moral reflections' 80 *California LR* 857.

Kamisar, Y. (1958) 'Some non-religious views against proposed "Mercy-killing" legislation' 42 (6) *Minnesota LR* 969.

—— (1995) 'Physician-assisted suicide: The last bridge to Active Voluntary Euthanasia' in Keown, J. (ed.) *Euthanasia Examined*, Cambridge: Cambridge University Press.

—— (1996) 'The reasons why so many people support physician-assisted suicide – and why these reasons are not convincing' 12 *Issues in Law and Medicine* 113.

Kass, L.R. (1989) 'Neither for love nor money: Doctors must not kill' 94 *Public Interest* 25.

Kelleher, M.J. (1997) 'Euthanasia and physician-assisted suicide' 2 (3) *Medico-Leg J Ireland* 77.

Kelly, B.J. and Varghese, F.T. (1996) 'Assisted suicide and euthanasia: What about the clinical issues?' 30 (1) *Australian and New Zealand Journal of Psychiatry* 3.

Kennedy, I. (1983) *The Unmasking of Medicine*, London: Granada Publishing Ltd.

—— (1994) 'Commentary on *Thor*' 2(2) *Med LR* 220.

—— (1995) 'Consent: Force feeding of prisoners' 3(2) *Med LR* 189.

Kenny, A. (1978) *Freewill and Responsibility*, London: Routledge & Kegan Paul.

Keown, J. (1995) 'Euthanasia in the Netherlands: Sliding down the slippery slope?' in Keown, J. (ed.) *Euthanasia Examined*, Cambridge: Cambridge University Press.

—— (1997) 'Restoring moral and intellectual shape to the law after *Bland*' 113 *LQR* 481.

Kugler, I. (2004) 'Necessity as a justification in *Re A (Children)*' 68 (5) *JCL* 440.

Kuhse, H. (1987) *The Sanctity of Life Doctrine in Medicine: A Criticism*, Oxford: Clarendon Press.

Lacey, N. (1993) 'A clear concept of intention: Elusive or illusory?' 56 *MLR* 621.

——, Wells, C. and Quick, O. (2003) *Reconstructing criminal law. Text and Materials*, 3rd edn, London: LexisNexis Butterworths.

Lanham, D. (1990) 'The right to choose to die with dignity' 14 *Crim LJ* 401.

Laing, J.A. (1990) 'Assisting suicide' 54(1) *JCL* 106.

Landsman, R.M. (1986) 'Terminating food and water: Emerging legal rules' in J. Lynn (ed.) *By no Extraordinary Means. The Choice to Forgo Life-Sustaining Food and Water*, Bloomington: Indiana University Press.

Latimer, E.J. (1991) 'Euthanasia: A physician's reflections' 6 (8) *J Pain and Symptom Management* 487.

Lawton, L.J. (1979) 'Mercy killing – the judicial dilemma' 72 *J Royal Soc Med* 460.

Legemaate, J. (2004) 'The Dutch Euthanasia Act and related issues' 11 *JLM* 312.

Lester, D. (1996) 'Psychological issues in euthanasia, suicide and assisted suicide' 52 (2) *J of Soc Issues* 51.

Lindsell, A. articles in *The Times*, 15 October 1997, 29 October 1997 and 6 December 1997.

Lineacre Centre for Health Care (1994) *Ethics Working Party Report on euthanasia and clinical practice* reproduced in L. Gormally, *Euthanasia, Clinical Practice and The Law*, London: The Lineacre Centre.

Ling, J.R. (2002) *The Edge of Life. Death, Dying and Euthanasia*, Epsom, Surrey: DayOne Publications.

Logue, B.J. (1996) 'Physician-assisted suicide: A social science perspective on international trends' in McLean, S. (ed.) *Death, Dying and the Law*, Aldershot: Dartmouth Pub. Co.

Louisell, D.W. (1973) 'Euthanasia and Biathanasia: On dying and killing' 22 *Catholic Uni LR* 72.

Lynn, J. and Childress, J.F. (1986) 'Must patients always be given food and water?' in J. Lynn (ed.) *By No Extraordinary Means. The Choice to Forgo Life-Sustaining Food And Water*, Bloomington: Indiana University Press.

Macdonald, W.L. (1998) 'Situational factors and attitudes toward Voluntary Euthanasia' 46 (1) *Social Science and Medicine* 73.

McCall Smith, A. (1999) 'Euthanasia: The strengths of the middle ground' 7(2) *Med LR* 194.

McCormack, P. (1998) 'Quality of life and the right to die: An ethical dilemma' 28 (1) *J Adv Nursing* 63.

McLean, S.A.and Maher, G. (1983) *Medicine, Morals and the Law*, Aldershot: Gower.

—— and Britton, A. (1996) *Sometimes a Small Victory*, University of Glasgow: Institute of Law and Ethics in Medicine.

Mann, P.S. (1998) 'Meanings of death' in M.P. Battin *et al* (eds) *Physician assisted suicide. Continuing the debate*, London and New York: Routledge.

Marcus, W.L. (1996) 'Regulatory issues in euthanasia, palliative care and assisted suicide' in M.P. Battin and A.G. Lipman (eds) *Drug Use in Assisted Suicide and Euthanasia*, Binghampton, New York: Pharmaceutical Products Press.

Mareiniss, D.P. (2005) 'A comparison of *Cruzan* and *Schiavo*' 26(2) *The Journal of Legal Medicine* 233.

Martel, J. (2001) 'Examining the foreseeable: Assisted suicide as a herald of changing moralities' 10 (2) *Social and Legal Studies* 147.

Martin, E.A. (ed.) (2003) *Oxford Dictionary of Law* (5th edn, reissued), Oxford: Oxford University Press.

Marzen, T.J. (1994) ' "Out, out, brief candle": Constitutionally prescribed suicide for the terminally ill' 21 *Hastings Constitutional LQ* 799.

Mason, J.K. (1993) 'Non-voluntary therapy under Lord Donaldson' *The Jur Rev* 115.

—— and Laurie, G.T. (1996) 'The management of the Persistent Vegetative State in the British Isles' *The Jur Rev* 263.

—— (2006) *Mason & McCall Smith's Law and Medical Ethics*, 7th edn, Oxford: Oxford University Press.

Mathews, M.A. (1987) 'Suicidal competence and the patient's right to refuse lifesaving treatment' 75 *California LR* 707.

Mathews, P. and Foreman, J. (eds) (1993) *Jervis on the Office and Duties of Coroners*, 11th edn, London: Sweet & Maxwell.

Meier, R.F. (1989) *Crime and Society*, Boston: Allyn & Bacon.

Meilander, G. (1986) 'Caring for the permanently unconscious patient. Why feeding is not medical care' in J. Lynn (ed.) *By no Extraordinary Means. The Choice to Forgo Life-Sustaining Food and Water*, Bloomington: Indiana University Press.

Meisel, A. (2004) 'Physician-assisted suicide shifting the focus from means to ends' in T.E. Quill and P. Battin (eds) *Physician-Assisted Dying. The Case for Palliative Care and Patient Choice*, Baltimore, Maryland: The Johns Hopkins University Press.

Meyers, D.W. and Mason, J.K. (2000) 'Physician assisted suicide: A second view from the Mid-Atlantic' *Anglo-American LR* 265.

Mitchell, B. (1998) 'Public perceptions of Homicide and criminal justice' 38(3) *BJ Criminology* 453.

—— (1999) 'In Defence of a Principle of Correspondence' *Crim LR* 195.

Miles, S.H. (1994) 'Physicians and their patients' suicides' 271 (22) *JAMA* 1786.

Moore, M. (1987) 'Intentions and *mens rea*' in R. Gavison (ed.) *Issues in Contemporary Legal Philosophy. The Influence of H.L.A. Hart*, Oxford: Clarendon Press.

Morgan, D. (1992) 'Whatever happened to consent?' 142 *NLJ* 1448.

Murphy, J.G. (1987) 'Mercy and legal justice' in J. Coleman and E.F. Paul (eds) *Philosophy and Law*, Oxford: Basil Blackwell.

National Council for Hospice and Specialist Palliative Care Services (1998) 'Voluntary Euthanasia: The Council's view' 5 (4) *Nursing Ethics* 371.

New York Multi Society Task Force on Life and the Law (1994) *When death is sought. Assisted suicide and euthanasia in the medical context* www.health.state.ny.us/nysdoh/ptovider/death/taskforc.htm

Norrie, A. (1986) 'Practical reasoning and criminal responsibility: A jurisprudential approach' in D.B. Cornish and R.V. Clarke (eds) *The Reasoning Criminal. Rational Choice Perspectives On Offending*, New York: Springer-Verlag.

—— (1989) 'Oblique intention and legal politics' *Crim LR* 793.

—— (1991) 'A critique of criminal causation' 54 *MLR* 685.

—— (1999) 'After *Woollin*' *Crim LR* 532.

—— (2001) *Crime, Reason And History. A Critical Introduction to Criminal Law*, 2nd edn, London: Butterworths.

O'Keefe, T.M. (July 1984) 'Suicide and self-starvation' *Philosophy* 349.

O'Rourke, K. (1991) 'Assisted suicide: An evaluation' 6(5) *Journal of Pain and Symptom Management* 317.

Orentlicher, D. and Callahan, C.M. (2004) 'Feeding tubes, slippery slopes and physician-assisted suicide' 4(25) *The Journal of Legal Medicine* 389.

Ormerod, D. (ed.) (2005) *Smith and Hogan Criminal Law*, 11th edn, Oxford: Oxford University Press.

Ost, S. (2005) 'Euthanasia and the defence of necessity: Advocating a more appropriate legal response' *Crim LR* 355.

Otlowski, M. (1994) 'Active Voluntary Euthanasia: Options for reform' 2(2) *Med LR* 161.

—— (2000) *Voluntary Euthanasia and the Common Law*, Oxford: Oxford University Press.

Owens, R.G. (1995) 'Legal and psychological concepts of mental status' in R. Bull and D. Carson (eds) *Handbook of Psychology in Legal Contexts*, Chichester: John Wiley and Sons.

Oxford Concise English Dictionary (1995) 9th edn, Oxford: Clarendon Press.

Oxford Dictionary of English (2003) 2nd edn, Oxford: Oxford University Press.

Pedain, A. (2003) 'The human rights dimension of the *Dianne Pretty* case' 62(1) *Camb LJ* 181.

Pellegrino, E.D. (1992) 'Doctors must not kill' 3 (2) *J Clin Ethics* 95.

—— (1996) 'The place of intention in the moral assessment of assisted suicide and Active Euthanasia' in T.L. Beauchamp (ed.) *Intending Death: The Ethics of Assisted Suicide and Euthanasia*, Englewood Cliffs, New Jersey: Prentice Hall.

Penrose, M.M. (1993) 'Assisted suicide: A tough pill to swallow' 20 (2) *Pepperdine LR* 689.

Pfeifer, J.E. *et al* (1996) 'Euthanasia on trial: Examining public attitudes toward non-physician-assisted death' 52(2) *J Social Issues* 119.

Phippen, L. and Radlett, D. (2005) 'Drugs and manslaughter' 155 (7184) *NLJ* 1054.

Portenoy, R.K. *et al* (1997) 'Determinants of the willingness to endorse assisted suicide. A survey of physicians, nurses and social workers' 38 (3) *Psychosomatics* 277.

Powell, T. and Kornfeld, D.B. (1993) 'On promoting rational treatment, not rational suicide' 4 *J Clin Ethics* 334.

Preston, T.A. (1998) Letter to the Editor: 'The rule of double effect' 338 (19) *NEJM* 1389.

Price, D.P.T. (1996) 'Assisted suicide and refusing medical treatment: Linguistics, morals and legal contortions' 4(3) *Med LR* 270.

—— (1997) 'Euthanasia, pain relief and double effect' 17 (2) *LS* 323.

—— (2001) 'Fairly Bland: An alternative view of a supposed new "Death Ethic" and the BMA Guidelines' 21 (4) *LS* 618.

Quill, T.E. (1991) 'Death and dignity. A case of individualized decision-making' 324 *NEJM* 691.

—— (1993) 'The ambiguity of clinical intentions' 329 *NEJM* 1039.

—— *et al* (1997) 'The rule of double effect – a critique of its role in end-of-life decision making' 337 (24) *NEJM* 1768.

Quinn, K.P. (1997) 'Assisted suicide and equal protection: In defence of the distinction between killing and letting die' 13 (2) *Issues in Law and Medicine* 145.

Rachels, J. (1975) 'Active and passive euthanasia' (1975) 292 *NEJM* 78.

—— (1986) *The End of Life. Euthanasia and Morality*, Oxford, Oxford University Press.

Randall, F. (1997) 'Why causing death is not necessarily morally equivalent to allowing to die – a response to Ferguson' 23 (6) *J Med Ethics* 373.

Reese, W.L. (1980) *Dictionary of Philosophy and Religion*, Englewood Cliffs, New Jersey: Humanities Press.

Rhodes, R. (1998) 'Physicians, assisted suicide, and the right to live or die' in M.P. Battin *et al* (eds) *Physician Assisted Suicide. Continuing the Debate*, London and New York: Routledge.

Robins, E. *et al* (1959) 'The communication of suicidal intent: A study of 134 consecutive cases of successful (completed) suicide' 115 *Am J Psych* 724.

Robinson, P.H. (1995) 'Should the criminal law abandon the *actus reus – mens rea* distinction?' in S. Shute, J. Gardner, and J. Horder (eds) *Action and Value in Criminal Law*, Oxford: Clarendon Press.

—— (1997) *Structure and Function in Criminal Law*, Oxford: Clarendon Press.

Rothschild, A. (2004) 'Oregon: Does physician-assisted suicide work?' 12 (2) *J of Law and Medicine* 217.

Rumley, P. (2001) 'Vegetative State – a better way eight years on?' 151 *NLJ* 1669.

Salako, S.E. (1998) 'Causation in criminal law: A new look at *Jordan, Smith, Blaue* and *Cheshire*' 62 (5) *JCL* 461.

Samuels, A. (2005) 'Complicity in suicide' 69 (6) *JCL* 535.

Sandak, L.R. (1978) 'Suicide and the compulsion of lifesaving medical procedures: An analysis of the refusal of treatment cases' 44 *Brooklyn LR* 285.

Schopp, R.F. (1998) *Justification, Defences and Just Convictions. Cambridge Studies in Philosophy and Law*, Cambridge: Cambridge University Press.

Scofield, G.R. (1995) 'Exposing some myths about physician-assisted suicide' 18 *Seattle ULR* 473.

Searle, J.R. (1983) *Intentionality: An Essay In The Philosophy of Mind*, Cambridge: Cambridge University Press.

Shaffer, C.D. (1986) 'Criminal liability for assisted suicide' 86 *Columbia LR* 348.

Sheldon, S. and Thomson, M. (eds) (1998) *Feminist Perspectives on Health Care Law*, London: Cavendish Pub. Ltd.

Shorter Oxford English Dictionary (1993) 3rd edn, Oxford: Clarendon Press.

Siegel, K. and Tuckel, P. (1984–5) 'Rational suicide and the terminally ill cancer patient' 15 (3) *OMEGA* 263.

Simester, A.P. (1995) 'Why omissions are special' 1 *Legal Theory* 311.

—— and Sullivan, G.R. (2003, revised 2004) *Criminal Law Theory and Doctrine*, 2nd edn, Oxford: Hart Publishing.

Singer, P. (1994) *Rethinking Life And Death. The Collapse Of Our Traditional Ethics*, Oxford: Oxford University Press.

Sistare, C. (1987) 'Agent motives and the criminal law' 13 (3) *Social Theory and Practice* 303.

Skegg, P.D.G. (1988) *Law, Ethics And Medicine. Studies In Medical Law*, Oxford: Clarendon Press.

Skene, L. (2005) 'The *Schiavo* and *Korp* cases: Conceptualising end-of-life decision-making' 13 (2) *Journal of Law and Medicine* 223.

Slovenko, R. (1997) 'Foreword' in S.I. Greenburg (ed.) *Euthanasia and Assisted Suicide. The Psychosocial Issues*, Illinios: Charles C. Thomas Pub.

Smith, A.T.H. (1978) 'On a*ctus reus* and *mens rea*' in P.R. Glazebrook (ed.) *Reshaping the Criminal Law. Essays In Honour of Glanville Williams*, London: Stevens and Sons.

Smith, C.K. (1996) 'Safeguards for Physician-assisted suicide: The Oregon Death with Dignity Act' in McLean, S. (ed.) *Death, Dying and the Law*, Aldershot: Dartmouth Pub. Co.

Smith, G.P. (1989) 'All's well that ends well: Toward a policy of assisted rational suicide or merely enlightened self-determination?' 22 *University of California LR* 275.

Smith, J.C. (1984) 'Liability for omissions in criminal law' 4 *LS* 88.

—— (1989) *Justification and Excuse in The Criminal Law*, London: Stevens and Sons.

—— (1996) 'Commentary on *R v Dear*' *Crim LR* 595.

—— (1997) 'Criminal liability of accessories: Law and law reform' 113 *LQR* 453.

—— (1998a) 'Commentary on *R v Woollin*' *Crim LR* 890.

—— (1998b) '*R v Rungzabe Khan and Tahir Khan*' *Crim LR* 830.

—— (2000a) 'A Comment on Moor's Case' *Crim LR* 41.

—— (2000b) 'Commentary on *R v Wright*' *Crim LR* 928.

Smith, S.W. (2005) 'Fallacies of the logical slippery slope in the debate on physician-assisted suicide and euthanasia' 13(2) *Med LR* 224.

Sneiderman, B. and Deutscher, R. (2002) 'Dr. Nancy Morrison and her dying patient: A case of medical necessity' 10 *Health Law Journal* 1.

Solomon, M.Z. *et al* (1993) 'Decisions near the end of life: Professional views on life-sustaining treatments' 83 (1) *American Journal of Public Health* 14.

Somerville, M. (1993) 'The song of death: The lyrics of euthanasia' 9 *J Contemporary Health Law and Policy* 1.

Stannard, J.E. (1992) 'Criminal causation and the careless doctor' 55 *MLR* 577.

—— (1993) 'Medical treatment and the chain of causation' 57 *JCL* 88.

Stauch, M. (1995) 'Rationality and the refusal of medical treatment: A critique of the recent approach of the English courts' 21 *JME* 162.

——, Wheat, K. with Tingle, J. (2006) *Text, Cases and Materials on Medical Law*, 3rd edn, Abingdon, Oxon: Routledge-Cavendish.

Steinbock, B. and Norcross, A. (eds) (1994) *Killing and Letting Die*, 2nd edn, New York: Fordham University Press.

Stell, L.K. (1998) 'Physician-assisted suicide. To decriminalize or to legalize, that is the question' in M.P. Battin *et al* (eds) *Physician Assisted Suicide. Continuing The Debate*, London and New York: Routledge.

Still, A. and Todd, C. (1998) 'When technical rationality fails. Thinking about terminally ill patients' 3 (1) *J of Health and Psychology* 137.

Stroud's Judicial Dictionary (1953) 3rd edn; (2002) 6th edn, London: Sweet & Maxwell.

Sugarman, D.B. (1986) 'Active versus Passive Euthanasia: An attributional analysis' 6 (1) *J Applied Social Psychology* 60.

Sulmasy, D.P. and Pellegrino, E.D. (1999) 'The rule of double effect. Clearing up the double talk' 159 (16) *Arch Int Med* 545.

The Sunday Times 15 November 1998.

Thomson, J.J. (1977) *Acts and Other Events*, Ithaca: Cornell University Press.

Thompson, I.E., Melia, K.M. and Boyd, K.M. (1994) *Nursing ethics*, 3rd edn, Edinburgh: Churchill Livingstone.

Tolle, S.W. *et al* (2004) 'Characteristics and proportion of dying Oregonians who personally consider physician-assisted suicide' 15 (2) *J Clin Ethics* 111.

Tur, R.H.S. (2002) 'The doctor's defence and professional ethics' 13 *KCLJ* 75.

Turner, A. article in *The Independent* 25 January 2006.

Valente, S.M. and Trainor, D. (1998) 'Rational suicide among patients who are terminally ill' 68 (2) *AORN Journal* 252.

Van Delden, J. *et al* (2004) 'Thirty years experience with euthanasia in the Netherlands' in T.E. Quill and P. Battin (eds) *Physician-assisted dying. The case for palliative care and patient choice*, Baltimore, Maryland: The Johns Hopkins University Press.

Van der Maas, P.J. *et al* (1992) 'Euthanasia and other medical decisions at the end of life', Vol.2 Health Care Policy Monographs, Amsterdam: Elsevier.

Velasquez, M.G. (1987) 'Defining suicide' 3 (1) *Issues in Law and Medicine* 37.

Vernaglia, L.W. (1999) 'Who killed Georgette Smith? Healthcare providers at the intersection of criminal law and patient care' 1 (4) *JONA's Healthcare Law, Ethics and Regulation* 12.

Wade, D.T. (2001) 'Ethical issues in diagnosis and management of patients in the Permanent Vegetative State' 322 *BMJ* 352.

Wall, P.D. (1997) 'The generation of yet another myth on the use of narcotics' 73 *Pain* 121.

Wanzer, S.H. *et al* (1984) 'The physician's responsibility toward hopelessly ill patients' 310 (15) *NEJM* 955.

Wasik, M. (1982) 'Cumulative provocation and domestic killing' *Crim LR* 29.

Watson, A. (1977) *Society and Legal Change*, Edinburgh: Scottish Academic Press Ltd.

Watson, M. (2000) 'A necessary death?' 108 *The Criminal Lawyer* 4.

Watts, D.T. and Howell, T. (1992) 'Assisted suicide is not Voluntary Active Euthanasia' 40 *American Geriatrics Society* 1043.

Weir, R.F. (1989) *Abating Treatment With Critically Ill Patients. Ethical and Legal Limits to The Medical Prolongation Of Life*, Oxford: Oxford University Press.

—— (1992) 'The morality of physician-assisted suicide' 20 (1–2) *Law, Medicine and Health Care* 116.

Wheat, K. (2000) 'The law's treatment of the suicidal' 8(2) *Med LR* 182.

White, R. and Haines, F. (2004) *Crime and Criminology: An Introduction*, 3rd edn, Oxford: Oxford University Press.

Williams, G. (1983) *Textbook of Criminal Law*, 2nd edn, London: Stevens and Sons.

—— (1987) 'Oblique intention' 46 (3) *Camb LJ* 417.

—— (1989) '*Finis* for *novus actus*?' 48 (3) *Camb LJ* 391.

—— (1991) 'Criminal omissions – the conventional view' 107 *LQR* 86.

Williams, G. (2001a) 'The principle of double effect and terminal sedation' 9 (1) *Med LR* 41.

—— (2001b) 'Case Note on *Re A (Children)* [2000] 4 All ER 961' 1(2) *Wales LJ* 183.

—— and Dingwall, G. (2004) 'Inferring intention' 55 (1) *NILQ* 69.

Williams, J. (2001) 'Hunger-strikes: A prisoner's right or a "Wicked Folly?"' 40(3) *Howard Journal* 285.

Wilson, J.Q. and Hernstein, R.J. (1986) *Crime and Human Nature. The Definitive Study Of The Causes Of Crime*, New York: Simon and Schuster.

Wilson, W. (1995) 'Is life sacred? 17 (2) *Journal of Social Welfare and Family Law* 131.

—— (1999) 'Doctrinal rationality after *Woollin*' 62 *MLR* 448.

—— (2002) *Central issues in criminal theory*, Oxford: Hart Publishing.

—— (2005) 'The structure of criminal defences' *Crim LR* 108.

—— and Smith, K.J. (1995) 'The doctor's dilemma: Necessity and the legality of medical intervention' 1 (4) *Medical Law International* 387.

Young, M.G. and Ogden, R.D. (1998) 'End-of-life issues: A survey of English-speaking Canadian nurses in AIDS care' 9 (2) *Journal of Assoc of Nurses in AIDS Care* 18.

Government reports

Advisory Council on the Penal System. Sentences of Imprisonment (1978) *A Review of Maximum Penalties*.

Criminal Law Revision Committee Working Paper (1976) *Offences Against the Person*.

Criminal Law Revision Committee 14th Report (1980) *Offences Against the Person* Cmnd.7844.

Government response to the HLSC Report on Medical Ethics (1994) Cmnd.2553.

HLSC (1988–9) *Murder and life imprisonment*, HL Paper 78–1 (the Nathan Committee).

HLSC (1993–4) *Medical Ethics*, HL Paper 21–I.

HLSC (2005) *Report on the Assisted Dying for the Terminally Ill Bill 2004*, HL Paper 86–I.

Law Com Working Paper No.55 (1974) *Codification of the criminal law. General principles and defences of general application.*

Law Com No.83 (1977) *Criminal law. Report on defences of general application.*

Law Com No.143 (1985) *Codification of the criminal law. A Report to the Law Commission.*

Law Com No.177 (1989) *A criminal code for England and Wales.*

Law Com No.218 (1993) *Legislating the criminal code. Offences against the person and general principles.* Cmnd.2370.

LC Report No.290 (2004) *Partial defences to murder* www/lawcom.gov.uk/docs/lc290 (2).pdf.

LCCP No.122 (1992) *Legislating the criminal code. Offences against the person and general principles.*

LCCP No.131 (1993) *Assisting and encouraging crime.*

LCCP No.139 (1995) *Consent in the criminal law.*

LCCP No.177 (2005) *A new Homicide Act for England and Wales?*

President's Commission for the Study of Ethical Problems in Medicine and Biomedical and Behavioural Research (1983) *Deciding to forgo life-sustaining treatment. A Report on the ethical, medical and legal issues in treatment decisions* Washington: US Government Printing Office.

Royal Commission on Capital Punishment (1949–53) Cmnd.8932.

Index